Music, Dance
and the Archive

INDIGENOUS MUSIC, LANGUAGE AND PERFORMING ARTS

Associate Professor Myfany Turpin, Series Editor

The many forms of Australia's Indigenous music and temporal arts have ancient roots, huge diversity and global reach. The Indigenous Music, Language and Performing Arts series aims to stimulate discussion and development of the fields of Aboriginal and Torres Strait Islander music, language and performing arts, in both subject matter and approach, as well as looking beyond Australia to First Nations cultures around the world. Proposals are welcomed for studies of traditional and contemporary performing arts (including dance), popular music, art music, experimental and new media, and the importance of First Nations languages for culture and empowerment, as well as theoretical, analytical, interdisciplinary and practice-based research. Where relevant, print and ebook publications may be supplemented by online or audiovisual media.

Archival Returns: Central Australia and Beyond
Edited by Linda Barwick, Jennifer Green and Petronella Vaarzon-Morel

For the Sake of a Song: Wangga Songmen and Their Repertories
Allan Marett, Linda Barwick and Lysbeth Ford

Music, Dance and the Archive
Edited by Amanda Harris, Linda Barwick and Jakelin Troy

Recording Kastom: Alfred Haddon's Journals from the Torres Strait and New Guinea, 1888 and 1898
Edited by Anita Herle and Jude Philp

Reflections and Voices: Exploring the Music of Yothu Yindi with Mandawuy Yunupingu
Aaron Corn

Singing Bones: Ancestral Creativity and Collaboration
Samuel Curkpatrick

Songs from the Stations: Wajarra as Sung by Ronnie Wavehill Wirrpnga, Topsy Dodd Ngarnjal and Dandy Danbayarri at Kalkaringi
Myfany Turpin and Felicity Meakins

Wurrurrumi Kun-Borrk: Songs from Western Arnhem Land
Kevin Djimarr

Music, Dance and the Archive

Edited by Amanda Harris, Linda Barwick
and Jakelin Troy

SYDNEY UNIVERSITY PRESS

We acknowledge the traditional owners of the lands on which Sydney University Press is located, the Gadigal people of the Eora Nation, and we pay our respects to the knowledge embedded forever within the Aboriginal Custodianship of Country.

Aboriginal and Torres Strait Islander readers are advised this publication contains names and images of people who have died.

Contents

List of figures

List of figures

List of tables

Editors' preface and acknowledgements

This book is an output of a four-year project on which the editors (and several chapter authors) have collaborated since 2018. Our project *Reclaiming Performance Under Assimilation in Southeastern Australia, 1935–75* was funded by the Australian Research Council's Discovery Project Scheme from 2018 to 2022 (DP180100943). It arose from conversations between Amanda Harris, Linda Barwick, Rachel Fensham, Tiriki Onus, Jakelin Troy, Jacqueline Shea Murphy, Matt Poll, Lyndon Ormond-Parker and Sally Treloyn about histories of the resilience of Aboriginal and Torres Strait Islander people and their practices of performing music and dance that deserve to be more widely known. We devised a project around detailed archival research, collaborative sharing and workshopping of materials, and creative methods of recuperation and reconnection. This book brings together some of the creative and scholarly work that has resulted.

Along with our initial project collaborators, we extend our thanks for research support to Sharon Huebner, Adnan Bhatti, Mujahid Torwali, Mahesh White-Radhakrishnan, and especially to Laura Case, whose editorial assistance has been vital to shaping this book. We also thank collaborators on workshops and engagement with archives over the course of the project: Adnan Bhatti, Lou Bennett, Tim Bishop, Nerida Blair, John Casey, Cameron Davison, Jason Fieldhouse, Luke Forbes, Payi Linda Ford and Emily Tyaemaen Ford, Shannon Foster, Michelle Francis, Dennis Fuller, Kaisi Fuller, Selme Fuller, Jennie Ginger, Anna Haebich, Lisa Haldane, Kevin Hunt, Carole Johnson, Regina Kantilla, Anthea Kerinaiua, Jo Kinniburgh, Cathy Mandile, Allan Marett, Sarah Muller, Francis Orsto, Gregoriana Parker, Frances Therese Portaminni, Jonathon Potskin, Augusta Puangatji, Nardi Simpson, Joe Sproats, Judy Sproats, Jacinta Tipungwuti, Jacinta Tobin, Lara Troy-O'Leary, Peter Waples-Crowe, Therese Webster. We thank Sydney University Press's editorial team Susan Murray, Jo Lyons, Nathan Grice and Naomi van Groll, Series Editor Myfany Turpin, and the peer reviewers whose expert comments helped to refine the volume. Finally, we thank all of the contributors to the book for the thinking, expertise, creativity and passion they have poured into their chapters.

A note on language and style

Throughout this book we capitalise terms Indigenous, Aboriginal, Native, Country, Elders, Dreaming, and render words in Indigenous languages in roman font (not-italicised), except where they are rendered as glosses on the main text.

About the contributors

Linda Barwick is a researcher and writer whose interests include nurturing creativity, honouring intergenerational wisdom and promoting diversity of thought and compassionate action. She enjoys gardening, bridge, grandchildren and cats, and is Emeritus Professor at Sydney Conservatorium of Music, University of Sydney, and a Fellow of the Australian Academy of the Humanities.

Clint Bracknell is a Nyungar singer/song-maker from the south coast of Western Australia and Professor of Indigenous Languages at the University of Queensland. He holds a PhD in ethnomusicology from the University of Western Australia and is Deputy Chair of the Australian Institute of Aboriginal and Torres Strait Islander Studies.

Genevieve Campbell is a musician and ethnomusicologist, working with senior Tiwi song custodians in the maintenance of performative knowledge transmission. She is an Honorary Fellow at Sydney Conservatorium of Music and the Sydney Environment Institute, with cross-disciplinary interests in performance, eco-musicology, and the impacts of environmental and social change on embodied culture in the context of cultural maintenance, artistic creativity and community health.

Chi-Fang Chao is a senior lecturer in the Department of Dance at the University of Roehampton, London. She has been trained in anthropology and dance studies. Her research interests include the anthropological study of ritual and dance, dance ethnography in Okinawa, Japan, and reflexive/post-colonial dance theatre of Indigenous people in Taiwan. She was invited to cooperate with the Formosan Aboriginal Song and Dance Troupe in producing two works of contemporary Indigenous people's dance and music theatre: *Pu'ing: Search for the Atayal Route* (2013) and *Ma'ataw: The Floating Island* (2016), both committed by the Council of Indigenous People and premiered in the National Theatre in Taiwan.

Amanda Harris is an Australian Research Council Future Fellow at Sydney Conservatorium of Music, University of Sydney, and Director of the Sydney Unit of digital archive Pacific and Regional Archive for Digital Sources in Endangered Cultures (PARADISEC). Amanda is interested in hearing the voices of those often excluded from conventional music histories through collaborative research focused on gender and intercultural musical cultures. Her monograph *Representing Australian Aboriginal Music and Dance 1930–70* was published by Bloomsbury Publishing in 2020.

Born in Auckland, Aotearoa, **Jack Gray** is a founding member and the Artistic Director of Atamira Dance Company since 2018. His independent arts practice engages diverse audiences in community-centred spaces of Indigenous knowledge exchange, such as Cultural Informance Lab (California), Transformation Lab (New York), I Moving Lab (USA, Australia, NZ), Indigenous Dance Forum (New York), I LAND (Hawaii, Seattle, Portland, Chicago, New York), Intentional Indigenous Artform Exchange (New York) and more. He was a Visiting Assistant Professor at University of California Riverside, Artist in Residence at New York University's Asian/Pacific/American Institute, Regents Scholar at UCLA World Arts and Cultures/Dance.

Cindy Jinmarabynana is a Marrarrich/Anagawbama clan woman from the An-barra language group of Arnhem Land in the Northern Territory of Australia. Her outstation is Ji-bena and she is a cultural manager for Gupanga. She lives in the Western Arnhem Land community of Maningrida, where she is a teacher and Lúrra Language and Culture team member at Maningrida College. She is co-chair of the Northern Land Council's Learning on Country Steering Committee, and a director of Bawinanga Aboriginal Corporation. Cindy is a dedicated mother and grandmother who is passionate about passing on language and knowledge for future generations to ensure the continuity of culture.

Jodie Kell is a PhD candidate, supervised by Professor Linda Barwick and Associate Professor Myfany Turpin. She works at PARADISEC as an audio engineer and co-producer of the podcast *Toksave: Culture Talks*. Her doctoral research focuses on the role of women in music making and the dynamics of gender in the music performance space through a participatory ethnography of the Ripple Effect Band – an all-women's rock band from the Western Arnhem Land community of Maningrida of which Jodie is the band manager, co-songwriter and lead guitarist.

Matt Poll is the manager of Indigenous programs at the Australian National Maritime Museum and previously worked as Curator of Indigenous Heritage collections of the Chau Chak Wing Museum at the University of Sydney, following more than a decade as repatriation project officer at the University of Sydney. Matt played an integral part in implementing an Acknowledgement of Country built into the architecture of the new Chau Chak Wing Museum, which opened in November 2020. Matt is also currently chairperson of Orana Arts in mid-western regional

NSW and is a long-term member of Aboriginal and Torres Strait Islander Advisory Board for Sydney's Museum of Contemporary Art.

Marianne Schultz holds a MLitt and PhD in History from the University of Auckland in addition to a MA in Performing Arts from Middlesex University, London. Marianne has danced and taught professionally in the United States and New Zealand, most recently with the Foster Group's production *Orchids*. She is the author of two books, *Performing Indigenous Culture on Stage and Screen: A Harmony of Frenzy* and *Limbs Dance Company: Dance For All People*. Her articles on dance and the performing arts have appeared in several peer-reviewed journals and in the volume *Staging the Other in Nineteenth-Century British Drama*.

Jacqueline Shea Murphy is a professor in the dance department at UC Riverside, where she teaches courses in critical dance studies and in Iyengar yoga. She is author of *"The People Have Never Stopped Dancing": Native American Modern Dance Histories* (University of Minnesota Press, 2007), and is founder and co-director of the Indigenous Choreographers at Riverside gathering project (https://icr.ucr.edu/). Her new book, *Dancing Indigenous Worlds: Choreographies of Relation*, is forthcoming from the University of Minnesota Press. It emerges out of relationships – including with Jack Gray – that have grown while she has been engaging with Native American and Indigenous dance in the US, Canada and Aotearoa over the past 20 years.

Rosy Simas is an enrolled member of the Seneca Nation. She is a transdisciplinary and dance artist who creates work for stage and installation. Simas' work weaves themes of personal and collective identity with family, sovereignty, equality and healing. She creates dance work with a team of Native and BIQTPOC artists, driven by movement-vocabularies developed through deep listening. Simas is a 2013 Native Arts and Cultures Foundation Choreography Fellow, 2015 Guggenheim Creative Arts Fellow, 2017 Joyce Award recipient from The Joyce Foundation, 2019 Dance/USA Fellow, 2021 Native Arts and Cultures Foundation SHIFT award recipient, 2022 USA Doris Duke Fellow, 2016 and 2022 McKnight Foundation Choreography Fellow, and multiple awardee from NEFA National Dance Project, the MAP Fund, and National Performance Network. Simas is the Artistic Director of Rosy Simas Danse and Three Thirty One Space, a creative studio for Native and BIPOC artists in Minneapolis, Minnesota, USA.

Jacinta Portaminni Tipungwuti is a senior culture woman and traditional owner of the Tiwi Islands, Northern Australia. She is a custodian and composer of the songlines of Wrangku Country on western Bathurst Island, she dances Ampiji (Rainbow) and Yirrikapayi (Crocodile) and she is a senior woman of the Lorringala (Stone) Skingroup. As a member of the Tiwi Strong Women's Group, she has performed at the Sydney and Darwin Festivals, the Sydney Opera House, the National Film and Sound Archive, and at music and language conferences around Australia.

Jakelin Troy (Jaky) is Ngarigu of the Snowy Mountains, called by Jaky's community Kunama Namadgi, in south-eastern Australia. She is Director, Indigenous Research at The University of Sydney and founded the Sydney Indigenous Research Network (https://bit.ly/3SpWQF1). Jaky is conducting research with Linda and Amanda into the use of historical records locked in the archives to support her own and other Aboriginal communities to recover and maintain language, cultural practices, performance and music. Recently she has been working with communities in north-west Pakistan to support their cultural activism as they document and share their language, music and performance.

List of abbreviations

ABC	Australian Broadcasting Corporation
AFL	Australian Football League
AGNSW	Art Gallery of New South Wales
AIAS	Australian Institute of Aboriginal Studies
AIATSIS	Australian Institute of Aboriginal and Torres Strait Islander Studies
AuSIL	Australian Society for Indigenous Languages
CAAMA	Central Australian Aboriginal Media Association
FASDT	Formosan Aboriginal Song and Dance Troupe
IFMC	International Folk Music Council
KMT	Kuomintang
LD&C	Language Documentation & Conservation
MAI	Montréal Arts Interculturals
MS	Melodic Sequence
NAA	National Archives of Australia
NFSA	National Film and Sound Archive of Australia
NGA	National Gallery of Australia
NLA	National Library of Australia
PARADISEC	Pacific and Regional Archive for Digital Sources in Endangered Cultures
PBS	Public Broadcasting Service
SLNSW	State Library of New South Wales

1

Embodied culture and the limits of the archive

Amanda Harris, Linda Barwick and Jakelin Troy

Records of music and dance held in archives and museums can take tangible forms – as audiovisual recordings, or as photographs and musical notation that capture performance. However, for these embodied forms of culture, an archival record can store only the shadow of a song or dance. In this book, we consider the ways that ephemeral cultural forms like these expose the limits of the archive. The contributing authors do this through collaborative and creative research that explores relationships between people and their material and ephemeral culture. In this introduction to the volume, we consider how embodied practice draws our attention to the limits of archival records, and to the aspects of performance, cultural maintenance and connection to culture *not present* in the archive. We also highlight the necessity of relationships, Country and creativity in practising song and dance, and in revitalising practices that have gone out of use. This thinking takes us beyond matters of access to archives and of democratising and decolonising the archive.[1] We begin this venture with a reflection on recent collaborative efforts to re-embody a Ngarigu song, involving the three editors as

---

1   Important recent work in this area includes Linda Barwick, Sharon Huebner, Lyndon Ormond-Parker and Sally Treloyn, "Reclaiming Archives: Guest Editorial". *Preservation, Digital Technology & Culture* 50, no. 3–4 (2021), 99–104; Indigenous Archives Collective, 2021, "The Indigenous Archives Collective Position Statement on the Right of Reply to Indigenous Knowledges and Information Held in Archives", *Archives and Manuscripts* 49 (3), 244–52, https://bit.ly/3RN3RPV; Kirsten Thorpe, Shannon Faulkhead and Lauren Booker, "Transforming the Archive: Returning and Connecting Indigenous Repatriation Records". in *The Routledge Companion to Indigenous Repatriation: Return, Reconcile, Renew*, eds Cressida Fforde, C. Timothy McKeown and Honor Keeler (Abingdon, Oxon: Routledge, 2020), 822–34; Beth Marsden, Katherine Ellinghaus, Cate O'Neill, Sharon Huebner and Lyndon Ormond-Parker, "Wongatha Heritage Returned: The Digital Future and Community Ownership of Schoolwork from the Mount Margaret Mission School, 1930s–1940s", *Preservation, Digital Technology & Culture* 50, no. 3–4 (2021), 105–15; Tiffany Shellam and Joanna Cruickshank, "Critical Archives: An Introduction", *Journal of Colonialism and Colonial History* 20, no. 2 (2019).

research partners.[2] We open with this case study to position ourselves within this research, to ground the introduction in our lived experience of co-designed arts practice, and to highlight similar approaches and methods that take form throughout the book.

Re-embodying a Ngarigu song

In April 2021, a renewal took place in the Snowy Mountains of New South Wales of the Ngarigu "song of the Menero women" whose archival traces in the form of a piano arrangement Jaky and Linda had spent some years reinterpreting as a Ngarigu-centred record of performance practice.[3] After considerable archival research, in December 2020, we (Jaky and Linda) had taken the next step in our process of enquiry by trying out the re-created snow increase ceremony song, feeling it in our mouths, throats and bodies as co-created vocalisation, with the assistance of percussion provided by Allan Marett. At this phase, each of us was tuned in to the other to find the tempo and tessitura that felt right and performable for us, that gave us strength to sing out and to imagine performing it with others – with the "Menero women" whose singing had inspired John Lhotsky to write the song down, and with the potential wider circle of contemporary Ngarigu people.

Jaky describes the ongoing resonances of the song as she returned to Canberra:

> During the flight home I could still feel the song playing through my body, not just in my head. The moves as Linda and Allan and I performed the song continued to animate my body and the sound of our music played in my mind. So much so that when I returned home, I felt compelled to share the song with my mother and daughter and it came out so clearly. Without needing to refer to my notes I sang that song. My mother was very moved and immediately connected to its purpose and meaning for our Country; for her it invoked the feeling of the cold in the mountains and that moment before it snows. My daughter was drawn to the song in spite of herself: she did not like the sound, she is a singer and loves sweetness in music. My low voice and the unfamiliar style of the music was not to her taste. Nevertheless, the song itself, its purpose and meaning drew her in and she also became fixed on this music, ultimately singing it for herself. In the end it was Lara

---

2   Paul Gilchrist, Claire Holmes, Amelia Lee, Niamh Moore and Neil Ravenscroft, "Co-Designing Non-Hierarchical Community Arts Research: The Collaborative Stories Spiral", *Qualitative Research Journal* 15, no. 4 (2015), 459.

3   John Lhotsky, *A Song of the Women of the Menero Tribe near the Australian Alps. Arranged with the Assistance of Several Musical Gentlemen for the Voice and Pianoforte, Most Humbly Inscribed as the First Specimen of Australian Music to Her Most Gracious Majesty Adelaide, Queen of Great Britain and Hanover* (Sydney: Sold by John Innes, Pitt Street. By commission at R. Ackerman's Repository of Arts, Strand [London], 1834); Jakelin Troy and Linda Barwick, "Claiming the 'Song of the Women of the Menero Tribe'". *Musicology Australia* 42, no. 2 (2020), 85–107.

Figure 1.1 Performance at Mutong of Ngarigu Snow Song. From left to right: Amanda Harris, Jacinta Tobin, Lara Troy-O'Leary, Linda Barwick, Peter Waples-Crowe and Jakelin Troy. Photo by Toby Martin.

who insisted we take the song to Country. It became important for her to sing the song where it was meant to be performed, in Ngarigu snow Country.

We all agreed that the next step was to take the song back to Country, and draw it into an "ever-widening circle" of community and kin.[4]

After the December 2020 imagining of how the song was performed in 1834, and an additional rehearsal at Sydney Conservatorium of Music in February 2021 joined by Lara Troy-O'Leary, the team decided to try to find the exact location suggested in the historical literature – Mutong.[5] It was with great excitement that Linda and Peter Waples-Crowe first walked onto the rural property on the bank of the Snowy River on 14 April 2021 and gazed at what is very likely the place where Ngarigu women performed the song and Lhotsky also felt the "majesty" of this music. It stayed with Lhotsky as it has stayed with us, who have performed it

---

4   Clint Bracknell and Kim Scott, "Ever-widening circles: Consolidating and enhancing Wirlomin Noongar archival material in the community", in *Archival Returns: Central Australia and Beyond*, eds Linda Barwick, Jennifer Green and Petronella Vaarzon-Morel. LD&C Special Publication 18. (Honolulu & Sydney: University of Hawai'i Press and Sydney University Press, 2020), 325–38, http://hdl.handle.net/10125/24890/.

5   Troy and Barwick, "Claiming the 'Song of the Women of the Menero Tribe'", 2020. On 12 February 2021, Jakelin, Lara and Amanda joined Graeme Skinner and Toby Martin to practise and talk about different versions of the song, some played through on a nineteenth-century square piano played by Graeme, and others sung with drumstick beats by Toby, and lap percussion by Jakelin, Lara and Amanda.

again, on Country. When the group, including Jaky, Linda, Peter, Lara, Amanda and co-researchers, Jacinta Tobin, Neal Peres Da Costa, Graeme Skinner and Toby Martin, convened there a day later in glorious autumn weather, it seemed as if everything just fell into place. With the graceful curve of the Snowy River at our backs, and the view of the High Country before us, over several rehearsals we negotiated a performance of the song that felt supported by the environment. The point at which it really came together as a performance was when Lara, the youngest Ngarigu singer, asked to be able to lead because she had a feeling for how the song should sound. When she began to lead and Peter accompanied us on boomerang clapsticks, we all fell into a groove that we were able to repeat with an ease and naturalness that gave us a sense of completion (Figure 1.1).

Most remarkable was the effect of the reimagined snow increase ceremony song; it invoked the biggest dump of snow in decades. In May, the *Sydney Morning Herald* reported that an early and snowy winter was coming and by June snow was predicted beyond the alpine region for a very cold winter 2021.[6] Winter 2021 continued to be the best cold season in long memory, powdery, beautiful, deep snow that many said was a miracle in the midst of climate change predictions of warmer alpine temperatures. This is what we imagined the song was meant to do and every time it has been sung by a community member since then it snows. To the Ngarigu, and other Aboriginal people involved in this project, bringing the snow is possibly the most important impact of this renewal of cultural practice.

The song, as published by Lhotsky, was not intended as a historical record, nor as a way for future generations of Ngarigu to understand it as an Indigenous cultural performance. It was to create an amusement for settler-colonists of his time with an engaging local flavour that drew lightly on the Ngarigu performance. However, it was in being faithful to that flavour that Lhotsky preserved so much of the original.[7] In our next iteration of the research project we turned to the parlour music of the nineteenth century to understand how this music was received and understood by a non-Indigenous audience. Lhotsky's parlour music was sung by Amanda Harris with Neal Peres Da Costa playing a nineteenth-century square piano in a concert at the Sydney Conservatorium of Music that brought to life archival records of music performed in Sydney in the 1820s and 30s.[8] In the same program the corroboree

---

6   Laura Chung, "'Winter is Coming': Snow and Strong Surf as Cold Front Moves Across the State", *Sydney Morning Herald*, 15 May 2021, https://bit.ly/3PqH9M3, accessed 4 November 2021; Sarah McPhee, "First Big Cold Snap of Winter: Snow Expected Beyond Alpine Areas", *Sydney Morning Herald*, 7 June 2021, https://bit.ly/3PExiSv, accessed 4 November 2021.

7   Troy and Barwick, "Claiming the 'Song of the Women of the Menero Tribe'".

8   "From the Sydney Amateur Concerts 1826", SCM Early Music Ensemble, Neal Peres Da Costa (director), Sydney Conservatorium of Music, 27 May 2021, https://hdl.handle.net/2123/28800. The concert placed the song alongside repertoire performed in 1826 Sydney concerts in a small hall, with historic instruments and interpretative techniques, with an image of Ngarigu Country projected in the background. After the piano-accompanied version, singing of the Ngarigu song was led by Jakelin and accompanied by Amanda with volunteer women students from the string orchestra.

version as performed by the research team in Ngarigu Country was again presented, this time in a public performance. The audience appreciation of both versions was resounding, but the corroboree song again worked its magic and stayed with people long after the performance, as reported back to the team.[9]

The song is now being embraced by Ngarigu of the High Country who see it as an important continuing connection with ancestral practices that are focused on caring for Country. Bringing the song back into Ngarigu cultural practice has been a very moving experience. Jaky, Linda and Amanda held a meeting online with the Tumbarumba Kunama Namadgi Indigenous Corporation in September 2021, and a further community workshop with the Ngarigo Nation Indigenous Corporation in April 2022.[10] For some in the meetings it was a remembered song, and the experience transported them to a moment when Ngarigu corroboree practice was still a lived experience. One Elder, Uncle John Casey, spoke of having witnessed the song sung by women at a corroboree held to coincide with the drowning of Old Adaminaby for Eucumbene Dam in 1957, during the construction of the Snowy Mountains Hydro-Electric Scheme. Uncle John remembered that the song had been sung at a fast tempo, faster than how Amanda and Jaky first sang it for the meeting. When Linda sang it again at a faster tempo Uncle John commented, "You nailed it", and there was a sense of real joy in the whole group that an Elder had embraced the song. In this way the song can now go forward into renewed practice, a process that was also discussed in that meeting. Ngarigu community members are looking forward to continuing to perform the song on Country in the early autumn, at the time of year when it was heard by Lhotsky so long ago.

The song will not necessarily have an easy path back into community use. In renewing a practice from archival records, the experience will always be one that has different meaning for individuals across a community. A collective sense of identification with a song such as this does not ensure it will have a collective practice for its future performances. Some are concerned that it may only be a song for women, as suggested in its published title "Song of the Women of the Menero Tribe". Others would have it performed as Lhotsky witnessed it, likely men leading the song and accompanying on percussion with women singing as a group.[11] Archival records become contested objects in community politics, open for interpretation and potential dispute. Nevertheless, from the point of view of the Aboriginal researchers and performers in this initial exercise there is great value in revealing archival records and ensuring community members are able to re-engage with and feel a sense of ownership of these hidden artefacts of cultural life that would otherwise remain just ink on paper.

---

9   Verbal and written feedback was provided to Neal Peres Da Costa and Matthew Stephens, including from Annette Lemercier, who stated that including Troy and Barwick's transcription of the song in the program "was a very exciting initiative", Lemercier to Stephens, 27 June 2021.

10   Graeme Skinner and Neal Peres Da Costa supported the April 2022 workshop as part of their collaboration with Jakelin and Amanda on the ARC Discovery Project *Hearing the Music of Early NSW*.

11   Troy and Barwick, "Claiming the 'Song of the Women of the Menero Tribe'".

Embodied research beyond the archive

These efforts to bring the song back into an embodied form through connections to widening circles of community have drawn our attention to a number of themes, many of which are explored later in the book. The first theme highlights how collaborative practices shape our understanding of embodied culture. As the initiators of singing this song, and as Ngarigu women, Jakelin Troy and Lara Troy-O'Leary felt the weight of the task – the difficulty of knowing how to sing something that had gone unsung for so long, that carried with it the possibility that singing it might connect them to countrywomen and ancestors; the discomfort of using their voices in unfamiliar ways, and in an awkward vocal range. Through shared time, experimentation, laughter and collective fumbling attempts, singing this old-made-new song became an increasingly joyful experience, and a less uncomfortable one.

The second theme highlights the way written and archived renderings of ephemeral culture can alter and obscure meaning. Experimenting with the piano version of the Ngarigu song as a collaborative process between a singer (Harris) and a specialist in historical performance of nineteenth-century music (Peres Da Costa), playing a nineteenth-century square piano, confirmed the findings of earlier processes of singing through the Troy–Barwick version. In collaborative learning and performance of the song, previous singers had found the return to a different tonal centre after the C section almost impossible to accurately execute. For Harris and Peres Da Costa, too, singing and playing the piano version confirmed that this decorated final section made most musical sense when it was imagined as a coda after at least one repeat, rather than as a core part of the song. The song's structure in its piano form could be made sense of when brought back into sounding through the piano and through the bodies of the musicians interpreting it, in a way that its rendering on the page eluded.

The third theme concerns the assemblage of cultural objects for exhibition and the contextual layers that are overlaid through this process. The Ngarigu song was assembled in a new form through the meticulous work of Barwick and Troy in drawing together historical documentation, consulting moon records and maps, and applying their knowledge of musicological and linguistic principles to stripping back the overlaid European musical arrangement to its core elements. This work led to a new realisation of the song in the notation published in their 2020 article.[12] In order to be sung, this version had to be brought back into relationship with singers, with Country, and with a community of practice. What that community looks like is a complex story. The singing of a group of women to mark a full moon, to recognise the seasonal change, and to effect an ecological action of bringing snow was one context, the writing down of the song during explorations of the natural environment of alpine Ngarigu Country by a Polish scientist was another. An additional context was the environs of colonial Sydney where the song was notated

---

12 Troy and Barwick, "Claiming the 'Song of the Women of the Menero Tribe'".

and where accompaniment was created by European settler "musical gentlemen". Each context had a different kind of proximity to the cultural object of the song, both in geographical and temporal terms, and also in musical ones. The possibilities for making musical, cultural and artistic sense of this archival record of song then were multi-faceted, and our team's responses have also taken a number of forms. These various contexts could begin to be interrogated only by bringing the song back into relationship with place, with singing and music-making bodies, with the articulation of language words, and with the ears of listeners.

Embodied culture and the archive

The themes that have emerged from re-embodying the Ngarigu song have broader relevance for working with records of cultural practice held in archives. By prioritising embodied expressions of cultural practice, this work has led us to think as much about the *limits* of the archive, as about its *potentialities*. Embodied modes of enquiry repeatedly destabilise the very definition of "archives" and can reimagine different forms in which cultural knowledge can be held and conserved for current and future Indigenous stakeholders. Re-embodying historical performances creates another kind of store of songs, dances and stories that has the potential for long-term continuities and safekeeping, and that points to other ways that cultural heritage records are "archived". Some recent scholarly literature pushes the idea of archives in new directions, imagining archives that are interconnected places and bodies, that are inscribed in the senses, and that can be physically incorporated into creative art practices and take on entirely new forms.

In her chapter in a volume on Indigenous research methods, Māori literary scholar Alice Te Punga Somerville rethinks the forms that archives take in her field of Māori, Pacific and Indigenous writing. Evoking Epeli Hauʻofa's conceptualisation of Oceania as a connected "sea of islands" rather than as disconnected nations in a vast ocean, Te Punga Somerville articulates the forms an archive of Māori "texts" might take in a "sea of archives":

> An archive in my line of work is just as likely to be in a wardrobe, cupboard or meetinghouse; Indigenous texts might be carved, oral, written, sung, woven, danced and so on. Archives are places where things, people and ideas come together.[13]

Te Punga Somerville's reimagining of archives that might exist only in their embodied forms and in their gathering together of people, things and ideas aims

---

13 Epeli Hauʻofa, *We Are the Ocean* (University of Hawaiʻi Press, 2008), 32–33; Alice Te Punga Somerville, "'I Do Still Have a Letter': Our Sea of Archives", in *Sources and Methods in Indigenous Studies*, eds Chris Andersen and Jean M. O'Brien (London: Routledge, 2017), 121.

to foreground the ways that Indigenous people remain connected to their cultural heritage and each other, and to de-emphasise the idea that cultural heritage is scattered and disconnected in its archival housings.

This reinscription of records of culture onto bodies and places is also articulated by Achille Mbembe. Theorising South African archives, Mbembe emphasises the inscription of the archive in the senses. Archival objects are "removed from time and from life" and "have no meaning outside the subjective experience of those individuals who, at a given moment, come to use them".[14] In undigitised archives, the physical object is situated within "a tactile universe because the document can be touched, a visual universe because it can be seen, a cognitive universe because it can be read and decoded".[15]

Returning to Te Punga Somerville's evocation of texts that may also be sung, woven or danced, we are reminded of the ways in which not just text and visual records but also intangible culture can be archived. To add to Mbembe's sensory categories in archives of performance, archival objects can also be located in an auditory universe because they can be heard. But songs that are only heard and not sung undergo a shift in their mode of communication, in their culture keeping and interrelationship. We can listen to a recording of a song, and watch a performance of a dance, but these records remain disembodied unless they are, in turn, sung and danced.

The omission of the auditory from Mbembe's sensory universes is indicative of the nature of archives as primarily visual records of history and culture. Two of the co-authors of this chapter collaborate on a large audiovisual archive that makes sound and moving image available through digitisation and online delivery.[16] But audiovisual archives only partially supplement these lopsided sensory universes, which are made whole only by being reunited with people and their subjective uses of historical records. Te Punga Somerville's sea of archives weaves together the historical records' connected parts in order to restore the whole, or indeed to fashion new wholes. Mbembe and Te Punga Somerville's rethinking of what the archive is, what it does and how meaning is made of it shows that it is only in interaction with the archive that its holdings are rewoven into their stories and histories. No disembodied archive contains a complete record. Many of these visual and textual resources are, after all, the incomplete records of practised culture from societies where stories, histories, lineages and knowledges are passed down from voice to ear, and body to body. The embodiment of the stories builds a collective archive through the act of passing on knowledge from generation to generation.

---

14 Achille Mbembe, "The Power of the Archive and its Limits", in *Refiguring the Archive*, eds Carolyn Hamilton, et al. (Dordrecht: Springer Netherlands, 2002), 22–23.
15 Mbembe, "The Power of the Archive and its Limits", 20.
16 Amanda Harris, Nick Thieberger and Linda Barwick, eds, *Research, Records and Responsibility: Ten Years of PARADISEC* (Sydney: Sydney University Press, 2015).

Several scholars offer new creative responses to material archival records that bring them back into relationship to the body. Narungga poet and scholar Natalie Harkin builds on the practices of her ancestors to create new works of art from historical records, weaving shredded letters from her grandmother and great-grandmother into traditional Ngarrindjeri baskets. Harkin links her weaving of archived letters to the reclamation work of an international community of Indigenous artists:

> Weaving as praxis developed as a central conceptual metaphor and a literal cultural practice: to liberate these letters in ways previously unimagined, to free them from the state and weave them back into the world, into my family and into my body.[17]

This artistic practice not only makes sense of the incomplete, traumatic records of child removal and destruction of family and community relationships, but also interrupts the record keeping of the archive, weaving past, present and future into connection and continuity. It is:

> a new way for me to embody family, history, land and ancestors through these archival records. Here, weaving is a metaphor for family and culture because all things are connected and rely on one another. This practice acknowledges that strength resides in the interweaving of materials where new items can be incorporated and interpreted within stories told by the Old People.[18]

Flipping the perspective of historical cultural records as the starting point for connecting past, present and future cultural practices, Robert Lazarus Lane describes Yolngu cultural custodian Wukun Wanambi's "archival art". Lane explores performance of ceremony and art making in which "the artwork becomes not merely a way to document something but is itself another iteration of that which it is documenting".[19] Describing Wukun Wanambi's ceremonial activity, Lane upends the sequence of ethnographic documentation, arguing that ceremonial practice is already a practice of documentation and preservation:

> anthropologists who could film were of use to Indigenous ceremonial leaders because they provided another means to archive the specific expressions inherent in ceremonial activity. As an exchange process, ceremony's documentary modes and documentary's ceremonial modes served dual interests.[20]

---

17 Natalie Harkin, "Weaving the Colonial Archive: A Basket to Lighten the Load", *Journal of Australian Studies* 44, no. 2 (2020), 157.
18 Harkin, "Weaving the Colonial Archive: A Basket to Lighten the Load", 157–58.
19 Robert Lazarus Lane, "Wukun Wanambi's *Nhina, Nhäma ga Ngäma (Sit, Look, and, Listen)*", in *Indigenous Archives: The Making and Unmaking of Aboriginal Art*, eds Darren Jorgensen and Ian McLean (Crawley: University of Western Australia Press, 2017), 242.
20 Lane, "Wukun Wanambi's *Nhina, Nhäma ga Ngäma (Sit, Look, and, Listen)*", 236.

The idea that ceremonial practices are already modes of archiving culture renders records of these ceremonies mere snapshots of the complex temporal, interpersonal and physical act of documenting culture. Archives make fragments of cultural practice, and artistic practices can again make whole culture out of fragmented archival records through processes of re-embodiment. They also turn "collections" of archival objects into new kinds of assemblages made up of interconnected parts that bring together past, present and future. This re-embodiment has the effect of reconstituting "collections" so that they are no longer defined by their collector (often an individual bound up in processes of colonisation), and instead are re-embedded in community and practice. People's "belongings", collected and exhibited in institutions, are brought back into belonging to communities of cultural practice through music and dance. In this process, assemblages in both archives, and in museums, might usefully be brought into a single frame of reference. Music, dance and archives are then only part of the story, taking in a wide range of performed cultures and of historical records of both material and ephemeral cultures.

Summary of chapters

In the chapters that follow, practitioners and theorists have come up with a range of approaches to understanding archival records of music and dance, and enlivening them through re-embodying and re-embedding them in the communities they came from. The eight chapters have a strong emphasis on collaborative research. These co-authored and sole-authored chapters use the methods of history, ethnomusicology, dance theory, archival studies and creative practice to think through the uses of archival collections in historical and contemporary performances of music and dance by Indigenous people. The collection is strongly located in the Australian continent where the editors and many of the authors reside, with a focus on Aboriginal and Torres Strait Islander practices. This regional focus is complemented by contributions from authors across the globe, with chapters on Māori, Haudenosaunee and Indigenous Taiwanese music and dance. Though each chapter considers records from public and private archives, the living practice of music and dance is also strongly present across all chapters. These embodied performance practices draw on so much more than archives, showing that Country, place, ancestors go far beyond the fragmented records of culture in archival and museum collections.

In Chapter 2, Reuben Brown and Solomon Nangamu consider how archival recordings can sustain current practices of manyardi in Western Arnhem Land. They weave an intricate story of contemporary performances of manyardi, sung by Nangamu and his countrymen, that materialise ancestral practices and conjure connections between historical events, people and Country. They find that although archival recordings are often used to recall old songs and renew their practice, their use does not result in a homogeneity of musical style. And that while old recordings do prompt the singing of songs, singing is also refreshed by the presence of Country, gifting new songs and evoking old ones that can be passed down through subsequent generations.

In Chapter 3, Jack Gray and Jacqueline Shea Murphy's dialogue performs an exchange between dancer and scholar, Māori artist and non-Indigenous observer, colleagues and friends. They explore Gray's choreographic interactions with his ancestral house, Ruatepupuke, now in the Chicago Field Museum. In relating to Gray's wharenui through dance, Gray seeks to engage not just with the physical house, but also with the intangible spaces around it. By bringing living dance practice into dialogue with the ancestral house and its history of removal from an ancestral home into the museum, Gray and Shea Murphy explore the ways this creative work bridges a kinship of both time and space.

In Chapter 4, Genevieve Campbell, Jacinta Tipungwuti, Amanda Harris and Matt Poll look at histories of collecting material culture alongside records of performed culture from the Tiwi Islands. They show how "collections" by museums and archives caused records of culture to be dispersed rather than assembled. Tipungwuti and her countrywomen in the Strong Women's Group are re-assembling those disconnected parts of culture through renaming the material culture and by bringing their live performances back into dialogue with the material parts of cultural practice held in static museum displays.

Chapter 5 also brings performance into the space of museums and galleries. Rosy Simas describes her process of whole-body deep listening that awakens memory and evokes Haudenosaunee ancestors, culture and history. Simas theorises the Native body as an ever-evolving archive of genealogy, history, culture and creation. She details her creative work *We Wait In The Darkness*, a dance performance, gallery installation, and later museum exhibition that awakened collective memories stored in the body, allowing them to be communicated to a live audience. In this way, Simas conceptualises the body as archive for histories of performance.

In Chapter 6, Clint Bracknell describes a creative process of reanimating historical songs sung by the Nyungar ancestor Miago. Bracknell demonstrates the way that Nyungar song revitalisation is dependent on incomplete and fractured archives. Exploring his collaboration with Gina Williams, he offers a template for music revitalisation of endangered song traditions. Their work brings traditional song practice into relationship with contemporary creative practice.

In Chapter 7, Marianne Schultz also looks back at historical performance records, recounting two parallel histories of international performances of Māori music and dance. The two singers, Princess Iwa and Bathie Stuart, and their touring shows between 1910 and 1929 showcased hybrid performance to international audiences. One Māori and the other Pākeha, each singer represented the cultural practices of Aotearoa New Zealand on public stages. Interrogating these histories of performance, Schultz seeks to reimagine the sound and movement missing from static archival records to enliven historical music and dance.

In Chapter 8, Chi-Fang Chao shows how embodied theatrical performances create accounts of Taiwanese Indigenous cultures that provide an alternative interpretation to the archive, constituted by historical Chinese writings and illustrations, Japanese visual records and modern ethnographies. Chao suggests that the productions of the Formosan Aboriginal Song and Dance Troupe preserve cultural memories in a form imbued with all of the possibilities of sound and movement excluded from static archival objects. Through these performances, cultural revitalisation and resistance to archival representation is realised through powerful social action.

In the final chapter, Jodie Kell and Cindy Jinmarabybana analyse new and old interpretations of the "Diyama" song in the Burarra language of Arnhem Land. Kell and Jinmarabybana show that among the multiple varying accounts and stories present in archives and oral histories, contemporary singing continues to construct cultural identity. They suggest that the differing interpretations of the "Diyama" song's history by men and by women continue in contemporary realisations of song performance, and that both musical innovation and continuity of tradition make up the song's story.

References

Barwick, Linda, Sharon Huebner, Lyndon Ormond-Parker and Sally Treloyn. "Reclaiming Archives: guest editorial". *Preservation, Digital Technology & Culture* 50, no. 3–4 (2021): 99–104.

Bracknell, Clint and Kim Scott. "Ever-widening circles: consolidating and enhancing Wirlomin Noongar archival material in the community". In *Archival Returns: Central Australia and Beyond*, eds Linda Barwick, Jennifer Green and Petronella Vaarzon-Morel. LD&C Special Publication 18. Honolulu & Sydney: University of Hawai'i Press and Sydney University Press, 2020: 325–38. http://hdl.handle.net/10125/24890/.

Chung, Laura. "'Winter is Coming': Snow and Strong Surf as Cold Front Moves Across the State". *Sydney Morning Herald*, 15 May 2021. https://bit.ly/3PqH9M3.

Gilchrist, Paul, Claire Holmes, Amelia Lee, Niamh Moore and Neil Ravenscroft. "Co-Designing Non-Hierarchical Community Arts Research: The Collaborative Stories Spiral". *Qualitative Research Journal* 15, no. 4 (2015): 459–71.

Harkin, Natalie. "Weaving the Colonial Archive: A Basket to Lighten the Load". *Journal of Australian Studies* 44, no. 2 (2020): 154–66.

Harris, Amanda, Nick Thieberger and Linda Barwick, eds. *Research, Records and Responsibility: Ten Years of PARADISEC*. Sydney: Sydney University Press, 2015.

Indigenous Archives Collective. "The Indigenous Archives Collective Position Statement on the Right of Reply to Indigenous Knowledges and Information Held in Archives". *Archives and Manuscripts* 49, no. 3 (2021): 244–52, https://doi-org.ezproxy.library.sydney.edu.au/10.1080/01576895.2021.1997609.

Hau'ofa, Epeli. *We Are the Ocean*. University of Hawai'i Press, 2008. https://doi.org/10.1515/9780824865542.

Lane, Robert Lazarus. "Wukun Wanambi's *Nhina, Nhäma ga Ngäma (Sit, Look, and, Listen)*". In *Indigenous Archives: The Making and Unmaking of Aboriginal Art*, eds Darren Jorgensen and Ian McLean. Crawley: University of Western Australia Press, 2017: 227–49.

Lhotsky, John. *A Song of the Women of the Menero Tribe near the Australian Alps. Arranged with the Assistance of Several Musical Gentlemen for the Voice and Pianoforte, Most Humbly Inscribed as the First Specimen of Australian Music to Her Most Gracious Majesty Adelaide, Queen of Great Britain and Hanover*. Sydney: Sold by John Innes, Pitt Street. By commission at R. Ackerman's Repository of Arts, Strand [London], 1834.

Marsden, Beth, Katherine Ellinghaus, Cate O'Neill, Sharon Huebner and Lyndon Ormond-Parker. "Wongatha Heritage Returned: The Digital Future and Community Ownership of Schoolwork from the Mount Margaret Mission School, 1930s–1940s". *Preservation, Digital Technology & Culture* 50, no. 3–4 (2021): 105–15.

McPhee, Sarah. "First Big Cold Snap of Winter: Snow Expected Beyond Alpine Areas". *Sydney Morning Herald*, 7 June 2021. https://bit.ly/3PExiSv.

Mbembe, Achille. "The Power of the Archive and Its Limits". In *Refiguring the Archive*, eds Carolyn Hamilton, Verne Harris, Michèle Pickover, Graeme Reid, Razia Saleh and Jane Taylor. Dordrecht: Springer Netherlands, 2002: 19–27.

Shellam, Tiffany and Joanna Cruickshank. "Critical Archives: An Introduction". *Journal of Colonialism and Colonial History* 20, no. 2 (2019).

Somerville, Alice Te Punga. "'I Do Still Have a Letter': Our Sea of Archives". In *Sources and Methods in Indigenous Studies*, eds Chris Andersen and Jean M. O'Brien. London: Routledge, 2017: 121–27.

Thorpe, Kirsten, Shannon Faulkhead and Lauren Booker. "Transforming the Archive: Returning and Connecting Indigenous Repatriation Records". In *The Routledge Companion to Indigenous Repatriation: Return, Reconcile, Renew*, eds Cressida Fforde, C. Timothy McKeown and Honor Keeler. Abingdon, Oxon: Routledge, 2020: 822–34.

Troy, Jakelin and Linda Barwick. "Claiming the 'Song of the Women of the Menero Tribe'". *Musicology Australia* 42, no. 2 (2020): 85–107.

2

"I'll show you that manyardi": Memory and lived experience in the performance of public ceremony in Western Arnhem Land

Reuben Brown and Solomon Nangamu

Introduction

This chapter examines the role of archival recordings as an aid to revive and maintain song and dance practices and connections to ancestry and Country associated with the living performance tradition manyardi in the region of Western Arnhem Land, Australia. Specifically, it addresses the questions: How do performance traditions such as manyardi from Western Arnhem Land materialise ancestral connections in the present? And how do archival recordings of songs inform and sustain the practice of manyardi and composition of new songs?

In 2012, the co-authors of this chapter, musicologist Reuben Brown and songman Solomon Nangamu, travelled to Warruwi, South Goulburn Island, to make a trip with a group of dancers, singers and didjeridu players (see Figure 2.2). The trip arose from discussions Brown and Nangamu held while working together with Bininj at Gunbalanya (south of Warruwi on the mainland in Arnhem Land) and listening to a collection of archival recordings of manyardi, including Nangamu's Mirrijpu (seagull) songset.[1] As Nangamu puts it, "that song I sing, it's got meaning for all that sacred site around the island – those two islands, south and north".[2] "I follow all that song from my, like my own sacred … thing – sacred site, that's where I sing. I sing about the sea, about mother nature. The sacred site,

---

1 Following previous scholarship of Western Arnhem Land public ceremony, in this chapter we use the term "songset" to describe the named repertoires of songs handed down to songmen. See Reuben Brown, "Following Footsteps: the kun-borrk/manyardi song tradition and its role in Western Arnhem Land society" (PhD thesis, University of Sydney, 2016); Linda Barwick, Bruce Birch and Nicholas Evans, "Iwaidja Jurtbirrk Songs: Bringing Language and Music Together", *Australian Aboriginal Studies*, no. 2 (2007), 6–34.

2 Solomon Nangamu, RB2-20120609RB_v02.mp4 08:39-09:01, https://dx.doi.org/10.26278/FP7X-X254.

Figure 2.1 Warruwi, South Goulburn Island. Photo by Reuben Brown.

the crow that did cut that two islands – split it in half."[3] Nangamu suggested he accompany Brown to his ancestral Country of Goulburn Island, not only to make a recording of manyardi with countrymen there for future generations, but also to show Brown his songs, by going to the sacred site from where the songs emerged and where ancestral spirits reside.

The chapter draws together ideas about the performative power of manyardi. Firstly, through Nangamu's reflections about how the old people composed songs in order to capture the essence of things that sustain them, such as cockle, oyster and fish. Secondly, through the idea in anthropological and musicological literature that elements of the Dreaming can be conjured up in the here and now. In Western Arnhem Land, legacy song recordings are often used as an aid to revive songs for apprentice songmen, where an established arawirr (didjeridu) player and songman with expert knowledge are present to help guide their performance.[4] Brown

---

3   Solomon Nangamu, RB2-20110825-RB_02_edit.wav 26:37–27:06, https://dx.doi.org/10.26278/
     R4FY-AR35.

4   Repatriation or archival recordings is a common methodology in applied ethnomusicology, and
     examples of song and dance revival from Australia and elsewhere abound. For a description of
     the process of return of archival recordings and images to the Kimberley and their use by
     ceremony leaders to revive dormant song and dance repertories of junba, see Sally Treloyn,

compares the melodic sequences of the Marrwakara (M: goanna)[5] and Mirrijpu (M: seagull) songsets performed by the group in 2012 with legacy recordings made by Ronald Berndt of the same songs performed back in the 1960s by male relatives of the singers, analysing how manyardi is connected to the memory of performance events and particular singers, rather than learned from "authoritative" archival recordings. Nangamu demonstrates knowledge of how manyardi is passed on and sustained, with insights about kinship and song inheritance, song conception, vocal style, song text and the ancestral genesis of his own manyardi. Insights by participants assembled for the performance in 2012 at Amartjitpalk also reveal how performing manyardi at Goulburn Island is undertaken to conjure up connections between people, historical events, and ancestors in the Country, making Arrarrkpi and the Country feel alive and happy.

Memories of connection: The wurakak (M: crow) story

Arrarrkpi (M: Indigenous people) tell a story that has been handed down over many generations of a time before Arrarrkpi (M: humans), when the north and south islands were joined as one. Nangamu led a retelling of this story at Amartjitpalk, by way of explaining how his inherited songset named Mirrijpu (M: seagull)[6] came into existence. The mirrijpu was once Arrarrkpi, as were all the other birds that can be found on Goulburn Island. Korroko (K: long ago), during the period of the ancestors, they were spending their time on Weyirra (North Goulburn Island) fishing, when they had unwelcome company in the form of a waak waak/wurakak (K/M: black crow). Here is a version of the story Nangamu recorded prior to our trip:

> Yoh [yes] that mayhmayh, a long time [ago], that seagull he was like human too, like, long time. They used to see crow used to come, just asking around. The black crow, he was a Bininj (K: human) too. They used to tell him "no, you go, don't come here!" He was scratching around for a scrape of tucker. But they didn't even give it

Matthew Dembal Martin and Rona Goonginda Charles, "Moving Songs: Repatriating Audiovisual Recordings of Aboriginal Australian Dance and Song (Kimberley Region, Northwestern Australia)", in *The Oxford Handbook of Musical Repatriation*, eds Frank Gunderson, Robert Lancefield and Bret Woods (New York: Oxford University Press, 2019). See also Bracknell, this volume.

5   Throughout this chapter words in Kunwinjku (K) and Mawng (M) are indicated and English translations are glossed in brackets the first time the word appears in the text. Standard orthographies are used. The authors have chosen to include these words and translations to show how manyardi singers included both words from their first language Mawng and lingua franca Kunwinjku (which their interlocutor Reuben Brown could speak at conversational level). The Mawng term "Arrarrkpi" has a number of senses including "Indigenous", "human" and "male".

6   Mirrijpu in Mawng means both "seagull" in the broader sense and silver gull (*Chroicocephalus novaehollandiae*). Nangamu also identified the species of seagull after which his song is named as the roseate tern (*Sterna dougallii*).

Figure 2.2 The group at Amartjitpalk performing manyardi, Goulburn Island, 2012. From left to right: Brendan Marrgam, Sam Wees, Russell Agalara, Maurice Gawayaku and his son, Micky Yalbarr (didjeridu), Solomon Nangamu, Harold Warrabin. Photo by Reuben Brown.

to him. They said, "nah, we'll give you little rubbish" – bone or whatever. He said "alright", and that island it was only one big island, South Goulburn. So that crow went and got his axe, that big stone axe. Long time. And [he] split that island in two – North and South, but he's in the middle. That's my sacred site. Under the sea – that's the big stone axe inside. In the middle – South Goulburn and North Goulburn, but it's in the middle. You see that reef there – that's him there ... he talks too – at full tide he go "waak!" – you can listen. That one's from Mirrijpu now [that story]. They were too greedy for tucker, they never give him [any], and he told them all, "I'll teach you a lesson, so you'll be sitting separate, island to island." So, he made all of my [Manangkardi-speaking] tribe, all that Mirrijpu.[7]

Nangamu and others in the group including Russell Agalara and Harold Warrabin discussed how Mawng people's djang (K: sacred sites) are located not only on the islands, but also underneath the sea, where the trunk of a large paperbark tree that once stood on the united Goulburn Island fell, after the crow chopped it down.

---

7   Solomon Nangamu, RB2-20120609-RB_v01.mp4 08:46–10:56, https://dx.doi.org/10.26278/ 98XR-A024. For a longer version of the story, see Ruth Singer, "Agreement in Mawng: Productive and Lexicalised Uses of Agreement in an Australian Language" (PhD thesis, The University of Melbourne, 2006), 333.

When the water is calm, a whirlpool forms in between the islands, indicating the presence of the tree still growing at the bottom of the ocean floor:

> RA: They seen that satellite, that yemed [K: thing], leaf growing in the middle of that water, it's growing.
> SN: Underneath.
> RA: Yeah, that tree is still there.
> SN: Maybe it's going to connect those two islands?
> HW: Coming up, yoh growing.
> RA: They saw it with a computer, them scientist mob, they find a tree growing right in the middle.[8]

Linda Barwick observes how the practices of song, dance and visual art that make up Indigenous Australian performance traditions represent "interdependent parts of a complex whole", which are linked together through one's ancestral Country.[9] Understanding of this interconnectedness stems from the knowledge that individual songs, dances and designs drawn in the sand, painted on rock and on the body, were handed down first by creation spirits that shaped the Country, then carried on by ancestors over thousands of generations. For Arrarrkpi and Indigenous people elsewhere in Australia, the act of performing songs and dances that have been handed down expresses links between people and their ancestral Country. Through our reflection and analysis of the event at Amartjitpalk, we suggest that when Arrarrkpi perform manyardi at specific sites of significance on Goulburn Island, they re-activate their memories and regenerate their spiritual connections to ancestral Country.

The "interdependent parts" that made up this performance include: the memory of those people who passed on the songs to the current-day singers and their traditional Country and languages; the ancestral stories that link the Country and the songs together, and the feelings and associations that were conjured up during the performance. We analyse how two musically distinct songsets – Marrwakara/Mularrik (M: goanna/green frog) and Mirrijpu (M: seagull) – linked through Manangkardi traditional Country and language, were paired together in performance, and how this pairing reflects an awareness of "the complex whole".

---

8   Solomon Nangamu, Russell Agalara and Harold Warrabin, RB2-20121103-RB_01_edit.wav 16:20–16:47, https://dx.doi.org/10.26278/6C8F-4737. The research referenced is unknown to the authors.
9   Linda Barwick, "Song as an Indigenous Art", in *The Oxford Companion to Aboriginal Art and Culture*, eds Sylvia Kleinert and Margo Neale (South Melbourne, Australia: Oxford University Press, 2000), 328.

Regenerating ancestral connections by performing manyardi

> Any living thing they was eating, like kobah-kohbanj [K: old people], like korroko
> [K: a long time ago] – oyster, cockle, anything that lived in that sea – seafood,
> people who lived on this island, long time. They said, "ah, we can't just go eat food?
> How 'bout we make song about this tucker? Bush tucker." So, they made all this
> song now, that we're singing now. They talk about land, they talk about the seaside,
> any living creature that God made, and kobah-kohbanj they got that thing, and
> they passed it to me, and I try and pass it to my new generation …[10] (Nangamu)

Nangamu's explanation as to how it was that his manyardi came about – offered
during a discussion over lunch while the group took a break from singing and
dancing at Amartjitpalk – suggests that kobah-kohbanj were keeping alive the very
things that they treasured and that sustained them by putting them into a song. As
Nangamu suggests, "they got that *thing*" – that inspiration or life-force that has its
origins in the Dreaming – and fashioned it in musical form, and then they passed
it on so that it could continue to be nurtured. Nangamu alludes to the richness of
the manyardi tradition and the many named songsets that have been performed by
various songmen over the generations, all of which pay homage to various "living
creatures" of Western Arnhem Land. His reference to God as creator reveals the
way in which the Methodists' teachings of Christianity have been incorporated into
Arrarrkpi people's spiritual beliefs and understandings about the Dreaming.

Nangamu's insights also resonate with the observations on the performative
nature of the Dreaming by scholars such as Ronald Berndt, Fred Myers and
William Stanner. Stanner argued that stories from the Dreaming do not provide a
literal meaning, nor a definition or truth, but rather a "poetic key to Reality" or a
"key of Truth":[11]

> The active philosophy of Aboriginal life transforms this "key", which is expressed
> in the idiom of poetry, drama and symbolism, into a principle that the Dreaming
> determines not only what life is but also what it can be. Life, so to speak, is a
> one-possibility thing, and what this is, is the "meaning" of the Dreaming.[12]

The Dreaming which shaped the Country that people inhabit, and to which people
are linked through their ancestors who had lived on that Country since time
immemorial, manifests itself in the here and now in various forms. Living
phenomena such as birds (a crow or seagull) and the sea (the appearance of a
whirlpool) are interpreted as manifestations of the ongoing presence and power

---

10   Solomon Nangamu, RB2-20121103-RB_02_edit.wav 42:52–44:24, https://dx.doi.org/10.26278/
     TSRV-YY61.
11   William Edward Hanley Stanner, "The Dreaming", in *The Dreaming and Other Essays*
     (Collingwood, Victoria: Black Inc. Agenda, 1953), 61–62.
12   Stanner, "The Dreaming".

of the Dreaming. Songs, dances and ceremony passed on from ancestral spirits that still dwell in the Country of Western Arnhem Land such as mimih (K: stone Country spirits) or warra ngurrijakurr (M: mangrove-dwelling spirits or "little people") – are thought to "follow up the Dreaming", and re-enact its presence.[13] Fred Myers argues that it is precisely through the activities performed in the *present* that gives meaning to the Dreaming, and enables Aboriginal people to "hold" their particular ancestral Country:

> The meaning of these places, their value, must be understood as constructed – not by the application of some pure cultural model to blank nature … but in activities that constitute relationships within a system of social life that structures difference and similarity among persons.[14]

Ronald Berndt argues that artists (i.e. songmen such as Nangamu) play a vital role in this interpretation of the Dreaming, as re-activators of the spirits, "reviving the spiritual" through the paintings, songs, dance, carvings etc. that they create.[15] Berndt suggests that through metaphoric and symbolic meaning, Western Arnhem Land songs "guide us toward an intellectual appreciation of the world about us".[16] Discussing Marrwakara/Mularrik songs which are the focus of this chapter, he contends that by anthropomorphising natural species in song – investing them with "human characteristics" – Arrarrkpi perceive these animals not just as food, but understand their place within a broader ecology.[17]

Archival recordings of manyardi

The performance and recording of Marrwakara/Mularrik and Mirrijpu songs by the group at Amartjitpalk with Brown in 2012 followed a historical precedent. For many years, Arrarrkpi songmen have hosted and performed manyardi for other musicologists, linguists and anthropologists from outside their community. Many of the songmen recorded by Colin Simpson with the American-Australian Scientific Expedition to Arnhem Land at Oenpelli/Gunbalanya in 1948 were Arrarrkpi from Goulburn Island.[18] In 1961 and 1964, anthropologists Ronald and Catherine Berndt

---

13   Stanner, "The Dreaming".
14   Fred Myers, "Ways of Place-Making", *La Ricerca Folklorica* 45 (2002), 106.
15   Ronald Berndt, ed, *Australian Aboriginal Art* (Sydney: Ure Smith, 1964), 24.
16   Ronald Berndt, "Other Creatures in Human Guise and Vice Versa: A Dilemma in Understanding", in *Songs of Aboriginal Australia*, eds Margaret Clunies Ross, Tamsin Donaldson and Stephen Aubrey Wild (Sydney: University of Sydney, 1987), 189.
17   Berndt, "Other Creatures in Human Guise and Vice Versa: A Dilemma in Understanding".
18   This included Nakangila Tommy Madjalkaidj (senior), a Mawng speaker who came from the Mandjurngudj clan, who plays didjeridu on "cut 7" of the Simpson recordings at Oenpelli/Gunbalanya and Nabulanj Namunurr from North Goulburn Island, who sings on "cut 1". For further discussion, see Brown, "Following Footsteps", 246–50.

recorded Harold Warrabin's father – Joseph Gamulgiri (see Table 2.1) – performing songs from the Marrwakara/Mularrik songset with songman John Guwadbu[19] "No. 2" at Warruwi. Gamulgiri, who was also the brother of Nangamu's father,[20] was one of many Arrarrkpi who assisted Berndt with his research, from the time of Berndt's first visit to the island in 1947.[21] To complete this intergenerational picture, Phillip Magulnir[22] – the brother of John Guwadbu and father of current manyardi didjeridu player Alfred Gawaraidji – also played didjeridu for Guwadbu, Gamulgiri and others during this time.[23] As Nangamu explained:

> old man John, and his brother that Alfred [Gawaraidji], his father – old Philip Magulnir – he was didj man, he was number one, he played different kind of manyardi like for them, that old fella. That's why you see Alfred he go play didjeridu anywhere![24]

Another songman – Nanguluminy[25] – was also recorded singing Marrwakara by Sandra Le Brun Holmes in 1964.

In his 1987 article, Ronald Berndt transcribes the Marrwakara/Mularrik songs he recorded with Gamulgiri and Guwadbu, and sets out a narrative that explains the songs, based on interviews with the singers elicited after the recording.[26] In 2006–7, Linda Barwick and Isabel O'Keeffe made a series of recordings of Warrabin and Nangamu singing two Marrwakara/Mularrik songs and Mirrijpusongs at Warruwi, including didjeridu accompaniment by Micky Yalbarr, Alfred Gawaraidji and Nangamu (see Table 2.1).[27] Based on discussions with contemporary consultants, Linda Barwick, Isabel O'Keeffe and Ruth Singer examine the "dilemmas of interpretation" in Berndt's original transcriptions (most of which were remarkably accurate) and his narrative for the Marrwakara/Mularrik songset, and transliterate Berndt's transcriptions into Mawng orthography.[28] In July 2012, some months prior

---

19   Sometimes spelled "Gwadbu".
20   Solomon Nangamu, RB2-20120729-RB_09_edit.wav, 09:57.850–10:12.950, https://dx.doi.org/ 10.26278/QDQH-P258.
21   In January 1948, a year after his visit to Goulburn Island, Ronald Berndt wrote to the superintendent at Warruwi, Reverend Alf Ellison, requesting portraits of a number of Mawng men and women with whom he had collaborated, including "Gamulgiri", to incorporate in his 1951 publication. Ronald Berndt, Letter to Alf Ellison, 15 January 1948, Item 4.3.6. NTRS 38, Location 142/2/4, Northern Territory Archives.
22   Spelled elsewhere as "Mankowirr".
23   Solomon Nangamu and Harold Warrabin, RB2-20121103-RB_01_edit.wav, 07:23–07:48, https://dx.doi.org/10.26278/6C8F-4737.
24   Solomon Nangamu and Harold Warrabin, RB2-20121103-RB_01_edit.wav, 07:23–07:48, https://dx.doi.org/10.26278/6C8F-4737.
25   Spelled elsewhere as "Nanguluminj" and "Nangolmin".
26   Berndt, "Other Creatures in Human Guise".
27   For further details of Marrwakara and Mirrijpu recordings made by Berndt, Barwick, O'Keeffe and others referenced in Table 2.1, see Appendix 1.2. in Brown, "Following Footsteps".
28   See Linda Barwick, Isabel O'Keeffe and Ruth Singer, "Dilemmas in Interpretation: Contemporary Perspectives on Berndt's Goulburn Island Song Documentation", in *Little*

Figure 2.3 Photo of Joseph Gamulgiri (left) and his son Harold Warrabin (right). Photo of Gamulgiri held by Martpalk Arts and Crafts (original photographer and date unknown); photo of Harold Warrabin by Martin Thomas, 2012.

to the recording at Amartjitpalk, Nangamu and Gawaraidji also made a recording with Brown of Warrabin singing at Gunbalanya (2012d in Table 2.1). The presence of Nangamu, Gawaraidji and Brown as recordist (a student of previous recordist Barwick) once again provided the singers with an opportunity to revisit the songs and regenerate their memories of their fathers who taught them the songs when they were growing up.

Manyardi and memory

The performance of manyardi relies on a select group of expert musicians who are familiar with one another's repertories. Performing engages the collective memory, and part of the joy of performing is allowing the songs to evoke memories of people and Country, including memories of previous occasions when the musicians came together to perform the songs. On both occasions at Gunbalanya and Amartjitpalk in 2012, Nangamu practised the songs with Warrabin first to help him remember the songs. As the songmen were remembering how the tune went, Nangamu

---

Paintings, Big Stories: Gossip Songs of Western Arnhem Land, ed. John Stanton (Nedlands: University of Western Australia, Berndt Museum of Anthropology, 2013).

Year	Songset(s)	Songs	Recordist	Performers
1961 1964	Marrwakara/ Mularrik	12	Berndt	John Guwadbu ("No. 2") Joseph Gamulgiri Phillip Magulnir
1965	Marrwakara	1	Le Brun- Holmes	Nungolomin [Nanguluminy], didjeridu player unknown
2006a 2006b 2006c	Mirrijpu	4 5 4	O'Keeffe Barwick O'Keeffe	Solomon Ganawa, Johnny Namarruda (didj) Micky Yalbarr (didj), William Mulumbuk (didj) Alfred Gawaraidji (didj)
2006d	Marrwakara/ Mularrik and Mirrijpu	2,7	O'Keeffe	Harold Warrabin Solomon Nangamu Mickey Yalbarr (didj)
2007	Mirrijpu	8	Barwick	Solomon Nangamu Micky Yalbarr (didj) Henry Guwiyul (didj)
2011a 2011b	Mirrijpu	4 4	Brown	Solomon Nangamu, Russell Agalara (2011a) Alfred Gawaraidji (didj)
2012a 2012b 2012c	Mirrijpu	7 13 2	Brown	Solomon Nangamu, Russell Agalara Harold Warrabin Alfred Gawaraidji (didj)
2012d 2012e	Marrwakara/ Mularrik and Mirrijpu	2 2,7	Brown	Solomon Nangamu, Russell Agalara Harold Warrabin, Maurice Gawayaku, Micky Yalbarr (didj), Alfred Gawaraidji (didj)

Table 2.1 Summary of recordings of Marrwakara/Mularrik (M: goanna/green frog) and Mirrijpu (M: seagull) at Goulburn Island and Gunbalanya.

announced that he would "change" his voice, to sound like the old men who used to sing the song (Guwadbu No. 2 and Gamulgiri).[29] He sang with a soft legato-like quality, imitating Guwadbu's voice on Berndt's recording, which features on the cassette *Songs of Aboriginal Australia* that accompanies an edited volume of the same name.[30] Warrabin's voice, by contrast, has a rougher, more strained timbre, perhaps following the vocal style of his father ("second singer" Gamulgiri).[31]

In preparation for the performance at Amartjitpalk, Nangamu and Warrabin requested that Brown burn them a copy of Berndt's recordings of Guwadbu and Gamulgiri singing Marrwakara/Mularrik, so that they could listen to the old people, and refresh their memory of the songs.[32] Interestingly, these recordings are by no means identical to contemporary versions performed by Warrabin: the former includes a number of Marrwakara/Mularrik songs that Warrabin no longer sings.[33] Warrabin's current repertory consists of two songs: MK01 – which can be performed on its own – and MK02, which is sometimes joined on (i.e. the didjeridu accompaniment continues uninterrupted) to song MK01 as one song item. While MK01 remains relatively true to the Berndt recording, there are several differences in contemporary versions of MK02, including subtle variations in the melody and the way that the song text (Figure 2.4) is pieced together. The three different recorded versions of MK02 are transcribed in Figure 2.5, Figure 2.6 and Figure 2.7 (listen to SAA-B-06-MK02.mp3, 20061013IB02-05-MK02.mp3 and RB2-20121103-RB_01_03_MK01_MK02.wav).[34]

---

29 RB2-20121103-RB_02_12_MK01_practice.wav. https://dx.doi.org/10.26278/2Q12-MW41.
30 Margaret Clunies Ross, Tamsin Donaldson and Stephen Aubrey Wild, eds, *Songs of Aboriginal Australia* (Sydney: University of Sydney, 1987).
31 Western Arnhem Land songmen often make the distinction between the current composer and "main" singer of a songset who directs the performance in ceremony ("number one" singer) and other male relatives/singers who are considered apprentices to the main singer (the "second" singer/s).
32 For details, see recording sessions 19610301MK and 19640224MK detailed in Appendix 1.2. of Brown, "Following Footsteps".
33 It is not uncommon for certain songs to be left out of a songset over the passage of time; sometimes entire songsets are no longer performed when the main songman passes away and male relatives cannot or do not wish to carry on singing the songs. For example, the wardde-ken songset Kurri (blue-tongue lizard) was performed as part of an elicited recording in 2006 by Simon Bidari for recordist Isabel O'Keeffe, but was no longer being performed during Brown's fieldwork at Gunbalanya during the period of 2011–15.
34 For the music transcription analysis Brown referred to the following recordings: SAA-B-06-MK02 (1964) in Stephen Wild (1990). Songs of Aboriginal Australia [audio cassette] Canberra: Australian Institute of Aboriginal and Torres Strait Islander Studies, AIAS 17; 20061013IB01-04-MK02, 20061013IB01-05-MK02, 20061013IB02-04-MK02, 20061013IB02-05-MK02 (2006) in Linda Barwick, Allan Marett, Nicholas Evans, Murray Garde, Isabel O'Keeffe and Bruce Birch (2012). Western Arnhem Land Song Project data collection. The University of Sydney. http://elar.soas.ac.uk/deposit/arnhemland-135103; RB2-20121103-RB_01_03-MK01_MK02.wav, https://dx.doi.org/10.26278/G9SR-AX36; RB2-20121103-RB_02_07_MK01_MK02.wav (2012), https://dx.doi.org/10.26278/ABMD-3N38. In 2006, the singers "practise" the song for the first two recordings, as Nangamu helps Warrabin to sketch out the melodic contour. The melody then takes shape in the third and fourth recordings of the song, which forms the basis of the 2006 transcription. See Appendix 1.1

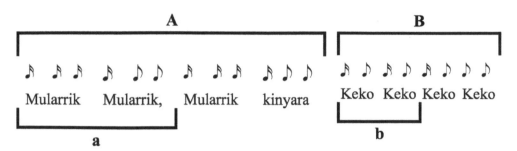

Figure 2.4 Song text of MK02.

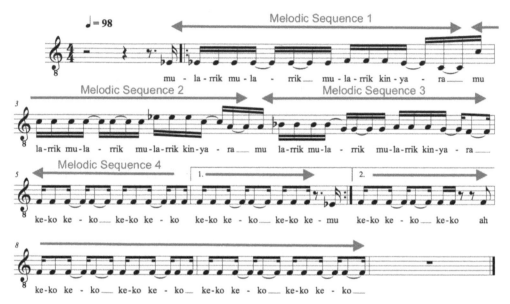

Figure 2.5 Music transcription of vocal part of MK02, performed by John Guwadbu "No. 2" and Joseph Gamulgiri in 1964 SAA-B-06-MK02.mp3. (Recorded by Ronald Berndt in 1964. Transcribed by Reuben Brown, based on rhythmic transcription by Isabel O'Keeffe.)

Stable and adapted aspects of manyardi

A comparison of recordings of MK02 performed by Guwadbu and Gamulgiri in 1964 with versions performed by Warrabin and Nangamu in 2006 and in 2012 reveals the extent to which aspects of a song are adapted while others remain stable over time, as it is passed on to different songmen (see Table 2.2). While the basic song text and melodic contour remain stable, aspects such as the text configuration, tempo and melody vary, and have been adapted or reinterpreted

and Appendix 1.2 of Brown, "Following Footsteps" for further details of these recording sessions. Thanks to Linda Barwick who assisted with the analysis in Table 2.2.

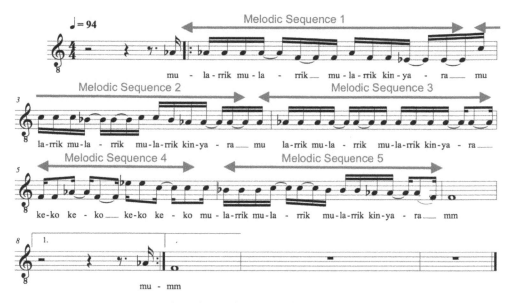

Figure 2.6 Music transcription of vocal part of MK02, performed by Harold Warrabin and Solomon Nangamu in 2006, transposed down a major 2nd from G to F (20061013IB02-05-MK02.mp3). (Recorded by Isabel O'Keeffe in 2006 20061013IB02-05-MK02 in Linda Barwick, Allan Marett, Nicholas Evans, Murray Garde, Isabel O'Keeffe, and Bruce Birch (2012). Western Arnhem Land Song Project data collection. The University of Sydney. http://elar.soas.ac.uk/deposit/arnhemland-135103).

over time. The main difference between Guwadbu's and Warrabin's versions relates to the melodic contour and melodic mode. Whereas Melodic Sequence 1 (MS1) in the 1964 version begins on a flattened 7th degree of the scale, the 2006 and 2012 versions start on a flattened 3rd degree of the scale, followed by an ascending Dorian sequence. The song text is also realised differently in all three versions, in particular Text Phrase B (the vocables: "keko keko, keko keko" – which imitate the sound of the mularrik [M: frog]). In the 1964 version Gamulgiri repeats Text Phrase A three times, followed by two repeats of the vocables (BB) and three repeats in the final version (BBB), sung on the 1st scale degree. In the 2006 version (AAAbA) the vocables are sung to a rising and falling melodic contour – MS4 (based on MS1 in the 1964 version) – and joined with Text Phrase A – MS5 (based on MS3 in the 1964 version). The 2012 version follows the 2006 version, but adds another section of song text A (truncated) at the end (AAabAa). Finally, whereas the 1964 version remains on the 1st degree of the scale during the vocables (B) section, the contemporary versions sing the vocables to a different melodic sequence (MS4) $1-3^b-1-7-5$, which also features in song MK01 (see Figure 2.11).

There are a number of possibilities that may explain the above variations: Warrabin's 2006 and 2012 versions of MK02 may well be based on his understanding of song MK01, which shares the same melodic sequence. It is also possible that the contemporary version of MK02 is based on a version/versions

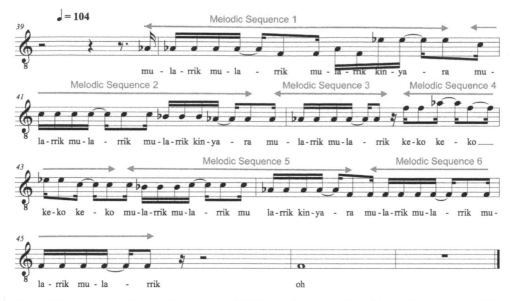

♩ = 104

mu - la - rrik mu - la - rrik mu - la - rrik kin - ya - ra mu -

la - rrik mu - la - rrik mu - la - rrik kin - ya - ra mu - la - rrik mu - la - rrik ke - ko ke - ko___

ke - ko ke - ko mu - la - rrik mu - la - rrik mu la - rrik kin - ya - ra mu - la - rrik mu - la - rrik mu-

la - rrik mu - la - rrik oh

Figure 2.7 Music transcription of vocal part of MK02, performed by Warrabin and Nangamu in 2012 (RB2-20121103-RB_01_03_MK01_MK02.wav). (Recorded by Reuben Brown in 2012, https://bit.ly/3AxjrYl.)

1964 SAA-B-06-MK02	MS1	MS2	MS3	MS4 (1.)	MS4 (2.)	
	7^b-1-7^b-5	5-7^b-5-3	4-2-3-2-1	1_____	1_____	
	A	**A**	**A**	**BB**	**BBB**	
2006 200610131B02-05 -MK02	MS1	MS2	MS3	MS4	MS5	
	3^b-1-3^b-1-7^b	5-4-5-4-3^b	3^b_____	1-3^b-1-7-5	4-5-4-3^b-1	
	A	**A**	**A**	**b**	**A**	
2012 RB2-20121103RB _01_03_MK01_MK02	MS1	MS2	MS3	MS4	MS5	MS6
	3^b-1-3^b-1-7^b	5-4-3^b	3^b_____	1-3^b-1-7-5	5-4-3^b-1	1_____
	A	**A**	**a**	**b**	**A**	**a**

Table 2.2 Comparison of the three recordings of MK02. Table shows Melodic Sequence (MS) number, scale degrees of the melodic sequence and corresponding Text Phrase (A, a, B, b, etc.).

of the song sung by Gamulgiri (rather than Guwadbu) that were not recorded by Berndt. In any event, the variations demonstrate that kun-borrk/manyardi songmen take a creative approach to song identity. In spite of the availability of older recordings in this instance, and their usefulness as an aid to manyardi performance – the song is ultimately held in the memory of the current songman, who inherits it and makes it his own through constant *re*interpretation in performance.

Vocal quality and realisation of song text

Returning to Nangamu's imitation of Guwadbu's voice in 2012, it appears this was not a one-off, but rather a convention observed of kun-borrk/manyardi and some wangga repertories, to imitate or retain the vocal timbre and style of the songman who composed the songs in the songset.[35] This fits with the degree of agency that singers attribute to past songmen, who continue to give them new compositions in their dreams. The imitation of voices ensures that even once the main songman dies, those who were familiar with his voice would still hear the spirit of the songman singing through the current singer/composer.[36] At the same time, the more frequently that current songmen sing songs from their repertory, and the more widely they perform their songs, the more they are likely to establish themselves as the "number one" singer of that songset and newly conceived songs, which may deviate slightly in vocal style and timbre or in the realisation of the melody and tempo, compared with previous versions performed by former songmen.

This is the case with the Mirrijpu songset, which was led by Nangamu's brother, Solomon Ganawa, until 2006 when he passed away, not long after Isabel O'Keeffe and Linda Barwick recorded Ganawa singing at Warruwi. After a period of one year in which the songs were not performed, Nangamu took over as the "number one" songman and has been a prolific performer of the songset, recording Mirrijpu on nine separate occasions, each time performing a variety of songs, including new songs he has since received in his dreams. As a result, Nangamu's recordings of Mirrijpu and his style of singing are now very well known in Western Arnhem Land, particularly among Bininj/Arrarrkpi living at Gunbalanya and Goulburn Island. Comparing recordings made by Nangamu in 2007 – the first time the songset was performed after the death of Ganawa – with recordings made by Ganawa in 2006, one hears minimal variation in tempo, and a similar realisation of the melody. For recordings of Nangamu made some years later in 2011 and 2012, however, notable differences can be observed in tempi (Nangamu's preferred tempo is slightly faster),[37] melody (Nangamu's realisation of the melody is more

---

35 O'Keeffe comments that Kun-barlang, Mawng and Kunwinjku people identify Kaddikkaddik songs in archival recordings "by recognizing the timbre of the voice of the Kaddikkaddik songman Frank 'Kaddikkaddik' Namarnangmarnang". Isabel O'Keeffe, "Kaddikkaddik Ka-wokdjanganj 'Kaddikkaddik Spoke': Language and Music of the Kun-Barlang Kaddikkaddik Songs from Western Arnhem Land", *Australian Journal of Linguistics* 30, no. 1 (2010), 59. Of course, this convention is not culturally unique to Western Arnhem Land.

36 For a detailed discussion of the significance of imitating the voice quality of earlier, often deceased singers in wangga repertories, see Allan Marett, *Songs, Dreamings, and Ghosts: The Wangga of North Australia* (Middletown, Connecticut: Wesleyan University Press, 2005); Allan Marett, "Ghostly Voices: Some Observations on Song-Creation, Ceremony and Being in North Western Australia", *Oceania* 71, no. 1 (2000), 24; Allan Marett, Linda Barwick and Lysbeth Ford, *For the Sake of a Song: Wangga Songmen and Their Repertories* (Sydney: Sydney University Press, 2013), 56.

37 Whereas Ganawa's preferred tempo for moderate rhythmic mode songs is 105–109 bpm, Nangamu's is 105–131 bpm. See Appendix 3 in Brown, "Following Footsteps".

Mirrijpu/yalarrkuku songset (seagull)
20060613IB-06-MP03_MP04
Transposed up maj 2nd

MP04

Sung by Solomon Ganawa
Transcribed by Reuben Brown

Nigi (M: mother song)

Figure 2.8 Music transcription of vocal melody of MP04 (nigi), performed by Solomon Ganawa in 2006, transposed up major 2nd from 20060613IB-06-MP03_MP04 in Linda Barwick, Allan Marett, Nicholas Evans, Murray Garde, Isabel O'Keeffe and Bruce Birch (2012) Western Arnhem Land Song Project data collection. The University of Sydney. http://elar.soas.ac.uk/deposit/arnhemland-135103. (Brown's musical transcriptions here and elsewhere in the chapter were based on listening to the recordings.)

embellished compared with Ganawa's) and vocal style (while Ganawa slides into the notes, Nangamu pitches the notes more precisely). A comparison of the Mirrijpu nigi "mother song" performed by Ganawa in 2006 (Figure 2.8) with a version performed by Nangamu in 2011 (Figure 2.9) neatly illustrates these differences. Nangamu's tempo (87 bpm) is faster than Ganawa's (73 bpm) and there are added notes in Nangamu's melody (highlighted in box outlines) compared with Ganawa's. In measure 9, where Ganawa slides from A to F while singing the vocables, Nangamu instead pitches the note F precisely; his realisation of the song text and vocables is also slightly different ("latpa" rather than "latma"; "o" rather than "e"; extra syllable "inyalat" rather than "yalat", etc.).

The conservatism of melodic contour from one generation to the next accords with observations in the literature about North-East Arnhem Land manikay. Peter Toner, analysing the correlation between melody and social structure and the way in which singers articulate connections to Country through their choice of melody in performance, observes that:

Figure 2.9 Music transcription of Solomon Nangamu's version of
MP04nigi (RB2-20110719-RB_04_06_MP19_MP04.wav, https://dx.doi.org/10.26278/KXKQ-X317).

> Yolngu singers use melody as a key means of constructing their identities as the
> outcome of the interaction of their social theory and social practice. Dhalwangu
> singers go into ritual musical performances with a diverse set of ideas about what
> it is to be Dhalwangu. These ideas, different (but probably overlapping) for every
> Dhalwangu person, are based on what an individual knows about cosmology,
> land tenure, genealogy – traditional grist for the anthropological mill – but also
> idiosyncratic personal and family histories, friendships, the events of everyday life
> and what they remember about previous ceremonies and musical performances.[38]

Many kun-borrk/manyardi repertories, such as Mirrijpu, Inyjalarrku and
Karrbarda, have been passed down to several male relatives of the same generation.
As discussed earlier, certain versions of a song remain associated with previous
songmen even after these songmen pass away, particularly the versions that were
conceived by those individuals. Figure 2.10 shows inheritance of the Mirrijpu
songset across four generations, from Tom Namagarainmag to his sons Michael
Nawudba, Solomon Ganawa and Solomon Nangamu, and from Nawudba to his
daughter, Mary, to her son, Russell Agalara (thus, inheritance is not strictly
patrilineal). Agalara is the "second singer" for the Mirrijpu songset, in the sense
that he is still apprenticing Nangamu, but he has already commenced leading the
ceremony in Nangamu's absence. Agalara learned the songs from his mother's

---

38   Peter Toner, "Melody and the Musical Articulation of Yolngu Identities", *Yearbook for
     Traditional Music* 35 (2003), 89, https://doi.org/10.2307/4149322.

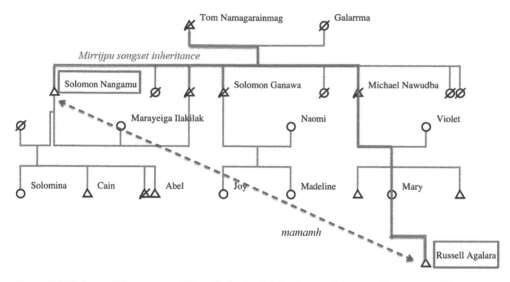

Figure 2.10 Solomon Nangamu and Russell Agalara's inheritance of the Mirrijpu songset. Figure represents song inheritance with black line, while dotted line shows mamamh relationship between Nangamu and Agalara. Names used with permission.

father, Michael Nawudba (Nangamu's older brother, now deceased), and recalls sitting with Nawudba as a toddler and listening to the songs. This means that although Agalara is younger than Nangamu, he is still familiar with the "old" songs from the repertory that Nawudba used to sing, and his interpretation of those songs is influenced by his memory of Nawudba's singing style and performance. Agalara and Nangamu call each other mamamh, which is a reciprocal kinship term for one's mother's (classificatory) father or mother's father's sister and conversely, one's daughter's daughter or daughter's son. (In the kinship system of Western Arnhem Land, one's father's brothers are all considered "father", and one's mother's sisters considered "mother".) Nangamu and Agalara therefore also refer to one another using the English terms "grandson" and "granddad".

Manyardi and Country

The juxtaposition of Mirrijpu and Marrwakara/Mularrik songs in the performance at Amartjitpalk brought up connections not only with people in living memory (i.e. Gamulgiri, Guwadbu) but also with Country and ancestors. After the group warmed up, Nangamu began blowing a slower-tempo rhythm on the didjeridu and Agalara led the singing of a Mirrijpu song with Warrabin and Yalbarr backing. They repeated the song three times, finding a meeting point with one another's voices. When this song had finished, Nangamu asked us if we had heard that "sweet sound", and the other musicians nodded in agreement. It was as though the sound that came out of their mouths, blended with the arawirr (M: didjeridu) and the nganangka (M: clapsticks), was not entirely of their making, but a part of the environment around them, which was also making the music and responding to their performance. Later on, while listening back over the recording, Nangamu commented that he felt "nice and good" to sing, as though a "whole orchestra" were backing him up.[39] At another stage of the performance after the men had got up to dance, Yalbarr remarked that the waves had swelled, to which Nangamu responded: "kunak-apa hapi kangmin … (the land/Country is happy …)" and Marrgam added, "eh hapi kangmin (yes it's happy) – on the right track!"[40]

After playing the didjeridu for the first Mirrijpu song, Micky Yalbarr pointed across the sea to North Goulburn Island, and told us that the song reminded him of a hunting area where he would go fishing and catch "trevally, skinny fish, any kind".[41] Nangamu then explained that both the Marrwakara and Mirrijpu song texts refer to this place, which belongs to the Country of Manangkardi-speaking people of the Majakurdu clan:

> Any song [with] "Inyalatpa" … that's one for us, like all the manyardi – "Linya" too … Same like Marrwakara [songset], "Linya". And Mirrijpu [songset] too, we go same, "Linya" … That's kunred (K: Country/home) – "Linya".[42]

> It's in … Marrwakara, it's in Mirrijpu – in Yalarrkuku – Milyarryarr and Manbam [songsets] – one. We talk about that one kunred (K: home).[43]

Nangamu explained that Linya is the "short name" for the place name "Parlalinya" – a Dreaming site on Weyirra associated with the lightning ancestral spirit called Namarrkon in Kunwinjku, who today assumes the form of a grasshopper. Place names such as these are significant because they are the same both in the spoken language (of Madjukurdu clan Manangkardi speakers who lived on Weyirra) and the spirit language (originally named by the spirit ancestors). As Nangamu explained to Brown: "we can record it, but the word [in the song] is like spiritual language, from the dead people to us then we pass it to a new generation and it goes on and on".[44]

---

39 Solomon Nangamu, conversation with the author. See recording session https://dx.doi.org/10.26278/E1CZ-4E20.

40 Brendan Marrgam, Solomon Nangamu and Micky Yalbarr, RB2-20121103-RB_03_edit_01.wav, 00:24:49–00:25:44, https://dx.doi.org/10.26278/64HC-GZ26.

41 Micky Yalbarr, RB2-20121103-RB_01_edit.wav, 11:04, https://dx.doi.org/10.26278/6C8F-4737.

42 Solomon Nangamu, RB2-20121103-RB_02_edit.wav 36:40–37:14, https://dx.doi.org/10.26278/93HZ-H861. It was not clear from our discussion whether "Inyalatpa" is a specific place name in Manangkardi, or a Manangkardi term for "home/county", which Nangamu suggests through his translation using the Kunwinjku word kunred. "Inyalatpa" also resembles another Mawng place name "Inyalatparo" on South Goulburn Island.

43 Solomon Nangamu, RB2-20121104-RB_01_XX_edit.wav, 00:05:20–00:05:30, https://dx.doi.org/10.26278/1TQK-Z450.

44 Solomon Nangamu, RB2-20110825-RB_02_edit.wav 28:37–29:00, https://dx.doi.org/10.26278/R4FY-AR35.

The singers also explained that the Marrwakara/Mularrik songs (MK01 and MK02) "go together" because the goanna Dreaming and the green frog Dreaming are connected by Mularrik Mularrik Creek on Goulburn Island, which runs through the town of Warruwi.[45] The pair of songs is contrasting in tempo and rhythmic mode (listen to RB2-20121103-RB_01_03_MK01_MK02.wav, where MK02 begins at 01:10).[46] The songs are also contrasting in the way they mix languages: MK01 is in Manangkardi spirit language and has the Manangkardi place name Parlalinya; MK02 is in Mawng and has the song text: "mularrik mularrik, mularrik, mularrik k-i[ny-a]ja-ka" [sung as kinyara], translated as "Frog, she keeps calling out". (See Figure 2.11.)[47]

Conclusion

The performance, discussion and insights from manyardi songmen and dancers at Amartjitpalk illustrate that to perform kun-borrk/manyardi is not merely to sing songs, but also to make connections to recent, historical and ancestral events, significant places, previous songmen etc., and to sustain these connections by involving everyone in the performance. Experienced and expert songmen such as Solomon Nangamu play an important role in leading the performance of kun-borrk/manyardi, and yet the success of the performance relies on the equal participation of members of the group, rather than the efforts of any one individual.

Perhaps contrary to expectations, the existence of older recordings of both the Mirrijpu and Marrwakara songsets has not resulted in a homogeneity of vocal or musical style in the performance of these songsets, based around the qualities of one songman. Rather, current songmen look to old recordings to assist their

---

45 Solomon Nangamu and Harold Warrabin, RB2-20121103-RB_02_edit.wav, 26:10, https://dx.doi.org/10.26278/93HZ-H861.

46 https://dx.doi.org/10.26278/G9SR-AX36. The pairing of fast and slow songs that are thematically linked is a feature of Aboriginal music which has been discussed in relation to junba music from the Kimberley and yawulyu/awelye (women's ceremony) music of Central Australia, and in relation to lirrga from the Daly region. See Treloyn's discussion of song "mates" in Scotty Martin's junba repertory. Sally Treloyn, "'When Everybody There Together … Then I Call That One': Song Order in the Kimberley", *Context* 32 (2007), 116. See also Linda Barwick's discussion on the paralleling of slow and fast Mangamunga songs: Linda Barwick, "Performance, Aesthetics, Experience: Thoughts on Yawulyu Mungamunga songs", in *Aesthetics and Experience in Music Performance*, eds Elizabeth MacKinlay, Denis Collins and Samantha Owens (Newcastle UK: Cambridge Scholars, 2005), 8, and her analysis of paired items in lirrga, Linda Barwick, "Tempo Bands, Metre and Rhythmic Mode in Marri Ngarr 'Church Lirrga' Songs", *Australasian Music Research* 7 (2002), 81–83. Brown's analysis of five contemporary kun-borrk/manyardi performance events found that songmen performed more than two song items with similar tempo or the same rhythmic mode in sequence, starting from slow tempo songs and moving to fast, then returning to slow at the end of the performance. See Brown, "Following Footsteps", 315.

47 This song text transcription is based on discussions with Harold Warrabin and Solomon Nangamu and on previous transcriptions informed by the singers discussed in Barwick, O'Keeffe and Singer, "Dilemmas in Interpretation", 55.

20121103RB01-03-MK01_MK02

Figure 2.11 Music transcription of Marrwakara songs MK01 and MK02 "joined together", performed by Harold Warrabin at Amartjitpalk, 2012 (RB2-20121103-RB_01_03_MK01_MK02.wav, https://dx.doi.org/10.26278/G9SR-AX36). (Transcriptions of didjeridu rhythms are to be taken as indicative; the aim here is to show how the clapstick, didjeridu and vocal parts interact and how the music is organised, rather than provide a detailed musical transcription of the recording for performance.)

memory of manyardi, and, in the case of Nangamu's Mirrijpu songset, consciously make new and different versions of the songs that they record in order to leave another permanent record for the next generation. Singers nevertheless recognise the musical authorship of the songs that they have learned from their male relatives. Analysis of the same song item in a songset realised by two different singers reveals both innovation and stable elements such as conservatism of melodic contour, song text and rhythmic mode. The current generation of manyardi songmen pays tribute to previous songmen by juxtaposing recently dream-conceived songs with the songs they have inherited, following the principles the old people taught them relating to song order and tempi, and continuing to teach the didjeridu accompaniment and song-leading to younger performers.

Rather than relying purely on the recording then, manyardi is collectively remembered, re-created and passed on through performance by a group of expert songmen and countrymen. Country also plays an active role in the process of refreshing memories of the old songs and conceiving new ones. Nangamu sums up this relationship with an anecdote about receiving a new song upon returning from his ancestral Country of Goulburn Island to Gunbalanya:

> Myself, I can listen to that clapstick. Somebody watch me, but they sing it for me. They give me that song [in a dream] and I sing that song. I got a couple of new songs now, when I was living there [in Goulburn Island]. And I got it in my dream, my ancestors they talked to me, and I listen, that they're going to give me something – a present, like a gift. Then I have that song and I pass it to my son and my grandchildren, pass it on to them, and on and on.[48]

References

Barwick, Linda. "Song as an Indigenous Art". In *The Oxford Companion to Aboriginal Art and Culture*, eds Sylvia Kleinert and Margo Neale. South Melbourne: Oxford University Press, 2000: 328–35.

Barwick, Linda. "Tempo Bands, Metre and Rhythmic Mode in Marri Ngarr 'Church Lirrga' Songs". *Australasian Music Research* 7 (2002): 67–83.

Barwick, Linda. "Performance, aesthetics, experience: thoughts on Yawulyu Mungamunga songs". In *Aesthetics and Experience in Music Performance*, eds Elizabeth MacKinlay, Denis Collins and Samantha Owens. Newcastle UK: Cambridge Scholars, 2005: 1–18.

Barwick, Linda, Bruce Birch and Nicholas Evans. "Iwaidja Jurtbirrk Songs: Bringing Language and Music Together". *Australian Aboriginal Studies* no. 2 (2007): 6–34.

Barwick, Linda, Isabel O'Keeffe and Ruth Singer. "Dilemmas in Interpretation: Contemporary Perspectives on Berndt's Goulburn Island Song Documentation". In *Little Paintings, Big Stories: Gossip Songs of Western Arnhem Land*, ed John Stanton. Nedlands: University of Western Australia, Berndt Museum of Anthropology, 2013: 46–71.

---

48 Solomon Nangamu, RB2-20120609-RB_v02.mp4, 00:00–01:50, https://dx.doi.org/10.26278/FP7X-X254.

Berndt, Ronald. Letter to Alf Ellison, 15 January 1948, Item 4.3.6. NTRS 38, Location 142/2/4, Northern Territory Archives.

Berndt, Ronald, ed. *Australian Aboriginal Art*. Sydney: Ure Smith, 1964.

Berndt, Ronald. "Other Creatures in Human Guise and Vice Versa: A Dilemma in Understanding". In *Songs of Aboriginal Australia*, eds Margaret Clunies Ross, Tamsin Donaldson and Stephen Aubrey Wild. Sydney: University of Sydney, 1987: 169–91.

Berndt, Ronald. SAA-B-06-MK02 (1964), in Stephen Wild (1990). Songs of Aboriginal Australia [audio cassette] Canberra: Australian Institute of Aboriginal and Torres Strait Islander Studies, AIAS 17.

Brown, Reuben Jay [recordist]. RB2-20121103-RB_01_03_MK01_MK02.wav (2012) at https://catalog.paradisec.org.au/collections/RB2/items/20121103/essences/1364365.

Brown, Reuben Jay. "Following Footsteps: The Kun-borrk/Manyardi Song Tradition and its Role in Western Arnhem Land Society". PhD thesis, University of Sydney, 2016.

Marett, Allan. "Ghostly Voices: Some Observations on Song-Creation, Ceremony and Being in North Western Australia". *Oceania* 71, no. 1 (2000): 18–29.

Marett, Allan, Linda Barwick and Lysbeth Ford. *For the Sake of a Song: Wangga Songmen and Their Repertories*. Sydney: Sydney University Press, 2013.

Marrgam, Brendan, Solomon Nangamu and Micky Yalbarr. RB2-20121103-RB_03.wav 00:24:49–00:25:44 at https://catalog.paradisec.org.au/collections/RB2/items/20121103/essences/1364706.

Myers, Fred. "Ways of Place-Making". *La Ricerca Folklorica*, no. 45 (2002): 101–19.

Nangamu, Solomon. RB2-20110825-RB_02.wav. 26:37–27:06 at https://catalog.paradisec.org.au/collections/RB2/items/20110825/essences/1357033.

Nangamu, Solomon. RB2-20120609-RB_v01.mp4 08:46–10:56 at https://catalog.paradisec.org.au/collections/RB2/items/20120609/essences/1360639.

Nangamu, Solomon. RB2-20120609-RBv_02. 08:39–09:01 at https://catalog.paradisec.org.au/collections/RB2/items/20120609/essences/1360602.

Nangamu, Solomon. RB2-20120729-RB_09_edit.wav. 09:57.850–10:12.950 at https://catalog.paradisec.org.au/collections/RB2/items/20120729/essences/1364600.

Nangamu, Solomon. RB2-20121103-RB_01_edit.wav. 07:23.200–07:48.200 at https://catalog.paradisec.org.au/collections/RB2/items/20121103/essences/1364620.

Nangamu, Solomon. RB2-20121103-RB_02_edit.wav 42:52–44:24 at https://catalog.paradisec.org.au/collections/RB2/items/20121103/essences/1364708.

Nangamu, Solomon. RB2-20121104-RB_01_XX_edit.wav. 00:05:20–00:05:30 at https://catalog.paradisec.org.au/collections/RB2/items/20121104/essences/1365978.

O'Keeffe, Isabel [recordist]. [20061013IB02-05_MK02], (2006) in Linda Barwick, Allan Marett, Nicholas Evans, Murray Garde, Isabel O'Keeffe and Bruce Birch (2012) Western Arnhem Land Song Project data collection. The University of Sydney. http://elar.soas.ac.uk/deposit/arnhemland-135103.

O'Keeffe, Isabel. "Kaddikkaddik Ka-wokdjanganj 'Kaddikkaddik Spoke': Language and Music of the Kun-Barlang Kaddikkaddik Songs from Western Arnhem Land". *Australian Journal of Linguistics* 30, no. 1 (2010): 35–51.

Ross, Margaret Clunies, Tamsin Donaldson and Stephen Aubrey Wild, eds. *Songs of Aboriginal Australia*. Sydney: University of Sydney, 1987.

Singer, Ruth. "Agreement in Mawng: Productive and Lexicalised Uses of Agreement in an Australian Language". PhD thesis, The University of Melbourne, 2006.

Stanner, William Edward Henry. "The Dreaming". In *The Dreaming and Other Essays*. Victoria: Black Inc. Agenda, 1953: 57–73.

Toner, Peter. "Melody and the Musical Articulation of Yolngu Identities". *Yearbook for Traditional Music* 35 (2003): 69–95.

Treloyn, Sally. "'When Everybody There Together ... Then I Call That One': Song Order in the Kimberley". *Context* 32 (2007): 105–21.

Treloyn, Sally, Matthew Dembal Martin and Rona Goonginda Charles. "Moving Songs: Repatriating Audiovisual Recordings of Aboriginal Australian Dance and Song (Kimberley Region, Northwestern Australia)". In *The Oxford Handbook of Musical Repatriation*, eds Frank Gunderson, Robert Lancefield and Bret Woods. New York: Oxford University Press, 2019: 591–607.

Warrabin, Harold. RB2-20121103-RB_01_03_MK01_MK02.wav at https://catalog.paradisec.org.au/collections/RB2/items/20121103/essences/1364365.

3

Ruatepupuke II: A Māori meeting house in a museum

Jack Gray and Jacqueline Shea Murphy

Introduction: Converging platforms – zoom in to enter the room

This is a weaving of transcripts from a Zoom call that took place on 15 May 2021 between Jack Gray, director of Atamira Dance Company in Aotearoa,[1] and Jacqueline Shea Murphy, critical dance studies professor at the University of California, Riverside, USA.[2] Our contribution to this volume is not written in the same form as most academic articles, but rather as a kōrero – a term in Te Reo Maōri that is sometimes translated into English as narration, talk, discourse, account, conversation, and is also used as a verb, or something one does.

To kōrero is to dialogue, converse, address, speak truth. The kōrero that follows is a sharing of thoughts and ideas that, like all kōrero, may or may not conclude with a clearly stated argument, and which requires from the reader active listening and trust that, in the act of our speaking together, meaning is being made. Their kōrero refers to engagements that Gray had in August 2017, with his father's ancestor/ancestral whare (house), named Ruatepupuke II, currently held in the Field Museum in Chicago, Illinois, USA. These engagements, which Shea Murphy witnessed, involved Gray and several dancers visiting with Ruatepupuke, dancing in and with it,[3] and then presenting these movement engagements in a dance work at a theatre across town in Chicago.

---

1   Atamira Dance Company, https://www.atamiradance.co.nz/about, accessed 19 November 2021.
2   University of California, Riverside Department of Dance, "Jacqueline Shea Murphy, Associate Professor Profile", https://dance.ucr.edu/faculty/jacqueline-shea-murphy/, accessed 19 November 2021.
3   Jack Gray, *Field Museum*, 14 April 2021, https://www.youtube.com/watch?v=CGEQRod_fnA, accessed 19 November 2021.

Figure 3.1 Jack Gray wearing his father's painting overalls entering Ruatepupuke II, while video repeats its welcome, at Field Museum, Chicago. Photo by Jacqueline Shea Murphy.

Mihimihi: acknowledgements and welcoming

To enter the wharenui, a recorded American voice mispronounces the following greeting on a loop:

> Kia ora! Welcome to Rua-te-pu-puke, a Māori meeting house, out of respect please take your shoes off. (Ding)
> Kia ora! Welcome to Rua-te-pu-puke, a Māori meeting house, out of respect please take your shoes off. (Ding)
> Kia ora! Welcome to Rua-te-pu-puke, a Māori meeting house, out of respect please take your shoes off. (Ding)

JSM: Hey, Jack, nice to see you! I'm here in Huichin, which is sometimes called Oakland, California, on Lisjan Ohlone territory. So delighted to talk with you in this realm of the cyberworld about archives, and dance, and Ruatepupuke. Thanks for making time for this.

JG: Kia ora, Jackie. So good to see you and to have the opportunity to explore these things. I'm looking forward to giving life to this present moment as it helps us look into what has already been and what will come.

JSM: Great. So, when discussions around archives were happening in the research group we're part of, which this volume has come out of, I kept thinking about Ruatepupuke. There have been so many vibrant discussions about archives in Indigenous studies and in dance studies. A lot of these discussions circulate around the body as an archive of knowledge, as a way of holding knowledge that hasn't been allowed into institutions such as libraries or museums or history books because it a) isn't understood for the knowledge and power that it holds, and b) if it did, it wouldn't have been wanted there. So, the body has been understood in both fields as itself a kind of archive: as a repository for knowledge, and as a location or source of it. And bodies have also been understood as active in researching the archived knowledges they hold: the body as an archive can locate what might be called historical knowledge – in what has been bodily archived. Of course, there are lots of other ways of thinking about archives in both fields too.

Objects, beings, carvings: Ruatepupuke stories

JSM: In Indigenous studies, from what I've understood from my engagements with it, there is a disconnect between how Western colonising cultures archive what are seen as objects – by putting things into museums as artefacts to be seen and preserved – and how in many Indigenous cultures, these so-called objects are known and understood to be sentient beings.[4] These are radically different ways

---

4   The way entities seen as "objects" are in sentient relationship (in ways outside of a Western alive/ dead dichotomy) is articulated frequently and abundantly by Indigenous artists and scholars, and addressed regularly in Indigenous studies scholarship. A few (of many possible) examples include Tsimshian scholar Mique'l Askren's (now Dangeli's) discussion of the "tangible manifestations" of "supernatural power that are known as nax nox and halaayt" in Tsimshian epistemology, which are "commonly referred to as 'objects' or 'artifacts' in museum terminology" (Mique'l Askren, "Dancing Our Stone Mask Out of Confinement: A Twenty-first-Century Tsimshian Epistemology", in *In Objects of Exchange: Social and Material Transformation on Northwest Coast*, ed. Aaron Glass (New York: Bard Graduate Centre, 2011), 37). In Alutiiq artist and writer Tanya Lukin Linklater's discussion of visiting with cultural belongings from Kodiak Island and the Aleutian Chain of Alaska that have been "incarcerated or not allowed to rest" in university and museum holdings, Lukin Linklater writes how even if they "are no longer nourished within their life in their homelands, this does not negate their capacity for awareness, sentience, and agency", noting how, in travelling far distances to honour, visit and be in relation to these cultural belongings, she chooses "to look with compassion, kindness, and reverence" and to focus on how "these visits nourish them and reciprocal exchange takes place" (Tanya Lukin Linklater, "Indigenous Objects and Performance: Toward Insistence, Repair and Repatriation Otherwise in Three Parts" (PhD thesis proposal, Queens University, 2020) 20, cited with permission); Osage scholar George "Tink" Tinker writes about consciousness in all beings, including rocks (George "Tink" Tinker, "The Stones Shall Cry Out: Consciousness, Rocks, and Indians", *Wicazo Sa Review* 19, No. 2 (Fall 2004)); Māori

of understanding what it is to hold knowledge, and what it is to be a being. In colonising cultures, the binary distinction between life and non-life has imposed itself onto the putting-into-museum archives of so-called objects for display and preservation. So, while museum archives see archival knowledge held in objects, not bodies, dance and Indigenous studies see the body as a site of holding what might be considered archival knowledge. Another difference lies in the varied ways of understanding what *has* been put in the museum archive. In Indigenous studies, what is put into a museum is a location of knowledge, yes, but not in the preservative contained sense that the museum might be expecting to hold it in; rather, holding knowledge in a very different way that involves a kind of sentience. And this sentience requires engagement and nourishment. So – how does this all play into what I saw and in your work with Ruatepupuke in Chicago at the Field Museum in 2017? Can I ask you to talk a bit about the story of your voyages with and to your ancestor? Then perhaps we can address some of these issues.

JG: The ancestor's story that we're going to discuss today comes from my father's side and is related to our tribal house, or wharenui. The house has a name, which is Ruatepupuke II. Now, I'll give a shortened story of the old traditions around Ruatepupuke, which is synonymous with what we now know as whakairo or carving. Our ancestor dove down into the ocean domain of Tangaroa, the god (atua) of the sea, to rescue his son who had been taken (for transgressing a sacred protocol). He returned to the world of light, to Te Ao Marama (our reality here on "earth"), holding a broken piece of the wharenui of Tangaroa. This fragment of carving informs the cosmology around our carving traditions. One of the exciting things is that these carvings depicted half-human/half-oceanic forms in the form of taniwha or guardian spirits. Under the ocean, these carvings were moving and alive and would shapeshift in and on the walls. They would speak, look and engage with everything, and be the embodied consciousness of the ocean. The carving was broken off from the house and brought up into this world. However, the carvings ceased to move, and so now we see carvings as static. They are ancestral deities, and there is a notion already that there was a transition from the realm under the

---

performance scholar Te Ahukaramū Charles Royal's articulations of how "Māori knowledge builds upon and continually refers to ancestors – both human and non-human – as living presences existing beyond a metaphysical and real veil". He adds: "ancestors are also the phenomenon of the natural world" (Charles Royal Te Ahukaramū, "Ārai-te-uru: 'Through the Veil' – Traditional Māori Storytelling and Transformation". Keynote lecture at 2016 IFTR/FIRT conference, Stockholm, Sweden, 16 June 2016. https://www.iftr.org/conference/keynote-speakers, 8). See also: Kim TallBear, "Beyond the Life/Not-Life Binary: A Feminist-Indigenous Reading of Cryopreservation, Interspecies Thinking, and the New Materialisms", in *Cryopolitics: Frozen Life in a Melting World*, eds Joanna Radin and Emma Kowal (Cambridge, Massachusetts and London: MIT Press, 2017), 179–202; Kim TallBear, "Caretaking Relations, Not American Dreaming", *Kalfou* 6 no. 1 (2019), 24–41; and Amiria Henare, "Taonga Māori: Encompassing rights and property in New Zealand", in *Thinking Through Things: Theorising Artefacts Ethnographically*, eds Amiria Henare, Martin Holbraad and Sari Wastell (New York: Routledge, 2007), 47–67.

ocean where they had a life as opposed to the realm of humankind where they don't. So that's one story about Ruatepupuke I've learned as a result of exploring my whakapapa, or genealogy, and inherited stories of my people.

Another story is that an original wharenui (Ruatepupuke I) was built back in the day. Though there was a lot of intertribal fighting, our tribe decided to keep our carving sacred by dismantling the first house and hiding it under the mud of the riverbank (at Waipiro Bay). They tell a story that once that skirmish with the other tribe had finished, they no longer knew exactly where the carving of the first house was. They say the river changed, and the location of their carvings disappeared. They then made a second house. And this house, Ruatepupuke II, is the one that I've spent the most time contemplating and engaging and interacting with. This house was sold by a family member to a curiosity collector. They dismantled the wharenui against the tribe's wishes and took the house on a journey to London and Germany. Inside the museum the house itself was too big and was cut to accommodate the size of the exhibition room.

Wharenui from a Māori perspective: The ancestor's body

Now to discuss some elements or aspects of the wharenui from a Māori perspective. We named them after an ancestor, but they are themselves an ancestor. So we see the top of the roof that runs across the whare as the backbone. We see the rafters as the rib cage. We see and denote other aspects of how the house helps us as Māori to understand the pathway into the world and the exit out of it through life and death. To think about the ancestor's body being cut and humbled in many ways brings about emotions and feelings of distress and concern as you would imagine. The house was given to the museum after the world fair in Chicago, Illinois, and it was presented to the world alongside many other exotic gatherings (belongings) of Indigenous peoples. It was put into what is now known as the Field Museum.[5]

---

5   The Field Museum originated from the artefacts displayed at the 1893 World's Columbian Exposition, which was produced to celebrate the 400-year anniversary of Spanish coloniser Christopher Columbus's landing in what is today called the Caribbean (John Flinn, *Official Guide to the World's Columbian Exposition, Full Information Respecting All Features of the Exposition*. Issued under authority of the World's Columbian Exposition (Chicago: The Columbian Guide Company, 1893), https://bit.ly/3uwIFno, accessed 19 November 2021). This Exposition included many exhibits and performances designed to show the superiority of whites in relation to Indigenous peoples. The Field Museum was thus founded out of an Exposition that enacted discursive and epistemic violence towards Indigenous peoples by collecting and displaying living Indigenous "artefacts" – human and more-than-human – in celebration of white supremacy and US colonisation, and in attempts to solidify US imperialism. Over the next century, the Field Museum's roots have continued to grow out of this seed. (The Field Museum, https://www.fieldmuseum.org/about, accessed 19 November 2021.) The museum's depiction of Ruatepupuke echoes colonising histories in which Indigenous people are depicted welcoming white visitors with open arms. (The Field Museum, *Maori Meeting House, Ruatepupuke II*, https://bit.ly/3ee8fZi, accessed 19 November 2021.)

It stayed inside the basement, where it was forgotten and dismantled. Decades later it was resurrected inside the museum alongside many other Indigenous people's homes and belongings, staying for a couple of decades without the tribe knowing where it had ended up and people not knowing the main stories around what this wharenui represented. In the 1980s when *Te Māori* was shown at the Metropolitan Museum of Art in New York City, it became the very first exhibition of Māori-curated Māori art internationally. It was a milestone for Indigenous art to be curated through the Indigenous lens and for our storytelling instead of a non-Indigenous perspective to bring artefacts together.[6]

Soon after the rediscovery, there were delegates from Aotearoa New Zealand, Māori museum curators, who eventually, after hearing about the house, were able to engage in a long process of figuring out what to do. The tribe decided that the house would remain in Chicago, but elements of the house would be taken to Aotearoa and reinvigorated. Things were rewoven, things were re-carved, remade and represented with the Mana or the spiritual authority, the cultural authority of our tribe in a ceremony that happened at the museum.[7]

Encounters in relationship with the Field Museum

I came into this knowledge while based in the US, particularly during a time (Spring 2015) at the Asian/Pacific/American Institute at NYU.[8] I asked myself how I could align some of the practices and processes that I was looking at regarding how we recognise land as inherently Indigenous? How do we uncover and bring forth the memories, the stories, the knowledge, the names, the ancestors in places, and how might we mitigate the sense of loss, erasure and disruption to those pathways? That exploration led me to the facilitation of several encounters in relationship with the museum. My story thread was interweaving more as a cultural facilitator, enabling and empowering different ways for institutions to be educated and informed by the communities activating around them, and was also opening doors to knowledge keepers. We discovered that there were Māori people in Chicago who have genealogical lineages to the wharenui and could bring some of those different threads together. I've always journeyed knowing that this intactness is fluid and moving and constantly shapeshifting around all the various ideas and notions of belonging, identity and power. There are stories within the body to be

---

6   New Zealand History, *Te Maori Exhibition Opens in New York 10 September 1984*, https://nzhistory.govt.nz/te-Māori-exhibition-opens-in-new-york, accessed 19 November 2021.

7   New York Times, *Travel Advisory: Maori Art Comes to Chicago*, https://www.nytimes.com/1993/02/28/travel/travel-advisory-maori-art-comes-to-chicago.html?smid=url-share, accessed 18 August 2022.

8   Asian/Pacific/American Institute at New York University, *Jack Gray (2016)*, https://apa.nyu.edu/jack-gray-2016/, accessed 19 November 2021.

uncovered as a result of that reconnection. Some perspectives can render artistically and creatively to support the next generation to understand what it is to have a house in another land and continue the work of thinking through institutions and methodologies of preservation, and then adding an Indigenous performative and contemporary perspective on present and future moments.

Indigenous dancers as archival activators

JSM: Thank you. That is a very beautiful and intense and complicated story, in the best way, and painful. It's painful to hear and I can see that it's painful to tell, as well as inspiring. At the end you spoke of the possibilities of it and I appreciated that as well. What I hear in what you're saying is the story of how your ancestor was turned from being something that, if I'm understanding right, was a carving that was alive – that had an aliveness in it. That aliveness was contained in the carving. But in the process of being collected by a "curiosity collector", the ancestor was transformed from being a carving-containing-aliveness, into being an archival object that could be treated as such: that could literally be objectified, and cut, and treated as a thing. You've narrated the voyages and stories of that really powerfully. What I'm also thinking about, listening to you, is how your body, as it engages with the archive the museum is holding, enacts the beingness of it again. I ask that in part because as you were telling the story over Zoom, your arms and movements were really active and the movements were beautiful. You were – it seemed to me, as you told the story of the underwater underworld and the coming into being held in a carving – yourself showing motion and movement and aliveness. So I wanted to ask about your body operating in that way, as an archival activator. Can you talk a bit about what your movement as a dancer, as it engages with the objectified ancestor collected in a museum, does? What do you see it doing? I'm also interested in the connections between what you see it doing and the way you ended your discussion: how Ruatepupuke is now doing the work of bringing knowledge, bringing support, to the next generation of tribal members. So I'm curious about both of those things: how your body engages with what it does, and what the effects of that are.

JG: Wonderful, thanks, Jackie. I'm going to start at the point before I first met the house. I remember flying very early from Newark airport to Chicago, and the feeling of butterflies inside my stomach, I actually feel it right now and it, wow, it was amazing to reconnect with that. I'm thinking about the possibility of multiple lineages coming back together again and what that feels like inside, and I guess it was a type of excitement that I was going to meet something that was already inside me and that I would have a tangible body to reflect the feelings upon. I guess it must be the same feeling when meeting family for the first time, the excitement of that balanced with the pain of that separation. The surprise of what it feels like to want a connection that you've never physically had. I remember the night before, I found it difficult to settle in myself. There are many layers and many lineages, maternal and paternal, in our understanding, working through us. Coming into a space where the energies are at their peak velocity is an overwhelming physical (spiritual) experience. I haven't thought about all this before and so to know that I can recall this again shows it's deeply rooted. Yeah, there were a lot of tears. I felt very inconsolable, as I also thought a lot about my father, who relates to the house and who has departed this planet for quite some time (he passed away in 2003). I guess to know that the pieces could come together and the transmission that I need as a Māori man to grow could come by going to their house and having the abilities and capabilities to make that happen and the courage to make that happen was a force, an incredible physical force. My partner and I did a lot of ceremony including a lot of prayer by the water. Lake Michigan was a man-made lake which is pretty funny because it didn't look "man-made" to me, and there was washed up on the concrete a skeleton of a bird, which we wrapped in seaweed that we found. It was, I guess, a gesture of the ocean of Tangaroa (as we understand koha, or reciprocity) in a way – reclaiming those bits from under the sea to above the ocean. And then there we were taking it into this gigantic building.

Exclusionary processes and upholding tikanga

I've noticed so many times in America that the amount of security in these institutional places is quite phenomenal and brings a powerful sense of defensiveness – as if the defence is *against* you *coming into* the house. I think about this house and what it is for and that it's the body of the ancestor (inside this other house that is so unwelcoming), and I don't think people understand that because they are acclimated to homes keeping us outside. I struggle culturally to deal with those exclusionary processes (safety measures) because it's the antithesis (in Aotearoa) of what we expect when we come into relation with our ancestors. I met the house, and my first response was to express all the knowledge I was gifted growing up: sing, dance, chant, talk, and let it all pour out of me. This is making me think a lot about what is performance and what is pure expression. I'm trying to think about America's ongoing imperialism as something that usurps the agency of the house. Placing outsider thinking around a cultural object that has its own inherent world of meaning, and calling that an archive, is really limiting and complicated. Considering it as an archive doesn't take into account the living continuum of cultural relationship. The two worldviews present two different facets of relationship. So I want to throw those ideas into the mix of thinking around [the] archive to question seeing it as something static or separated, and instead suggest seeing it as something that is relative to where it is situated. My body as an archive brings about memories from ancestors past. It brings about a responsibility to uphold tikanga (or the protocols of our culture in the here and now). It supports the notion of transferring cultural thinking from so far away into a space that is already problematic because of others lack of understanding. Some themes include

Indigenous sovereignty, the grieving body and desiring the reconstruction of pathways for energy to flow. I found this feeling recognisable, and I'm sure that it would be to another Māori person doing the same thing (of asserting the Mana).

I do also want to move into some of the creative interventions that we did. I am a trained contemporary dancer used to working inside studios and theatres and spaces that are makeshift spaces for what eventually became the performance space, and the illusions created through that. I was able to go with a group of dancers (in Chicago) to explore what it meant for each of us to journey across the threshold of human conflict and meet what is most calling us to a traditional form. I suppose, in a way, from an architectural point of view, it wasn't just the "physical" house that I had to acknowledge. It was the intangible spaces outside of it, around it and before it. The grief of seeing our taonga – treasured entities with which, through intertwining lineages, one is in metaphoric and felt relation – unrepresented is felt in the emptiness in the energy around the house. When I was there as we moved in the place, people at the museum were walking and taking photos and talking loudly and doing lots of things (breaking customs) that weren't their fault. I felt a pain at that, but I understood that too, so it's tense. In many ways, my being in the space was problematic for the museum because I was inciting energy that they couldn't "control". It becomes about activism instead of intimacy, I guess, when meeting "your" body with other people's projections of an archive.

Performance cartographies: Manifesting in movements

JSM: Beautiful, Jack. Your response is gorgeous and reminds me of one of the books I've been teaching lately, called *Spiral to the Stars,* by Laura Harjo, who is a Mvskoke geographer. Harjo writes about "felt knowledge", and about how the body operates as an archive and experiences and keeps "felt knowledge" embodied in practice. Specifically referencing "knowledge produced through music and movement", Harjo writes, "Mvskoke songs and dance are acts of performance that trigger memories. They are performance cartographies that hold memories, invoking knowledge and relationality and operating to open a range of kin-space-time envelopes to dancers and listeners."[9] I feel like that was what was happening when I saw you right then, talking about Ruatepupuke: you were experiencing that felt knowledge, and it was triggering memories and manifesting in your movements. I also heard you registering the pain not only of not having access to the physical house, but also to the energies around the house – and that the house gives – that haven't been able to be accessed or supported. I have so many questions and I know we don't have a lot of time, so maybe I'll just say a couple and you can choose which ones resonate. One is about time and space. Harjo uses the term "kin-space-time

---

9   Laura Harjo, *Spiral to the Stars: Mvskoke Tools of Futurity* (Arizona: University of Arizona Press, 2019), 84.

Figure 3.2 Dancers assembled to represent the way manuhiri (visitors) are traditionally welcomed to greet the house, from afar and awaiting a call. Photo by Jacqueline Shea Murphy.

envelopes". What I was hearing in your story was a kin-space-time envelope: in your engagements with Ruatepupuke, a cross-temporal kinship is being activated. This kinship is felt in grieving, as you said – but there is also something in the capacity for it to be felt as grieving, that is an activation of the possibility of what actually is there. That's one thought that I had that I wondered if you might comment on. And then the other is, just maybe to ask a bit more about you bringing the dancers into that space in 2017. I was able to join you and the dancers you'd brought to the museum, and to witness as you danced in the space before and into the whare. Can you talk about going into the space, and what we were doing there? And then also, could you talk about taking what had happened with these dancers in the Field Museum, with Ruatepupuke, and a couple of days later, staging it at the Jackalope Theatre across town? I'm just wondering if you would like to say anything about that movement, and perhaps about how Harjo's idea of the kin-space-time envelope relates to the movement of you and the other dancers into the museum to dance with Ruatepupuke, and then out of the museum across town to the theatre, and then to New Zealand as you were saying earlier – back to the communities that could engage with what the energy is, even if they can't engage with the whare.

Figure 3.3 Dancers crossing the atea (the area directly in front of the house is symbolic of the atua named Tūmatauenga – the entity of warfare and human conflict) a spatial threshold evoked during the process of cultural protocol, or pōwhiri. Photo by Jacqueline Shea Murphy.

JG: This is a fascinating conversation. I love it, thank you, Jackie, for grounding these thoughts and ideas and also making me understand the importance and significance of it as a response. Time and space are a powerful notion in Te Ao Māori worldview. We know it as wānanga, which contain multiple energies converging together, and what that does is remove reliance on Western time. It allows you to [be]come more strongly embedded in the unfolding of the experience and [feel] that every part dictates the next way in which the current will flow.

Regarding the dancers that I worked with, I understood they were there in solidarity with me as a Māori person exploring how to interact with my tribal house in Chicago physically. First of all, what connected us was tuning into our own cultural identities and shared sense of the conflict that resides in our own stories. Then we were able to understand better that institution's colonisation. There are overwhelming structures that obstruct our ability to access these felt bits of knowledge in the body, so the encounter felt staged. Anchoring into my relationship with the house was important, knowing that I don't live there and that I don't know when I might go back again. I fixated on getting as much of that information physically into my body for the future. I hadn't thought about that as an archive until

Figure 3.4 Jack Gray physically responding to the inner architecture of Ruatepupuke II as a way of spiritually embodying the carvings and woven universe. Photo by Jacqueline Shea Murphy.

just a second ago, but knowing that the house's purpose is for people to work out their pathways, I needed to figure out another way to bring Māori spatial elements of interaction, such as pōwhiri – a staged ritual encounter between people of the land and the house, welcoming guests with no conversation but through tribally specific, continually evolving, ingrained formats – into the space in Chicago. I had to translate the ritual context of a powhiri in this completely different environment, happening inside the museum, where the first part of the call, the karanga, tells you to look up at the sky – but you're inside and you can't see the sky. So I had to find a way to navigate moving through the ritualistic cultural thresholds of the house from a global Indigenous lens, reading it as a performance while also interpreting its coloniality. I'm caught somewhere between notions of therapy in the Western sense, and then notions of rongoa, which is a listening in the intuitive sense – and how I understand all of those things within the realm of what we know or call dance. That space was doing what the space required, which was being in the domain of listening and further knowledge-making. At the point when we extracted ourselves from our experience that day, we were able to continue our creative journeying, moulding that material through conversation, through physicalising, through intervening with lights or sound or AV, and through thinking both interdisciplinarily and interculturally. And we also had a Q&A, which you moderated and we recorded, and that recording still exists – again as an archive of that particular moment.[10]

"As much as my body could physically gather": Ongoing journeys

So, bringing it back to Aotearoa, I ended up going back to my tribal land and performing some of these dances with dear friends of mine. I was able to have a surprise experience because I'm used to being the only one who knows the story. So it was such an amazing thing to go back to my land and to see all of the Elders, mostly now just the grandmothers, sitting there at the back of the room where my father went to school. They sang with us and remembered people whose voice recordings were in the archival radio interview (which we used as our soundtrack).[11] So lots of things happened that day. I was able to find my own joy and peace with knowing that I had gathered as much as my body could physically gather. I could bring as much as I could through my own storytelling, through my dance on my whenua (land) with my people. I know that my tribe are very renowned for being creative, for being performers; some of the most famous songs come from my area. (Although you can probably have anybody say that to be honest!) What was interesting was that sometimes we stick to resolving feelings that make us uncomfortable. I felt that what was being told to me after the performance was, it's still an unresolved issue. People can say things (or they can't say things) out of respect for others and I feel like these mysteries continue to flow. I think that's okay. It's not about having the definitive story or feel-good ending.

I was always sure that the house should come back, yet the people there presented another reality. When the meatworks (the area's main source of employment) closed down – during 1950s postwar – everyone started moving away towards the cities for further education or a different life. My father joined the army, one of the only things that many Māori could do at the time. When I was there, the area had high unemployment rates and not as much sustenance (because we're not living in the same ways that we used to live. And there is a general sense of poverty in these areas), which means they can't afford to fix a broken window on one of the marae (meeting house) or paint the outside of the building. So one of the last things they said was we're glad the house is somewhere that it can be looked after. That's a bittersweet note to finish on, because I realised there's a reason for everything, and we have to go through the whole journey. I know that my journey is ongoing, and I have many creative inspirations that will come through a deeper investigation of

---

10   Mixing Lab, "Ruatepupuke – The Talk Back", on *Mix Cloud*, https://bit.ly/3OQ37Yw, accessed 19 November 2021.

11   Ngā Taonga Sound and Vision, *Mobil Radio Awards Entry 1994: Best Community and Access Programme, Best Spoken Programmes, Best Documentary or Feature Programme "Ruatepupuke"*, (Audio, Reference Number: 13924, 1994), https://www.ngataonga.org.nz/collections/catalogue/catalogue-item?record_id=153267, accessed 19 November 2021.

Figure 3.5 Jack and dancers performing at Jackalope Theatre, 30 August 2017. Two days of rehearsals, embodying the experiences felt in and around the city, and sharing movement transferred from I Moving Lab's pick-up projects around the world. Photo by Jacqueline Shea Murphy.

Figure 3.6 Post-rehearsal pre-performance release, exploring Skikako (Chicago) as part of I Moving Lab's I LAND project. Photo by Jacqueline Shea Murphy.

body expression, knowledge and practice. So, it's one of those ongoing things, and I'm really happy anytime that I'm asked to share this story with people, so thank you, Jackie.

JSM: Thank you so much, Jack. It has been wonderful to talk with you. So many memories and things to continue to work with and think more about. I think we've been needing to have this conversation for a while, and I'm so glad we made time to do it.

Special thanks to Magnolia Yang Sao Yia for transcription help.

References

Askren, Mique'l. "Dancing our Stone Mask Out of Confinement: A Twenty-First-Century Tsimshian Epistemology" in *In Objects of Exchange: Social and Material Transformation on Northwest Coast*, ed Aaron Glass. New York: Bard Graduate Center, 2011: 37–47.

Atamira Dance Company, https://www.atamiradance.co.nz/about, accessed 19 November 2021.

Flinn, John. *Official Guide to the World's Columbian Exposition, Full Information Respecting All Features of the Exposition*. Issued under authority of the World's Columbian Exposition. Chicago: The Columbian Guide Company, 1893: 1–192, https://bit.ly/3uwIFno, accessed 19 November 2021.

Gray, Jack. *Field Museum*, YouTube video, uploaded 14 April 2021, https://www.youtube.com/watch?v=CGEQRod_fnA, accessed 19 November 2021.

Harjo, Laura. *Spiral to the Stars: Mvskoke Tools of Futurity*. Arizona: University of Arizona Press, 2019.

Henare, Amiria. "Taonga Māori: Encompassing Rights and Property in New Zealand". In *Thinking Through Things: Theorising Artefacts Ethnographically*, eds Amiria Henare, Martin Holbraad and Sari Wastell. New York: Routledge, 2007: 47–67.

Lukin Linklater, Tanya. "Indigenous Objects and Performance: Toward Insistence, Repair and Repatriation Otherwise in Three Parts". PhD thesis proposal, Queens University, 23 February 2020.

Mixing Lab. "Ruatepupuke – The Talk Back", on *Mix Cloud*, https://bit.ly/3OQ37Yw, accessed 19 November 2021.

New York Times. *Travel Advisory: Maori Art Comes to Chicago*, 28 February 1993. https://nyti.ms/3arRqsg, accessed 18 August 2022.

New Zealand History. *Te Maori Exhibition Opens in New York 10 September 1984*, https://nzhistory.govt.nz/te-maori-exhibition-opens-in-new-york, accessed 19 November 2021.

Ngā Taonga Sound and Vision. *Mobil Radio Awards Entry 1994: Best Community and Access Programme, Best Spoken Programmes, Best Documentary or Feature Programme "Ruatepupuke"*. (Audio: Reference Number: 13924, 1994), https://www.ngataonga.org.nz/collections/catalogue/catalogue-item?record_id=153267, accessed 19 November 2021.

Royal, Te Ahukaramū Charles. "Ārai-te-uru: 'Through the Veil' – Traditional Māori Storytelling and Transformation". Keynote lecture at 2016 IFTR/FIRT conference, Stockholm, Sweden, 16 June 2016. https://www.iftr.org/conference/keynote-speakers.

Tallbear, Kim. "Beyond the Life/Not-Life Binary: A Feminist-Indigenous Reading of Cryopreservation, Interspecies Thinking, and the New Materialisms". In *Cryopolitics: Frozen Life in a Melting World*, eds Joanna Radin and Emma Kowal. Cambridge, Massachusetts, and London: MIT Press, 2017: 179–202.

Tallbear, Kim. "Caretaking Relations, Not American Dreaming". *Kalfou* 6, no. 1 (2019): 24–41. Regents of the University of California, https://bit.ly/3QWnC6Z, text about podcast released 29 October 2018, accessed 25 October 2019.

The Asian Pacific American Institute at New York University. *Jack Gray (2016)*, https://apa.nyu.edu/jack-gray-2016/, accessed 19 November 2021.

The Field Museum, https://www.fieldmuseum.org/about, accessed 19 November 2021.

The Field Museum. *Maori Meeting House, Ruatepupuke II*, https://www.fieldmuseum.org/exhibitions/maori-meeting-house-ruatepupuke-ii, accessed 19 November 2021.

Tinker, George "Tink". "The Stones Shall Cry Out: Consciousness, Rocks, and Indians". *Wicazo Sa Review* 19, no. 2 (Fall 2004).

University of California, Riverside Department of Dance. *Jacqueline Shea Murphy, Associate Professor Profile*, https://dance.ucr.edu/faculty/jacqueline-shea-murphy/, accessed 19 November 2021.

4

Animating cultural heritage knowledge through songs: Museums, archives, consultation and Tiwi music

Genevieve Campbell, Jacinta Tipungwuti, Amanda Harris and Matt Poll

Introduction

> Ceremony [is how] young people start to learn about this singing and dancing – how you dance your own Dreaming dancing. All sort – like, you know, everyone has their own dancing from their grandfather, down to their fathers. That's where we get that. It's time for them to listen, to learn. It's time now, never too late ... Parlingarri [long ago]. Way back, from the past – and today. It's a bit different. Parlingarri, old people used to have that knowledge – the words and the song written in their pungintaga [head], brain.
>
> Jacinta Tipungwuti[1]

Throughout the twentieth century, intangible (recorded song and dance) and tangible (photographs, painted, carved and woven) Tiwi cultural items were collected by (non-Tiwi) observers, researchers and collectors. These often began as private collections, with many recordings of intangible culture making their way to public archives, while tangible culture ended up in museums and galleries. Oral and written evidence confirms that ceremony[2] on the Tiwi Islands was discouraged and disapproved of, both passively and actively, by missionaries through the early-to mid-twentieth century and this had a marked impact on performed cultural practice. Senior Tiwi women and men have described their experiences of being brought up in the Catholic mission school, removed from family, ceremony and

---

1   Mrs Tipungwuti, co-author on this paper, is directly quoted throughout. Her thoughts and opinions as representative of the group involved in viewing the material are incorporated in the body of the text. All quotations are from conversations led by Jacinta with the Strong Women's Group, in Sydney in March and May 2019 in Wurrumiyanga, Bathurst Island, reflecting on the visit to Sydney.

2   Here we refer to the Kulama rituals, which formed the basis of education and initiation for young Tiwi people, and Pukumani-associated ceremonies and rituals related to death and mourning.

language. Current Tiwi Elders were leaders in reclaiming cultural rights and ownership through the 1970s and 1980s and have continued to dance ceremony, compose traditional song and create painted, carved and woven art[3] while negotiating changing social and cultural motivations and pressures. Throughout the ebb and flow of these cultural, political and social shifts, the collected culture has remained in place, artificially separated into material and intangible culture. It is only through speaking with current Tiwi culture and knowledge holders that the interconnectedness of performance and artefact is now being added to the record.

This chapter deals with a series of consultations between Amanda Harris, Matt Poll, Genevieve Campbell, Jacinta Tipungwuti and additional Tiwi cultural custodians at the Sydney Conservatorium of Music and at the Sydney University Museum Collection store in March 2019 during a visit to Sydney by a small group of Tiwi singers for a performance at the Seymour Centre[4] and in follow-up discussions on the Tiwi Islands.[5] The Tiwi custodians included Jacinta Tipungwuti, Regina Kantilla, Augusta Punguatji,[6] Anthea Kerinaiua, Frances Therese Portaminni and Gregoriana Parker, who identify as members of the Strong Women's Group, so named for their roles as cultural leaders and holders of song knowledge. They were accompanied by Francis Orsto, an emerging songman and authority of cultural practice. They (henceforth the Strong Women's Group[7]) had travelled to prepare for a performance, and this context created an opportunity for active agency and rich engagement with the historical record of Tiwi culture held in the collections.

Ethnomusicologist Genevieve Campbell travelled with the Strong Women's Group and participated in all the consultations. In this chapter, Campbell has contributed the broad context for understanding Tiwi historical collections and present interpretations in collaboration with Jacinta Tipungwuti as a representative of the group. Cultural historian Amanda Harris provided historical context for the audiovisual materials that were watched with the group and reflections on how they are viewed now and curator Matt Poll has documented the history of the Macleay Collections and reflections on the contemporary consultations.

Senior Tiwi woman Jacinta Tipungwuti had viewed the Macleay Museum Collection back in 2009[8] with a group of Tiwi delegates who travelled to Sydney and

---

3   This includes making artefacts for local ceremonial and utilitarian use, as well as creating art for external sale and/or display.
4   A performance by the collaborative group Ngarukuruwala (we sing songs) was presented by the Sydney Environment Institute at the Sound Lounge, Seymour Centre, 15 March 2019.
5   The films (and photographs) of the museum collection were shown to other Tiwi individuals with particular family connection to and cultural knowledge of the material.
6   Mrs Punguatji passed away in August 2022. Her name is included here with the knowledge and permission of her family.
7   For the purposes of this chapter, Mr Orsto is happy for us to refer to the group as the Strong Women's Group on the reader's understanding that he was also present.
8   Regina Kantilla and Francis Orsto were also among the group in both 2009 and in 2019. Regina, Augusta Punguatji and Frances Therese Portaminni returned again in 2021.

Canberra as part of the repatriation process of the ethnographic Tiwi recordings held at the Australian Institute of Aboriginal and Torres Strait Islander Studies (AIATSIS). That also included viewing the Tiwi collections at the National Museum of Australia in Canberra and the National Film and Sound Archive and the Art Gallery of NSW (AGNSW) in Sydney.[9] Jacinta contributed to this chapter as a representative of senior Tiwi culture and knowledge custodians. Through the process of assessing and consulting on the collections, she (and the others in the group) articulated the sense that the material and the information embedded in them were "owned" not by individuals, but by kinship and Country groups and that those credited as the singers, dancers, painters or carvers were, at the time, the current custodians of those songs, dances and designs. This raises questions for archivists and historians around reclamation, ownership and agency of Indigenous stakeholders in the presentation of their cultural heritage. In their recent reflection on digital archival returns, Barwick, Green, Vaarzon-Morel and Zissermann state: "Even where intellectual property rights can be said to be held by Indigenous contributors to research, such rights can only be held individually (not collectively). This does not properly reflect Indigenous law and practices regarding the custodianship and intergenerational transmission of knowledge".[10] Jacinta's words quoted at the start of this chapter give a sense of this cross-generational and communal custodianship of collective knowledge that informed all of our consultations.

This chapter builds on other recent scholarship that has sought to think about the ways "collections" can disperse records of culture across institutions and pose challenges to cultural custodians seeking to reassemble fragmented records. Often the result of collaborative work, this scholarship has begun to highlight the ways the priorities of archives and those of communities may differ. Barwick et al. also identify a tension between the archive's emphasis on "products" and living communities' emphasis on "process"; in other words, a contrast between archives as "the documentary by-product of human activity" and "knowledge management systems that depend on face-to-face communication as the primary means of cultural transmission".[11]

In the same volume, Gibson, Angeles and Liddle explore the challenges faced by contemporary language custodians of archival records whose historical

---

9   It also included performances at the Conservatorium of Music and the National Film and Sound Archive, both of which were informed by the discoveries the group had made in the collections.

10   Linda Barwick, Jennifer Green, Petronella Vaarzon-Morel and Katya Zissermann, "Conundrums and Consequences: Doing Digital Archival Returns in Australia", in *Archival Returns: Central Australia and Beyond*, eds Linda Barwick, Jennifer Green and Petronella Vaarzon-Morel (Honolulu & Sydney: University of Hawai'i Press and Sydney University Press, 2019), 10. See also: Michael Christie, "Digital Tools and the Management of Australian Desert Aboriginal Knowledge", in *Global Indigenous Media: Cultures, Poetics, and Politics*, eds Pamela Wilson and Michelle Stewart (Atlanta: Duke University Press, 2008), 270–86; Terri Janke, "Indigenous Knowledge and Intellectual Property: Negotiating the Spaces", *The Australian Journal of Indigenous Education* 37, no. S1 (2008), 14–24.

11   Barwick et al., "Conundrums and Consequences", 2.

orthographies remain in a static past, written down a century ago. As orthographies have varied across the archives and in the labelling of collections, they are, while highly valued records of language and stories, simultaneously disconnected from those of the younger generation trying to learn.[12] Both Barwick et al. and Gibson et al. show the considerable challenges posed by assemblages of cultural materials in archives that are disconnected in complex ways from the contexts for culture among contemporary custodians. In another recent volume on repatriation of music, Daniel B. Reed describes repatriation as the "moment when archival memory and human memory" meet. Reed suggests that memory is preserved in different forms in oral traditions and in archives, but that connecting the two through repatriation brings the archive into its context as "part of the processes of human life".[13]

Visual art and material culture in museums and galleries are often regarded as separate from these records of song and language preserved in archives. The fraught histories of museum collections of Aboriginal and Torres Strait Islander material culture have been the topic of considerable scholarship. Scholars including Nicholas Thomas, Ian McLean, Sandy O'Sullivan and Sally K. May have interrogated the complex histories of collection of this tangible culture and the delineation of some objects as museum pieces and others as modern art.[14] The separation of historical materials across archives, museums, libraries, cultural institutions and private collections is addressed by Thorpe, Faulkhead and Booker in the context of larger agendas of repatriation of human remains. They show that different kinds of fragmented collections need to be brought into dialogue with one another to properly contextualise practices of collecting and to realise the potential for repatriation back to communities.[15]

---

12   Jason Gibson, Shaun Penangke Angeles and Joel Perrurle Liddle, "Deciphering Arrernte Archives: The Intermingling of Textual and Living Knowledge", in *Archival Returns: Central Australia and Beyond*, eds Linda Barwick, Jennifer Green and Petronella Vaarzon-Morel (Honolulu & Sydney: University of Hawai'i Press and Sydney University Press, 2019).

13   Daniel Reed, "Reflections on Reconnections: When Human and Archival Modes of Memory Meet", in *The Oxford Handbook of Musical Repatriation*, eds Frank D. Gunderson, Rob Lancefield and Bret Woods (New York: Oxford University Press, 2018).

14   We note that the opening chapters of McLean's recent book focus on performance rather than visual arts. However, McLean states that the outlawing of corroborees after the nineteenth century means that his focus shifts back towards his chief research topic – visual art practices rather than performative ones. Ian McLean, *Rattling Spears: A History of Indigenous Australian Art* (London: Reaktion Books Ltd, 2016); Nicholas Thomas, *Possessions: Indigenous Art, Colonial Culture* (New York: Thames & Hudson, 1999); Sandy O'Sullivan, "Reversing the Gaze: Considering Indigenous Perspectives on Museums, Cultural Representation and the Equivocal Digital Remnant", in *Information Technology and Indigenous Communities*, eds Lyndon Ormond-Parker, Aaron Corn, Cressida Fforde, Kazuko Obata and Sandy O'Sullivan (Canberra: AIATSIS Research Publications, 2013); Sally May, *Collecting Cultures: Myth, Politics, and Collaboration in the 1948 Arnhem Land Expedition* (Lanham, Maryland: AltaMira Press, 2009).

15   Kirsten Thorpe, Shannon Faulkhead and Lauren Booker, "Transforming the Archive: Returning and Connecting Indigenous Repatriation Records", in *The Routledge Companion to Indigenous*

In this chapter, we also highlight the dispersal of Tiwi records of cultural practice into "collections" held in different kinds of institutions. Like Thorpe et al. we aim to bring material and ephemeral cultural collections into dialogue and to highlight ongoing relationships between songs, cultural practice and material culture used in performance. We interrogate the notion of museum and archive "collections". Whereas the word implies a process of assembly, cultural objects have historically been separated and dispersed, not only from one another, but also from their cultural context, stripped of meanings and connections, and rendered inanimate. These assemblages are often categorised by a researcher or curator, or publishers' intentions, rather than an understanding and arrangement of information through the practice of culture. In photographic archives, for example, documentation of performances in the form of printed copies of photographic images are many times shuffled like a deck of cards, their numbering and ordering entirely arbitrary and their inherent archival value lost. We show how recent work with custodians of Tiwi culture reassembles parts of the cultural whole that have been fragmented by non-Indigenous collection practices that separate material culture and performance of dance and song into distinct categories.

The material and performed culture viewed by the Strong Women's Group (and the focus of this chapter) included:

- 1927–29 and 1942 collections of Tiwi artefacts at the Macleay Museum
- 1948 footage of a public corroboree in Darwin Botanic Gardens[16]
- 1963 Aboriginal Theatre performance, film and associated exhibition[17]
- 1964 film *In Song and Dance*[18]

Prompted by the participants, this also led to discussions about a further event:

- 1970 Ballet of the South Pacific

Returning to the University of Sydney in 2019 as invited consultants on research into historical public performances by Aboriginal people (represented by the film footage listed above) and the preparation of the Tiwi exhibit included in the Chau Chak Wing Museum's new permanent exhibition – *Ambassadors* – has confirmed for the Tiwi group their valid and valuable role in engaging with research, archives and museums. For those who had been to Sydney and Canberra in 2009 it was also

---

Repatriation: Return, Reconcile, Renew, eds Cressida Fforde, Timothy McKeown and Honor Keeler (Abingdon, Oxon: Routledge, 2020).

16   Courtesy NT Archives, *Darwin – Doorway to Australia* (1949), C809, 1139364, Northern Territory Archives, Darwin.

17   AIATSIS, "Songs and dances from Bathurst Island, Yirrkala and Daly River performed at the Aboriginal Theatre in Sydney in 1963", audio recordings, ELIZABETHAN_01; NFSA, *The Never Never Land*, film, Australian Elizabethan Theatre Trust, Artransa Park Film Studios, 1964, 10092, National Film and Sound Archive.

18   NFSA – Lee Robinson, *In Song and Dance*, Film Australia, 1964.

an opportunity to take a leading role in the ongoing story of the engagement and to be the latest holders of the responsibility for the items themselves.[19]

The interconnectedness of material pieces and recorded song and dance was apparent in all interactions with the collections. Songs mark totems, clans and Country groups just as painted designs do. Similarly, recorded songs – the recordings themselves – are tangible, and the reactions to the audio and visual items in the archive create a tangible experience in the same way as holding a century-old stone axe or ceremonial spear. Song becomes artefact in this context, as the voice, the words, the manifestation of the ancestor and the song subject all create a visceral experience to the Tiwi custodian and another – different, but equally meaningful – to the non-Tiwi observer, who is in turn invested with the importance of the archive, its content, and its potential value to the custodians.

> Those people in those days, they had to paint because the ceremony was coming. They kept them going. Each Dreaming has different paint. Different where we come from like totem. Great and grandfathers, fathers. It's sort of like we all Tiwi people from the two islands [but] different totem. It was passing down from the old people. Passing down the knowledge they had. Passing down to us, and us, we are passing down our knowledge to next generation, ongoing.
>
> Jacinta Tipungwuti

The Macleay Museum Collection of material culture

The University of Sydney has, for nearly a century, been custodian of a selection of objects from the Tiwi Islands. The assemblage contains four Tunkalinta and three Arawanikiri (types of spears), four Kurrujuwa (metal axes) and two Mukwani (stone axes), as well as a selection of around 60 photographs acquired by three different collectors between the 1920s and 1950s. The collections were transferred from the University of Sydney Department of Anthropology to the permanent collections of the Macleay Museum (now incorporated into the Chau Chak Wing Museum) between 1960 and 1964 and have been rarely exhibited.

The distance between the museum's location in south-eastern Australia and the Tiwi Islands off the coast of the Northern Territory means that there have been few opportunities for Tiwi people, who have significant personal and cultural connections to the items, to view the collection. In 2019, the Strong Women's Group's tour to Sydney for performances not far from the museum storerooms provided an opportunity to follow up on the previous visit more than a decade earlier and to start new conversations about what these objects mean for Tiwi today.

---

19 Although the AIATSIS recordings have been shared around the Tiwi community they were released to the 11 individuals in 11 hard copies and so those individuals are still regarded as the custodians of the material.

These conversations among the visiting Tiwi community would result in new interpretive layers being added to the objects' exhibition in the university's new Chau Chak Wing Museum (opened in November 2020), part of the transition from the older "natural history" style museum space into a new building designed to incorporate the multiple forms of collections across the University Art Collection and Nicholson Collection. The Tiwi group's visit to the collections enabled an entirely new way of thinking about positioning Tiwi exhibition objects in relation to each other that was not previously in the curatorial brief.

Several of the items that formed the basis of consultation with the Strong Women's Group were acquired by American anthropologist Charles William Merton Hart in the 1920s, as part of research funded by the Australian Research Council (ARC), administered via the University of Sydney Department of Anthropology. Hart conducted his research among Tiwi people between 1928 and 1929.[20]

Among the objects are two metal axes[21] with resin and plaited cane, decorated with alternating bands of yellow and white ochre, and two stone axes with similar production techniques but different patterning of the ochre. One of the stone axes is labelled as a "Koong Kwang". This bears no resemblance to Tiwi orthology but is in the group's opinion a rough transcription of an archaic word for stone axe or hammer – Mukwanga. Neither are names that the community use to discuss these objects in 2020. A modern (metal-headed) axe is Kurrujuwa or, less often used, the old word Walimani, a loan-word from Iwaidja. It was decided that Mukwani (a small stone axe) should be used in the exhibition to label the stone axes and Walimani to describe the metal axes.[22]

The original labelling of the Macleay Collection exemplifies past museum practices that were grounded in the science of anthropological research, but today these collecting purposes are entirely at odds with the ways that the community would represent themselves to the outside world. For example, very little was known about the provenance or function of the Tiwi spears, which form a centrepiece of the new museum display. While there is no way to be certain what degree of agency the Tiwi makers and owners of the spears had at the time they were collected, the 2019 Tiwi group were of the opinion that the spears provided

---

20 Charles William Merton Hart, "Fieldwork Among the Tiwi, 1928–1929", in *Being an Anthropologist*, ed. G. Spindler (New York: Holt, Rinehart & Winston, 1970).

21 These were made using found iron objects the Tiwi group recognised as coming from ships/ shipwrecks. They gave oral accounts of shipwrecks and of iron from Sulawesi being traded by Makassar peoples to the Tiwi since the seventeenth century, long before it was introduced by the British. Among the ethnographic recordings of Tiwi song are mentions of Makassan boats and the old Tiwi language includes some words likely borrowed from Portuguese via visitors from Indonesia.

22 These decisions were made referring to the current Tiwi Dictionary and opinions of speakers. Lee, Jennifer. "Tiwi-English Interactive Dictionary", from Australian Society for Indigenous Languages (AuSIL) Interactive Dictionary ed. Maarten Lecompte (for interactive version), 2011. http://203.122.249.186/TiwiLexicon/lexicon/main.htm. For more on lexical change, see Jennifer Lee, *Tiwi Today: A Study of Language Change in a Contact Situation* (Canberra: Australian National University, 1987).

to collectors in 1928 would have been free from ritual connections, having been retired from use.[23] There are numerous Tiwi words (many no longer in use)[24] describing many variations of spears, creating potential layers of meaning and impact for Tiwi viewers that the curators were unaware of when they relied only on the written catalogue documentation. The visiting Tiwi group was able to add rich information about their ritual use and gender associations, the meanings of their carved and painted designs, and the kinship groups to which their makers likely belonged. The degree of painted decoration and their carved design indicated to Tiwi cultural authorities that the spears were used in ceremony and in ritual/ mock fighting. Conversely, the axes were not considered ceremonial and there was speculation as to whether they perhaps had been painted at the request of collectors. All the items were confirmed to be free of any restrictions that would impede their public display.

The updating of historical documentation and language words for items such as these presents another opportunity to engage directly with current cultural custodians. The often-scant collection metadata represents another potential pitfall of museums presenting historical or archival information, reinforcing a hierarchy and imbalance between Tiwi community knowledge of these types of objects and the museums as authorities or primary sources of information. The simple process of renaming the spears and axes in the current Tiwi language and seeking accurate information and cultural context is a subtle shift in the process of museums recognising the agency and autonomy of community members in the consultation process.

The museum's Hart Collection was of particular interest to Tiwi singers when considered in relation to the audio recordings Hart made on the islands in 1928.[25] Several correlations were made between the song items and the tangible objects and photographs in the Hart Collection in terms of ceremonial context, likely artists and singers, and reference to kinship, Country identities and ancestral totems. Hart's photographs of ceremony being performed show particular dance gestures that match song items among the Hart recordings. Completing the circle, the photos show men carrying ceremonial spears which, while not the actual objects in the museum, confirm the performative context of the kinds of spears held in the collection.

Not all of the objects in the new Chau Chak Wing Museum Tiwi assemblage were acquired through anthropological research. One Tunkalinta/Numwariyaka (straight barbless spear) and three Arawanikiri (barbed spears) were acquired via private

---

23 There are references (Simpson 1951; Holmes 1995) to ritual paraphernalia being "sold" to visitors at the conclusion of ceremonies in which they were used. This correlates with traditions of creating ceremonial objects afresh for each event, and that spears were often used for non-ritual contexts (hunting or fishing) after they were created for ceremony.

24 Due to lexical change following Pukumani restrictions on words associated with the deceased and the impact of the introduction of English, the Tiwi language has undergone significant change over the past century. See Lee, *Tiwi Today*.

25 The Hart recordings were repatriated after the 2009 Tiwi delegation to Canberra.

collector Frank Delbridge in 1927 (and possibly purchased in Darwin) and by Cecil Blumenthal, who was based on Bathurst Island as a radar technician in 1942.

Continuities in song and material culture

An interesting link exists between Blumenthal's wartime collection activities, and local history and its documentation through performance. The Japanese air strike of Darwin in February 1942, which saw aeroplanes fly over and strafe the south-east of Bathurst Island, was documented in song within a Kulama[26] ceremony, most likely in around March that year. The song has entered the Tiwi repertoire with varying versions retelling (and enacting through dance) the story of the planes, the radio controllers' attempts to warn the mainland, the subsequent bombings and the killing of civilians.

The 1949 film *Darwin – Doorway to Australia* includes footage of a large public corroboree in Darwin's Botanic Gardens in April 1948 – the first such public event since the end of World War II. The film shows Tiwi Yoi (Dreaming) dances that are performed today, and the Strong Women's Group were particularly interested to hear mention of the Japanese air attack on Darwin during World War II in the film and suggested it is likely that this event might have been the first public performance on the mainland of a Tiwi Kulama "Bombing of Darwin" or "Air Raid" song.[27] The song has been performed many times since WWII, in the traditional Kulama musical and linguistic form as well as in the women's "modern" form with guitar. For older Tiwi people in particular this was an empowering event that signified the Tiwi's sense of being part of Australia and involved in the war, but mixed feelings remain about the warnings to Darwin going unheeded/ignored. "Bombing of Darwin" was performed at the Darwin Festival Closing Ceremony in 2009,[28] in an event quite similar to the 1948 corroboree. Presented on a prepared sand dance ground, it included groups from Beswick, the Tiwi Islands, Maningrida and Darwin (groups also represented in the 1948 footage) performing in a corroboree set up for a large public audience. During both the 1948 and 2009 events, performers grasped spears of the kind held in the museum's collection.

---

26 Kulama, traditionally held annually (at the beginning of the dry season) is an initiation and well-being ceremony. An explanation of Kulama's multi-layered and complex functions is beyond the scope of this chapter (see Genevieve Campbell, "Sustaining Tiwi Song Practice through Kulama", *Musicology Australia* 35, no. 2 (2013), 237–52). Pertinent here is that one of Kulama's ritual stages is the vehicle for marking current events and important news through song. Kulama songs among the recorded archive include topics such as Macassan boats, storms causing damage, mission houses being built and the moon landing in 1969.

27 "Aborigines Thrill Big Crowd with Dance and Ritual", *Northern Standard*, 23 April 1948, 5, http://nla.gov.au/nla.news-article49984700; "Death Dance Star Mobbed in Darwin", *Courier-Mail*, 19 April 1948, 3, http://nla.gov.au/nla.news-article49666240; "A Royal Tour Disappointment", *West Australian*, 20 April 1948, 6, http://nla.gov.au/nla.news-article46904700.

28 https://bit.ly/3czBMfs.

Figure 4.1 1948 Botanic Gardens corroboree – still from film *Darwin – Doorway to Australia* (1949), C809, 1139364, Northern Territory Archives, Darwin.

A turtuni or Pukumani pole is also visible in the 1948 footage.[29] Pukumani poles have been of particular interest to anthropologists, art historians and collectors due to their size and decoration and because they are unique to Tiwi mortuary ceremonies. The complexities of displaying mortuary-related material have made ethical collection and display a complex subject for Tiwi engagement with museums and archives for many years. Some of the earliest collections of Pukumani poles on record are those collected by government "protector" Herbert Basedow in 1911, and poles collected in 1924, held by the Vatican Ethnological Museum. Basedow's notes say the poles collected in 1911 were from a Pukumani Yiloti (Final) ceremony held for a baby some years before Basedow was there and that the body was exhumed but was deemed to be in too poor condition to collect (Basedow 1913). Basedow had the poles repainted by Tiwi men and then removed from the site and shipped to Adelaide, where they were eventually housed at the

---

29   The turtuni, more commonly referred to in the literature as Pukumani poles, are large decorative poles carved from tree trunks and painted with intricate ochre designs that form the centrepiece of mortuary-related Pukumani ceremonies. They stand as "grave poles" either at the actual site of burial or in the Country of the deceased (this having changed over the last century due to the logistics and regulations of townships and the introduction of Catholic cemeteries).

South Australian Museum in 1934. These circumstances have been particularly upsetting for Tiwi Elders.

The Vatican Ethnological Museum's description of its collection of Pukumani poles states that "traditionally the posts should be left to deteriorate; however, these were produced for display and are among the most ancient museum specimens in the world".[30] Whether the poles collected in 1924 were in fact "produced for display" (and not for an individual's mortuary ceremony) is questionable. There is some evidence that in the early contact era Tiwi people offered ceremonial paraphernalia (spears, baskets, and woven arm and head bands) in exchanges of goods with visitors to the islands (Venbrux 2008), but it is widely agreed among Tiwi people today that, as the process of harvesting, carving and painting the poles forms part of the ritual stages of Pukumani – the deceased's final, and most important, mortuary ceremony – they should never be removed. Moreover, the poles erected in the early part of last century were in the ancestral place of the deceased's Country; the poles symbolise the person and stand in their Country always, to slowly break down into the earth.

The first Pukumani poles to be commissioned as works of art (rather than objects for display in an ethnographic museum) were the 17 poles displayed in the AGNSW, acquired in 1958 by Dr Stuart Scougall and then gallery director Tony Tuckson.[31] It is significant that the Melville Island artists, knowing the poles were destined for exhibition and a non-ceremonial context, used ironwood rather than bloodwood, which was traditionally used for ceremony.[32]

These stories of collected Pukumani poles raised questions around the public display of objects and performances intended for ritual as the group watched two other excerpts of footage: one of the 1964 North Australian Eisteddfod, and another of a 1963 touring show called the Aboriginal Theatre, featuring 17 Tiwi performers among its cast.[33] A significant feature of the *Aboriginal Theatre's* staging for its

---

30 Ethnological Museum Anima Mundi, "*Pukumani* grave posts", accessed 24 June 2021, http://www.museivaticani.va/content/museivaticani/en/collezioni/musei/museo-etnologico/collezione/pali-funerari-pukumani.html.

31 In 2009, 87-year-old Margaret Tuckson († wife of the late Tony Tuckson) met with a Tiwi group at the AGNSW to view the poles together. It was a meaningful experience for the group and for Mrs Tuckson, who recalled the impact of the commission in 1958 and what it meant for the art gallery and for Indigenous Australian art in general. The group was able to make a couple of small corrections to the displayed information accompanying the exhibit, including correcting the attribution of one artist's name.

32 Wurringilaka (*Corymbia nesophila* – Melville Island bloodwood), endemic to the islands, has been replaced to some extent in recent years by Kartukini (*Erythrophleum chlorostachys* – ironwood) for carving due to its durability and accessibility.

33 The Tiwi performers were Christopher Tipungwuti, Bennie Tipungwuti, Valentine Pauitjimi, Daniel Pauitjimi, Barry Puruntatameri, Noel Puantalura, Declan Napuatimi, Conrad Paul Tipungwuti, Freddie Puruntatameri, Matthew Woneamini, Eddie Puruntatameri, Walter Kerinaiua, Hector Tipungwuti, Felix Kantilla, Raphael Napuatimi, Justin Puruntatameri, Timothy Polipuamini. Press Release: "45 Aborigines to arrive on Sunday for Sydney Presentation", 28 November 1963, Box 51, Folder 66/1 (Administration) Aboriginal Theatre & Exhibition, Records of the Australian Elizabethan Theatre Trust, MS 5908, NLA.

Sydney and Melbourne shows was the Pukumani poles around which the Tiwi performances revolved.

Looking at footage and listening to recordings of the *Aboriginal Theatre* as performers and ceremony leaders themselves, the group agreed that the dances and song texts were not altered, simplified or re-created in any way differently for the purpose of the non-Tiwi audience context. They recognised phrases and words that are still used in Pukumani and Kulama ceremonies on the islands and agreed that those songs would have been in the men's repertoire for (Tiwi) family and community events. The "Pukumani" segment of the concert comprised a selection of songs that would be performed as part of the (much larger) series of mortuary rituals and observances collectively known as Pukumani. The segment gave a demonstration of some elements of a mortuary ceremony, including the "Mosquito" and "Honey Bag" opening of ceremony, the calling of ancestral and Country names, and ritual wailing but, importantly, it did not refer to an actual deceased person. In a close parallel with the acquisition of the Pukumani poles in the AGNSW, the Tiwi listeners in 2019 told us that it was therefore fine to be performed in a public concert and that the words, the respect and the cultural meaning were intact. It was presented consciously as a piece of cultural heritage and art, as are the poles.

Among Tiwi consultants there have been widely differing opinions on the ethics surrounding the collection of some recorded material, especially the recordings of mourning songs. Some Tiwi people listen with interest to the performance elements that have been preserved for posterity, or with sentimental pleasure and pride – as did the group as they listened to the publicly staged performance of the *Aboriginal Theatre*, hearing the wailing and sung/intoned sighs of Amparru (grieving) songs as elements of ritual. Others heard, among the rest of the ethnographic recorded archive, personal grief and pain and thought it inappropriate for anyone other than close family to listen. There are ongoing discussions about the difference between singing for family and singing for visitors/researchers (in the context of ceremony), with many people concerned that singers might have been discomforted by the intrusion of the recorder (or not have been aware of its presence), or of the long-term ramifications of being recorded.

The complex circumstances of collected recordings are exemplified by a Pukumani ceremony recorded in 1966 with a very different context to the *Aboriginal Theatre*. Warabutiwayi Mungatopi (Allie Miller) played an important role as cultural ambassador and performer in the 1950s–1970s. In 1953 he was part of the group of Aboriginal dancers performing for Queen Elizabeth II's visit to Brisbane. He was one of ethnographer Charles Mountford's principal singers in 1954 and therefore a good deal of his vocal, linguistic and family history is recorded.[34] Mungatopi also led the Tiwi group sent to the North Australian

---

34 (Mountford 1958) and AIATSIS audio recordings C01-002916 through C01-002918.

Eisteddfod in Darwin in 1964 and the film[35] made about the event features him, as a white-haired Elder, dancing crocodile, his Yoi (Dreaming).

Allie Mungatopi/Miller and his wife Polly were also primary consultants for Sandra Holmes, who collected extensive field recordings of ceremonies as well as paintings and carvings in the 1960s.[36] It is perhaps then not a coincidence that, when the Pukumani ceremony for Polly and Allie Miller's deceased young son was held, in May 1966, at the then Bagot Aboriginal Reserve in Darwin,[37] it was presented to a non-Tiwi audience as an exhibition of sorts. The segment below, written by Holmes, indicates that the ceremony was seen by the government Native Welfare Branch as a good opportunity to give (white) people a new cultural experience. Unlike the consciously staged performances mentioned in this paper, it seems that on this occasion the Tiwi people were not necessarily given much of a choice in the matter. Allie is quoted as having been upset at the lack of understanding and respect for his son's ceremony: "Too many white people come ... we never ask them to come, only Welfare man can say."[38] In the following quotation Holmes makes the distinction between ceremony and performance:

> The Welfare Branch had declared an Open Day for tourists and locals ... Polly sang softly to the ghost of her dead son and signalled for me to record it ... Crowds of white visitors jostled each other for photo opportunities, staring expectantly up the hill to where the Tiwi mourners were assembled in full ceremonial regalia.[39]

By Holmes' accounts the ceremony was just as it would have been (in terms of structure and ritual) without any non-Tiwi onlookers. Clearly, though, they were being watched as spectacle. Holmes goes on to report:

> At this point a senior welfare officer stood up and made a speech to thank the public for attending the ceremony and the Tiwi people for the performance. By prior arrangement the sculptures and grave posts would be sold to various dealers and other outlets.[40]

The distinction between "ceremony" and "performance" in Holmes' reporting of the welfare officer's words implies there was a difference in perception between the audience's and the mourners' experiences of the event. The white audience was

---

35   Lee Robinson, *In Song and Dance*, Film Australia, 1964, courtesy of NFSA. Thanks to Colin Worumbu Ferguson and Jordan Ashley for identifying Rusty Moreen in the film.
36   AIATSIS audio recordings S02_000181A through S03_000187B and Sandra Le Brun Holmes, *The Goddess and the Moon Man: The Sacred Art of the Tiwi Aborigines* (Roseville East, NSW: Craftsman House, 1995).
37   The ceremony was held in Darwin because the child had died in Darwin en route to hospital.
38   Sandra Le Brun Holmes, *The Goddess and the Moon Man: The Sacred Art of the Tiwi Aborigines* (Roseville East, NSW: Craftsman House, 1995), 31.
39   Holmes, *The Goddess and the Moon Man*, 22.
40   Holmes, *The Goddess and the Moon Man*, 29.

watching a performance (with the added exoticism of knowing it was a ceremony) while the mourners were attempting to have ceremony for family, knowing they were being watched and photographed.

By contrast, in the 1964 eisteddfod film we see Allie speaking to the group (in Tiwi) saying, "We need to get ready and practise for this thing in Darwin. Ted Evans came across from Darwin to Snake Bay to tell us we are going in".[41] The Strong Women's Group viewed this as an indication that the performers' involvement was real and informed. Mary Elizabeth Moreen (Polly and Allie Miller's daughter and related by marriage to Rusty Moreen, who features in the film), now in her late sixties, was involved in her parents' consultations with Holmes. It is perhaps no coincidence that Mary is now a leader among the Strong Women's Group and has been proactive in reclaiming recorded collections and engaging with museums and archives.[42]

The songs and singers as animators of the archive

Way back they used the name of what they did in the past. We can name them because it's a bit similar to those in the past. The same sound. It's the way they used to say and hear somebody say and they put it in a song. It's like a good thing, saying and singing all these songs in the traditional way of singing. We all have different versions, different songs – it's all part of the good songs and the words' meaning.

Jacinta Tipungwuti

The body painting and feathered beards and headdresses worn by performers in the 1948 corroboree footage and the intricately painted spears in the Macleay Collection inspired much discussion about the perceived lost richness of ritual paraphernalia and preparation today. Tiwi viewers were also interested to see the paint on Eddie, a young boy featured in the *Aboriginal Theatre* film. The design is specific to a particular stage of initiation and is no longer used. Justin Puruntatameri, a leading song and culture man who passed away in 2012, aged 87, is shown as a much younger man, applying the design. Current Elders noted that this film shows that Mr Puruntatameri was continuing the practice of painting initiands in 1963 (more recently than people had thought) and it sparked discussion around the possibility of reintroducing the designs and some of the ceremonial dance and song events that involve young people.

---

41   Translation provided by Tiwi speakers (the film gives no translation). Ted Evans was the Northern Territory chief welfare officer at the time.

42   Mary Elizabeth Moreen was in the delegation to Canberra and viewed the Macleay Collection in 2009. Unfortunately she is now too unwell to travel but has been involved in discussions of the collection from her home.

The choice of participants in each of these performance events (based perhaps on cultural or socio-political authority) and the song choices they then made have had significant effect on which song types, which dances and which elements of the otherwise fragile song language have endured. In much the same way, the collection of certain artists' items have preserved particular designs and stories, with corresponding empowerment of individuals and of groups both at the time of collection or recording and recently, as they have become items of cultural heritage that add to the story of the museum collections.

While discussing the 1963 *Aboriginal Theatre*, Regina Kantilla talked about coming to Sydney to perform in a similar show – the 1970 Ballet of the South Pacific. Opening at Her Majesty's Theatre on 6 April 1970, the *Ballet of the South Pacific* brought together 20 Aboriginal performers from Northern Australia with dancers from the Cook Islands, directed by Beth Dean and Victor Carell.[43] The format of the *Ballet of the South Pacific* very closely mimicked the format of the 1963 *Aboriginal Theatre*, even to the extent of including some of the same musicians or dancers and many members of the same communities, though the production team was different. Members of the Bathurst Island Tipungwuti, Puruntatameri and Portaminni families were involved in both the 1963 *Aboriginal Theatre* and 1970 *Ballet of the South Pacific*.[44] The subject matter of songs featured in the *Aboriginal Theatre* and also in the Darwin eisteddfod are indicative of the Country and kinship affiliations of the performers involved in each.

In the 1970 shows, Tiwi women Regina Portaminni (now Kantilla) and Irene Babui presented a set of women's dances.[45] Regina was amused, in 2019, to see the photo of her younger self in this photograph. Their costumes were not Tiwi, but perhaps a choice made by the producers to portray an islander look since the Tiwi women's lack of "cultural dress"[46] necessitated creation of a "native" costume – Regina wasn't sure and didn't recall any discussion about costume choice. There

---

43 We had no footage of this, but Regina talked about coming to Sydney to perform in it, and we have since returned photos from her media interviews about the show to her. "Ballet of the South Pacific", *Australian Women's Weekly*, 1 April 1970, 25, http://nla.gov.au/ nla.news-article47814074. The full cast of Australian performers was: Irene Babui, Regina Portaminni, Simon Tipungwuti, Mathew Wonaeamirri, Edward Puruntatameri, Leon Puruntatameri, Frederick Nanganarralil, William Calder Nalagandi, Jackson Jacob, Larry Lanley, Gordon Watt, Arthur Roughsey, Yangarin Kumana, Nalakan Wanambi, Munguli Monangurr, Cyril Ninnal. Program for *Ballet of the South Pacific*, Subject file: Ballet of the South Pacific – Programs and Posters, Beth Dean and Victor Carell Papers, MLMSS 7804/10/7, SLNSW.
44 A Tiwi delegation also performed at the 1976 Pacific Arts Festival in Rotorua.
45 Program of *Ballet of the South Pacific* in James Cook M. Ephemera – Box 2 – (1900–), SLNSW; and Richard Beattie, "Aboriginal Girls to Dance in Sydney", *Sydney Morning Herald*, 21 March 1970, clipping in Carell, Victor – Proposed ballet of the South Pacific, A2354 1969/289, NAA, Canberra.
46 Tiwi men's ceremonial dress of nagas, loin cloths, was added in the early twentieth century with the arrival of the missionaries, while women and girls were put into skirts. European dress then became the norm. The establishment in 1969 of the Bima Wear screen printing and sewing cooperative on Wurrumiyanga (Nguiu), Bathurst Island, created dresses decorated with Tiwi designs that the Tiwi women wear today as a form of cultural dress, but in the 1960s there was no specific "traditional" dress for Tiwi women.

The Sydney Morning Herald 21/3/1970

Aboriginal girls to dance in Sydney

● By Richard Beattie

A ballet contrasting the dances of the Aborigines and the Cook Islanders will be seen in Sydney next month.

The show, called "The Ballet of the South Pacific," will open at Her Majesty's Theatre on April 6 with a cast of 18 Aboriginal men from many parts of the Northern Territory and two Aboriginal girls from Bathurst Island.

The other 40 members of the cast will be Polynesians from the Cook Islands.

Mr Victor Carell, the producer of the ballet, said that the popular idea that Aboriginal girls do not dance, spread through school textbooks, was wrong.

"They do dance, but usually more quietly and in a

more feminine and inconspicuous way when they are dancing with the men," he said.

Two Aboriginal girls, Regina Portaminni, 18, and Irene Babui, 22 (left and right in picture), both members of the Tiwi tribe, have been brought from Bathurst Island for the show.

The Aborigines will dance stories from their dream time legends and several camp fire dances, some of which are quiet and restrained.

The ballet will run for two weeks in Sydney before going to Brisbane and Melbourne and several large country towns.

Any profit made will be distributed between the Cook Islands National Arts Theatre Trust and the councils of the tribes from which the Aboriginal dancers come.

Figure 4.2 Regina Portaminni and Irene Babui, pictured in Richard Beattie, "Aboriginal Girls to Dance in Sydney", *Sydney Morning Herald*, 21 March 1970, clipping in Beth Dean and Victor Carell papers, MS 7804, Box 10. (State Library of NSW.)

was some offence taken by some of the wording in the newspaper article and the description of their performance as "primitive dances". Regina was not so concerned about this though and recalled the fun she and Irene had had on the tour and said "that's just how they talk about us back then … I don't know, it was cute those outfits we had … but I was very nervous too, but that's maybe why I learned how to do it. Now I'm so good on stage!"[47]

This costuming anachronism aside, there were many connections found between the archive collections and ongoing continuity of practice. In the context of the performers sharing their culture, the potential for the performances to be forward-looking and future-facing seems also to have been a key motivator. Most of the songs performed in the *Aboriginal Theatre* are performed today with the song texts varying slightly within the parameters of individuals' extemporisation and with accompanying dance and gestures unchanged. The opinion of the Strong Women's Group is that the song subject choices were also just like "the songs we show to people these days" with a combination of ancestral stories, the Yoi (Dreaming) of the participants and a recognition of the event itself through

47 Now, at the age of 67, Regina is the most outgoing of the women on stage, often taking lead dancing roles.

song. A song translating loosely as "Cars, Town Life, Aeroplane" in the 1963 *Aboriginal Theatre* program is considered by the group to be the performers' acknowledgement of their trip to Melbourne in the tradition of Tiwi songs that document current events for the social record.

> Maybe they sat down and talked about the program. Like we do with you sometimes. Choose some palingarri [old] stories, some Yoi for each person [totemic dances], some story songs. They sang that Nyingawi song to tell people about how we Tiwi learned to sing Kulama … and maybe "Bombing of Darwin" is interesting for white people to know those planes went over here, you know?
>
> Jacinta Tipungwuti

At their own performance in Sydney the week of viewing the footage, the group spontaneously inserted into the program a healing song to acknowledge the funeral of a Tiwi woman[48] being held that day. Knowing they would have been leading the healing stage of the funeral if they'd been attending, they sang because

> we were feeling bad not being at home and singing for her like we should be, so we sang it for her here. Share that sadness with friends in Sydney. Respect too. Showing respect for our sister.
>
> Jacinta Tipungwuti

A more generic version of a healing song would likely have been on the program anyway, just as in the "Pukumani" performance in 1963, and although they had a non-Tiwi audience, the cultural integrity and function of the song for the Tiwi participants overrode the fact that there was an audience.

Across the consultations, the principal connection between the group and the archives was the performance of culture. A core feature of Tiwi oral and embodied knowledge keeping is the creation of occasion-specific song text that acknowledges both the ancestral predecessors and the current knowledge holders. This makes fluid and transparent the boundaries between cultural artefacts (with their connections through designs to Country and kinship groups and ancestral stories) and sung artefacts (songs marking those same Country and kinship groups and ancestral stories). Just as Tungutalum sang "I am talking into the gramophone" for Hart's recorder in 1928,[49] and the Tiwi men in 1963 created a song to add their journey to Melbourne to the oral record, the Strong Women's Group in 2019 sang, among a program of ancestral and Country songs, a song to explain that they were in Sydney missing the AFL Tiwi Islands Grand Final. All are examples of the

---

48 The woman who died was the direct sister of one of the group and a classificatory sister to all of them.

49 C.W. Hart audio. AIATSIS collection C01-004240B-D33.

performance motivations for people to whom song is fundamentally a vehicle for knowledge transmission.

The 1928 recording of Tungutalum was played in the opening sequence of the 2019 performance in Sydney, completing a circle of animating culture in a tangible way. Having seen the objects collected by Hart at the time the recording of Tungutalum was collected, we then heard Tungutalum singing his own proactive engagement with the process of creating an archive that would then be re-engaged with nearly a century later.

Recordings among the archives of now-obsolete song forms (having not been performed in living memory), such as the "Mosquito" and "Honey Bag" calls and some dance gestures shown in the 1948 footage, have been cited by senior culture people as an important opportunity to reclaim cultural heritage – just one example of audiovisual archives having as tangible a presence as artefact. Like "corroborees" that have long brought people together in cultural exchange, the recordings of public performances, concerts and eisteddfods play an important role in supporting ongoing performance practices. The preparation of high-quality performances helped give validity to ongoing practice of traditions that might otherwise have been under pressure to fall away in favour of church hymns in language, or communication and adoption of teaching in English.[50]

When talking about the performances in the Botanic Gardens and the memories the Tiwi women had of being part of eisteddfods in Darwin and precursor competitions held on the islands, there is a sense of nostalgia for the experiences they had, and also a feeling that those events served a role in maintaining song culture, creating a goal and sense of pride in performing for an outside audience. That era has left a lasting impression on the culture now because it is the young women and men who had those experiences who have become the Elders holding onto culture. Jacinta Tipungwuti recalls learning these songs for the eisteddfod and remembers that it was only after they completed their schooling that they were able to develop knowledge in Tiwi song practice. Now children are able to learn Tiwi songs from their Elders as part of everyday life.

Cultural leaders and cultural ambassadors

They had that strong culture! And they left that for us … generation to generation … You know when old people pass away there'll be nobody there singing and dancing, but they have to know, have that knowledge … today and listen to the

---

50   See also Dunbar-Hall and Gibson's discussion (following Ellis) of hymns as a continuation of the sacred function of music in the cultural practice of many Aboriginal people. Peter Dunbar-Hall and Chris Gibson, *Deadly Sounds, Deadly Places: Contemporary Aboriginal Music in Australia* (Sydney: UNSW Press, 2004), 42.

Elders [in the footage] what they are singing about and the language that belongs to us.

Jacinta Tipungwuti

As language and music experts listening to the full audio of the Aboriginal Theatre performance, the Tiwi group was able to add song text, translations and some small corrections to song subjects mentioned in the film's narration and program – details that would not have affected the audience perception but that reiterate the value of information that those with cultural authority and knowledge can add to an archive. As experts in the performance of ceremony, the group also added value to the museum collection, organising Hart's photographs in sequence by recognising dances and gestures specific to certain ritual stages. It was clear that they saw the objects (in this case the photographs and the dance, gesture and spears they depict) not as inanimate, but as representations of performed culture. Each photograph was described in terms of the dance or the gesturing it had captured and the spears (both in the photographs and in the collection) were described by the way they were held and which part of ceremony they were used for. Here performance constituted the value of the archival objects, and the objects enabled a deeper understanding of the performative context and corrected some assumptions of the use of artefact. This series of photos was another example of a collection categorised by a researcher or curator rather than through the practice of culture. Reassembling them in their performed order has reanimated and enriched their meaning.

At the Macleay Collection viewing, the contrasting, yet equally meaningful, reaction to artefacts brought these differing and interconnecting agencies together as the group viewed the spears, the designs on which were known to Elders and family names attributed to potential individual makers. These designs were familiar and brought up emotions not only of interest from a heritage perspective but also of strong family pride and sentiment. They identified the idiosyncratic painted design elements of two distinct artists and designs connected to particular kinship groups. With this and the women's descriptions of how the spears are carried in ritual and dance in mind, the group and the curator developed the layout, order and positioning of the spears for the new display. This collaborative and participatory process of co-authoring display design and label information (where appropriate) reflects the expectations of contemporary community agency by retaining the autonomy of community opinion and authority.

A catalogue of designs and a length of fabric in the collection that is labelled as an example of one of the first designs from Bima Wear screen printing on Bathurst Island created a particularly strong point of collision between archive and living culture. Jacinta had a (newly made) skirt in her luggage in fabric of that same design. Some of the women present had worked at Bima Wear in the past and all have worn these fabrics daily since the 1970s. Not unlike the group's reaction to some of the songs in the audiovisual archive that were "just like we do now" and the grouping of spears by artist by identifying painted design elements used today, talk afterwards suggested the women were a little concerned that they might offend the people at the archives by saying that what they have been looking after so carefully is actually quite normal. On the other hand, as Augusta Punguatji said, "It is really good to let them know that we are still doing what those people did back then because our culture is so strong." These direct associations between current culture holders and their predecessors confirm their role not only as custodians of an ongoing culture but also as holders of knowledge that is of great value to museum curators and researchers.

Across the film material and the museum collection we also found that some items are no longer made or performed in exactly the same way, traditions having been modified through time and the creative idiosyncrasies of individuals, and so they have become important items of cultural heritage, preserved in the archive for both Tiwi and non-Tiwi viewers.

The following, from the promotional material associated with the Sydney performance in 2019, describes some of the motivation the Strong Women's Group share through their intangible cultural heritage:

> Ngarukuruwala means we sing songs. The Tiwi Strong Women's Group don't really "rehearse" or "perform" – they come together to sing. They don't really see themselves as a choir. They are a group of women who share a connection through the songs they know, create and sing together nearly every day.[51]

As the group have described their own approach towards the rehearsal process, which is not entirely different from the research process for museum exhibitions, it is not the end result – the performance or the exhibition itself – that is the main goal. It is in the process of coming together, the continuation of practice and the sharing of knowledge that the real cultural value of the items (tangible and intangible) is found.

Coda

> They carry [the spears] when they start to have the ceremony, coming in. The opening of the ceremony they carry this spear – the Elder of the ceremony.
>
> Jacinta Tipungwuti

In May 2021 eight Tiwi singers[52] performed in the new Chau Chak Wing Museum and viewed the Tiwi display for the first time. As they approached the case, senior

---

51   From promotional material prior to the Sound Lounge performance, http://sydney.edu.au/environment-institute/events/tiwijazz-ngarukuruwala-sing/.

52   Calista Kantilla, Elizabeth Tipiloura, Katrina Mungatopi, Frances Therese Portaminni, Gemma and John Louis Munkara, Regina Kantilla and Augusta Punguatji.

Figure 4.3 Gemma Munkara and Katrina Mungatopi viewing the Tiwi display; Chau Chak Wing Museum, May 2021.

songwoman Calista Kantilla called out the Tiwi ancestral Countries and kinship groups, acknowledging the group's presence as visitors to others' ancestral lands and as representatives of their own ancestors as current Elders. Just as they would in ceremony (and just as we had recently seen in the filmed and photographed archives) they carried spears – one a beautiful example of the broad-headed, double-barbed Arawanikiri ceremonial spear, made by Bede Tungutalum, a current senior culture man and artist and a direct male descendant of Tungutalum who was photographed and recorded by Hart in 1928.[53] Having spent time discussing the spears in the museum collection, gaining insights into the ochre designs and the ceremonial functions of the different types of spears in the display, it was a powerful moment then for the curators to witness the animating of what was previously merely collated data – the spears being used in contemporary, ongoing performative cultural practice. In real-time demonstration of their agency and engagement with the archives, the group read the object labels, and the spelling and the cultural information, and as the senior culture person present, Calista gave her official nod of

---

53 The two other spears have no confirmed artist or age. They are "very old" according to Calista. They bear a close similarity to those in the collection, which was of great interest to the group.

approval. In a symbolic gesture of acknowledgement and ratification of the display, the group then danced towards the display case, animating the cultural heritage in front of them and holding spears very closely resembling those made by their ancestors a century ago.

> It's hard to explain. The young people need to understand because in the future time they will make this place better for themselves and their families. It will strengthen them and give them more, like healing, and they will understand "who am I?" First thing they'll say to themselves. "Who am I, where I belong to?" which is the main identity. It's important for them to know their culture and the way they are living today.

Jacinta Tipungwuti

References

"A Royal Tour Disappointment". *West Australian*, 20 April 1948, 6. http://nla.gov.au/nla.news-article46904700.

"Aborigines Thrill Big Crowd with Dance and Ritual". *Northern Standard*, 23 April 1948, 5. http://nla.gov.au/nla.news-article49984700.

"Ballet of the South Pacific". *Australian Women's Weekly*, 1 April 1970, 25. http://nla.gov.au/nla.news-article47814074.

Barwick, Linda, Jennifer Green, Petronella Vaarzon-Morel and Katya Zissermann. "Conundrums and Consequences: Doing Digital Archival Returns in Australia". In *Archival Returns: Central Australia and Beyond*, eds Linda Barwick, Jennifer Green and Petronella Vaarzon-Morel. Honolulu and Sydney: University of Hawai'i Press and Sydney University Press, 2019: 1–27.

Basedow, Herbert. "Notes on the Natives of Bathurst Island, North Australia". *Journal of the Royal Anthropological Institute* 43 (1913): 291–323.

Campbell, Genevieve. "Ngarriwanajirri, the Tiwi Strong Kids Song: Using Repatriated Recordings in a Contemporary Music Project". *Yearbook for Traditional Music* 44 (2012): 1–23.

Campbell, Genevieve. "Sustaining Tiwi Song Practice Through Kulama". *Musicology Australia* 35, no. 2 (2013): 237–52.

Christie, Michael. "Digital Tools and the Management of Australian Desert Aboriginal Knowledge". In *Global Indigenous Media: Cultures, Poetics, and Politics*, eds Pamela Wilson and Michelle Stewart. Atlanta: Duke University Press, 2008: 270–86.

"Death Dance Star Mobbed in Darwin". *Courier-Mail*, 19 April 1948, 3. http://nla.gov.au/nla.news-article49666240.

Dunbar-Hall, Peter and Chris Gibson. *Deadly Sounds, Deadly Places: Contemporary Aboriginal Music in Australia*. Sydney: UNSW Press, 2004.

Gibson, Jason, Shaun Penangke Angeles and Joel Perrurle Liddle. "Deciphering Arrernte Archives: The Intermingling of Textual and Living Knowledge". In *Archival Returns: Central Australia and Beyond*, eds Linda Barwick, Jennifer Green and Petronella Vaarzon-Morel. Honolulu and Sydney: University of Hawai'i Press and Sydney University Press, 2019: 29–45.

Hart, Charles William Merton. "Fieldwork Among the Tiwi, 1928–1929". In *Being an Anthropologist*, ed. G. Spindler. New York: Holt, Rinehart & Winston, 1970.

Holmes, Sandra Le Brun. *The Goddess and the Moon Man: The Sacred Art of the Tiwi Aborigines*. Roseville East, NSW: Craftsman House, 1995.

Janke, Terri. "Indigenous Knowledge and Intellectual Property: Negotiating the Spaces". *The Australian Journal of Indigenous Education* 37, no. S1 (2008): 14–24.

Lee, Jennifer. *Tiwi Today: A Study of Language Change in a Contact Situation*. Canberra: Australian National University, 1987.

Lee, Jennifer. "Tiwi–English Interactive Dictionary", from Australian Society for Indigenous Languages (AuSIL) Interactive Dictionary, ed. Maarten Lecompte (for interactive version), 2011 http://203.122.249.186/TiwiLexicon/lexicon/main.htm.

May, Sally. *Collecting Cultures: Myth, Politics, and Collaboration in the 1948 Arnhem Land Expedition*. Lanham, Maryland: AltaMira Press, 2009.

McLean, Ian. *Rattling Spears: A History of Indigenous Australian Art*. London: Reaktion Books Ltd, 2016.

Mountford, Charles. *The Tiwi: Their Art, Myth and Ceremony*. London: Phoenix House, 1958.

Simpson, Colin. *Adam in Ochre: Inside Aboriginal Australia*. Sydney: Angus and Robertson, 1951.

O'Sullivan, Sandy. "Reversing the Gaze: Considering Indigenous Perspectives on Museums, Cultural Representation and the Equivocal Digital Remnant". In *Information Technology and Indigenous Communities*, eds Lyndon Ormond-Parker, Aaron Corn, Cressida Fforde, Kazuko Obata and Sandy O'Sullivan. Canberra: AIATSIS Research Publications, 2013: 139–49.

Reed, Daniel. "Reflections on Reconnections: When Human and Archival Modes of Memory Meet". In *The Oxford Handbook of Musical Repatriation*, eds Frank Gunderson, Rob Lancefield and Bret Woods. New York: Oxford University Press, 2018: 23–36.

Thomas, Nicholas. *Possessions: Indigenous Art, Colonial Culture*. New York: Thames & Hudson, 1999.

Thorpe, Kirsten, Shannon Faulkhead and Lauren Booker. "Transforming the Archive: Returning and Connecting Indigenous Repatriation Records". In *The Routledge Companion to Indigenous Repatriation: Return, Reconcile, Renew*, eds Cressida Fforde, C. Timothy McKeown and Honor Keeler. Abingdon, Oxon: Routledge, 2020: 822–34.

Venbrux, Eric. "Quite Another World of Aboriginal Life: Indigenous People in an Evolving Museumscape". In *The Future of Indigenous Museums: Perspectives from the Southwest Pacific*, ed. Nick Stanley. New York: Berghahn Books, 2008: 117–34.

5

The body is an archive: Collective memory, ancestral knowledge, culture and history

Rosy Simas

Positionality

In order to properly position myself within the context of this chapter, I need to introduce myself so that I might be recognised by other Native people, other Haudenosaunee, other Onöndowa'ga:' (Seneca), by the Creator and by the other living beings of this natural world. My name is Rosy Simas Dewadošyö' (get ready for winter). I am of the Joäshä' (Heron) clan of the Onöndowa'ga, who are one of the Six Native Nations of the Haudenosaunee.

As a Haudenosaunee, I am keenly aware that it is not my place to write or speak as an expert on our culture and customs. That is a role reserved for faith keepers, clan mothers, chiefs and scholars who have been given permission from Haudenosaunee leadership to do so. Rather, I describe in this chapter how the tradition of oral storytelling relates to wampum, and how my body is an archive. I call upon my first-person experience through a self-reflexive and autoethnographic approach and I cite those whose role it is to talk on Haudenosaunee culture with expertise.

It is my responsibility as a Haudenosaunee, a Seneca, as a Native artist and an independent scholar who is committed to living in relationship with the natural world to attend to the ways in which I engage with the institutional structures that exist within the world of the arts and academia. I do so by maintaining holistic and accountable relationships with other Native people, with my family and with my ancestors. As a result, this responsibility directly influences the ways in which I investigate, analyse, consider and conduct my research, both as an arts practitioner and an independent scholar. That responsibility and obligation is reflected here, within this chapter.

In addition, I want to acknowledge and thank those who have helped me think on this subject and encouraged me through the process of writing this chapter: editors Amanda Harris and Jakelin Troy, dance scholars Ananya Chatterjea, Sam Aros Mitchell and Jacqueline Shea Murphy.

Introduction

I consider my body to be an ever-evolving archive. I am a Native artist who generates performance and visual artwork from intersensory listening, to create transdisciplinary art to intentionally connect with audiences through movement, images, sound, metaphor and narrative. I also believe that this kind of work I do, an approach I liken to other Indigenous transdisciplinary artists, is paramount to the survivance of Indigenous people. Gerald Vizenor, in his book *Manifest Manners: Narratives on Postindian Survivance*, describes survivance as an "active sense of presence, the continuance of Native stories, not a mere reaction, or a survivable name. Native survivance stories are renunciations of dominance, tragedy and victimry".[1]

I propose here that Haudenosaunee knowledge and storytelling–imparting practices, by Haudenosaunee and for Haudenosaunee, are complete sensorial experiences which are critical to the cultural revitalisation and survival of communities. In this chapter, I will explore how these sensorial practices are a holistic part of growth of the familial, ancestral, historical and cultural archive within the physical bodies of the community. I describe how longstanding Haudenosaunee knowledge–imparting practices, which include oratory, wampum, oral storytelling and recitation, are all repetitive energetic forms for telling, sharing and understanding. In the writing of this chapter, I have considered the differences between scholarly archives that have been violent towards Indigenous peoples and the Indigenous archive, which, through a process of conceptualisation, re-Indigenises space and builds possibility for connection and healing for and between Indigenous bodies. Lastly, I describe how my work has oscillated between the archive/archives, the colonial archive and the Indigenous archive, and how this has manifested sites for healing and connection, both for me and for the communities with whom I share these practices.

Archive/archives

This concept of my body as an ever-evolving archive presents several challenges within the world of academia and art. Here I use the word and concept of "archive" as a way of defining the source of resilience and healing, and yes, survivance that comes from the wisdom, strength and empathy of our ancestors, family and community. I recognise that many scholars have written about the "archive" and the subsequent relationship to the body. For one, Diana Taylor in *The Archive and the Repertoire: Performing Cultural Memory in the Americas*[2] has illuminated the repeated scenarios of settler-colonial discovery and conquest, which continue to

---

1   Gerald Robert Vizenor, *Manifest Manners: Postindian Warriors of Survivance* (Hanover: Wesleyan University Press, 1994), 12.
2   Diane Taylor, *The Archive and the Repertoire: Performing Cultural Memory in the Americas* (Durham: Duke University Press, 2003).

haunt the Americas to this day. Taylor has called to attention the polarities that exist between the written word and embodied practice as well as between the settler valorisation of the textual body and the Indigenous understanding of the body. Yet these concepts remain stuck, trapped behind a binary that allows for little intervention.

I also recognise Ohlone Costanoan-Esselen and Chumash poet and scholar Deborah A. Miranda has even stated in her poetry that "My body is an archive". In her book *Bad Indians: A Tribal Memoir*[3] Miranda performs an intervention between the colonial archive and the Indigenous archive, drawing attention to the ways in which the Indigenous archive carves out space for Native artists and scholars to continue to be in an intrinsic cultural and radical relationship with the world.

I am aware that within this globalised society, dance has recently gained prominence in academia, especially in the field of performance studies. Performance studies research of dance regards the conveyance of bodily knowledge and looks to the body as a fertile site of research engagement. As an art form, Western dance is bound up by Western cultural and educational ideologies. Researching Indigenous dance/movement art practices, contemporary or otherwise, through this research methodology just doesn't work. What kinds of bodies in motion constitute "knowledge" when this art form is examined through these specific lenses? Whose bodies of work (and bodies, for that matter) are produced, valorised, researched and conveyed? Whose bodies are made invisible, excluded and forgotten?

My body/my archive

As an act of self-determination and resilience, I posit here that my Native body is indeed an archive, an ever-evolving part of the Native physical, spiritual and intellectual world. This archive or codex lives in relationality to the natural world and holds the power to decolonise, to heal bodies of land and water, while also possessing the ability to shift and change the contemporary spaces that we currently occupy.

In his book *Hungry Listening* xwélméxw (Stó:lō/Skwah), writer and scholar Dylan Robinson discusses the reclamation of Indigenous authority over scholarship through refusal. This refusal performs as a way to discontinue the contribution to limitations of settler-colonial views of Indigenous scholarship. In Robinson's words: "This refusal functions as a corrective to the history of Indigenous knowledge extraction, misrepresentation and claiming of authority by settler scholars. In doing so, it returns authority to Indigenous people and re-emphasises the importance of language in the construction of knowledge".[4]

---

3   Deborah Miranda, *Bad Indians: A Tribal Memoir* (Berkeley, CA: Heyday, 2013).
4   Dylan Robinson, *Hungry Listening* (Minnesota: University of Minnesota Press, 2020), 22–23.

The Indigenous body is not an archive to be "extracted" from, as has been the historical practice from Western scientists, scholars and those who settled on Turtle Island (North America) to steal from Indigenous people and return to Europe with their treasures. Despite settler colonialism's multiple attempts to extrapolate the intellectual and spiritual resources of Indigenous people, the approach I take here stands steadfast as a refusal to those extractions.

It's critical here to note the differences between "archive" and "archives" as constructed repositories of knowledge that contain historical documents and records. The "colonial archive" contains documents, maps and records produced by state or institutional agencies. My body as an archive represents my own experience, my own phenomenological encounters and my own histories, from a deeply corporeal space. By calling attention to these various *archives*, the capacity to create contemporary frameworks might be transformed through fostering an Indigenous holistic worldview, which ultimately can positively impact and influence all peoples.

The development of my creative process

About 10 years ago, I first came to understand that my body is an ever-evolving vibrant archive of genealogy, history, culture and creation. I realised how the movements of my childhood, of play, dance, ritual and ceremony – movements deeply connected to the earth – informed the very architecture of my body. As my bones were shaped by gestures, my senses became developed to receive and perceive information in culturally specific ways. Neurological pathways formed throughout my body, from experiences with family and with Elders. I found myself in a different relationship to nature than from those I was in school with. These movements were first imitated and then embodied. The origin, however, was from a deep cultural and physical groundedness.

Over the past two decades I have researched and developed methods to continue cultivating this deep relationship among my senses, physical experiences and nature as a means to create movement, images, text, sound and objects. I have performed this research myself as well as with others. My 2014 work, *We Wait In The Darkness*, exemplifies these claims and recuperates the Indigenous archive through this combined approach of deep listening, living in relationality with nature and intentional awakening of cultural memory.

From this work, memories awakened, my ancestors were evoked, and the rich culture and history of my people became revitalised through the act of deep listening. I contend here that it was through these multilayered sites of performance work, installations of visual art and immersive sound environments that an invitation came forth for deeper engagement. Through the process of creating this performance, past events were summoned, realised and understood. These events were ultimately transformed to become an act of healing and connection.

Haudenosaunee scholar Susan Hill (Wolf Clan, Mohawk Nation) and resident of Ohswe:ken (Grand River Territory) explains, "One of the Kanyen'keha words for clan is Otara; when one asks another what clan they belong to, the question literally translates to 'what clay are you made of?'"[5] Whether a Haudenosaunee knows the saying "what clay are you made of" or not, if they have learned movements passed down the generations through dance, games and physical work with family and community, those movements are powered by the force of gravity and its relationship with the substance of the earth.

In my dance workshops, I ask participants to use their imaginations to sense the fluid organic matter of their bodies that are made of the same substance as the earth. I ask them to imagine, through these sites of intentional communication, that the substances of their body can talk with and draw groundedness through the connection of reciprocity with the earth.

The archive of my body is also embedded with inherited historical trauma, epigenetic events that left chemical markers on my DNA from my grandmother and her grandmother. I have intuitively known that the memories I hold are not just my own. These memories are awakened through movement because they live within my body. Creating, for me, is a part of growing, understanding and healing.

Resmaa Menakem, an African American author, artist and psychotherapist who specialises in the effects of trauma on the human body and relationships, explains that painful memories are passed from generation to generation and that "these experiences appear to be held, passed on, and inherited in the body, not just in the thinking brain".[6] Through generative and grounded movements, these memories can be, as Menakem describes, "metabolized" and transformed.

For me, this "metabolization" becomes movement, gestures and expressions that inform all that I create and share with audiences.

The conceptual and physical process of working towards decolonising my practice includes an integration and utilisation of my somatic and contemporary dance training.

In teaching and creating dance, I work intersensorily and with movement that engages the whole person. This allows me to work with dancers holistically and develop movement that conveys directness, connectedness and strength. I contribute this connectedness in myself to my body's archive that was encoded with memories of my ancestors, voices of my Elders, groundedness of those who taught me to dance around a pow-wow drum and the embrace of my mother, who was held by her mother, who was held by her mother.

When I bring these ideas into my work with others, I begin with the senses of touch, hearing and sight. By bringing awareness to these senses, I draw attention to

---

5   Susan Hill, *The Clay We Are Made Of* (Manitoba, Canada: University of Manitoba Press, 2017), 5.
6   Resmaa Menakem, *My Grandmother's Hands: Racialized Trauma and the Pathways to Mending Our Hearts and Bodies* (Las Vegas, NV: Central Recovery Press, 2017), 68.

their interconnectedness. I illustrate how this interconnectedness then becomes the body's mechanism for listening.

In her chapter titled *Intimate Strangers: Multisensorial Memories of Working in the Home*, Paula Hamilton writes on "intersensoriality" and "that it is rare to experience only one sense at a time". Hamilton quotes sensory scholar Steven Connor who argues that our senses are "inherently relational"; for instance, "the evidence of sight often acts to interpret, fix, limit and complete the evidence of sound".[7]

Through the process of working intersensorily, this can be attended to. As movement engages the whole person, I have been able to work with dancers holistically, developing movement that conveys directness, connectedness and strength.

When one begins to explore a radical relationship with nature and other living beings, these "metabolised" memories can become expressions, gestures, healing and grounding movements. Within my creative work, and the work I do with others, this is shared with audiences.

Longstanding Haudenosaunee knowledge-imparting practices

Oratory speech, oral storytelling and recitation are all practices that are performed, repetitive, energetic forms for telling, sharing and understanding. These practices have been shared among the Haudenosaunee in Turtle Island since "the beginning time", which is placed at the moment when Skywoman fell from the sky onto the turtle's back.[8] The Haudenosaunee oral transmission of stories is through the sensorial experiences of hearing, seeing, smelling, touching and tasting. Oratory speeches that share stories and histories from memory recur to be remembered and shared. This cultural practice is a complete intersensorial experience that works to embed meaning into the listener on a physical, spiritual and intellectual level.

The Haudenosaunee utilise wampum to interpret our stories, treaties and laws. Iakoiane Wakerahkats:teh, a Condoled Bear Clan Mother of the Kanien'kehá:ka (Mohawk) Nation, describes the significance of wampum in Haudenosaunee history: "Wampum means white shell beads, which were originally used as a medium to console oneself in grief. Later, wampum belts were made to record and recognise agreements made by the Europeans."[9] Belts of wampum are considered

---

7   Paula Hamilton, "Intimate Strangers: Multisensorial Memories of Working in the Home", in *A Cultural History of Sound, Memory, and the Senses*, eds Joy Damousi and Paula Hamilton (New York: Routledge, 2016), 200.

8   Joanne Shenandoah and Douglas M. George-Kanentiio, *Skywoman: Legends of the Iroquois* (Santa Fe: Clear Light Publishers, 1998).

9   Jeanette Rodriguez and Iakoiane Wakerahkats:teh, *A Clan Mother's Call: Reconstructing Haudenosaunee Cultural Memory* (Albany: State University of New York Press, 2017), 22.

living objects that need to be seen and physically touched by our communities in order to be alive.

As Haudenosaunee, we practise collective remembering, learning and creating through the senses. We need to touch the wampum and hear in Haudenosaunee languages the teaching/story of each belt or strand to ignite our collective memory. The whole body receives the experience and is changed. Collective memory is stored within the body of individuals within Native communities. As I have described Resmaa Menakem's theory on metabolising inherited memories so we can heal from them, I suggest here that we inherit and can ignite intergenerational memories, which, in turn, may guide us to continually evolve our culture and connect to our ancestors, which ultimately is and always has been the key to Indigenous survivance.

Tying Haudenosaunee wampum interpretation practice to my own experience of awakened memory through my relationship with objects and artefacts for *We Wait In The Darkness* has brought up further questions for me. Looking at my own work and the work of other Native artists, I wonder how Native practices continue to awaken collective memory and move through the relationship with objects/materials, and how this might render the physical body as an archive of knowledge, wisdom and culture. How can a Native artist's body also be a vehicle for healing and connection? How can such a body, living in radical relationality to the natural world, shift, change and decolonise performance, academic and institutional spaces?

Here I look to Indigenous studies scholars Melanie Yazzie and Cutcha Risling Baldy and their introduction to a special issue of the journal *Decolonization: Indigeneity, Education & Society*, which describes "radical relationality" as a growing web that "blankets the world in stunning beauty and restores the balance that our stories and prophecies have always foretold".[10] I turn to Indigenous studies scholar and Goenpul woman of the Quandamooka Nation, Aileen Moreton-Robinson, who has described Indigenous methods of "relationality" as being "grounded in a holistic conception of the interconnectedness and inter-substantiation between and among all living things and the earth, which is inhabited by a world of ancestors and creator beings".[11] This holistic connectedness requires that we, through our bodies, have been and continue to be in relationship to our environment and other beings. We experience life via our senses, which inform our every physical, spiritual and intellectual move. It follows then that body-based artists, through developed methodologies, can create artwork intrinsically tied to, in response to, and with bodies sensorially in relation with the

---

10   Melanie Yazzie and Cutcha Risling Baldy, "Introduction: Indigenous Peoples and the Politics of Water", *Decolonization: Indigeneity, Education & Society* 7, no. 1 (2018), 11.
11   Aileen Moreton-Robinson, "Relationality: A Key Presupposition of an Indigenous Social Research Paradigm", in *Sources and Methods in Indigenous Studies*, eds Chris Anderson and Jean O'Brien (New York: Taylor & Francis, 2017), 71.

natural world, by weaving and connecting the legibility of the Native body between land and constellations, between story and body.

In the urban intertribal community in which I live, I have witnessed over many years radical relationality at work in the art practice of Native artist Dyani White Hawk (Lakota). In the 2017 TPT Minnesota Original documentary *The Intersection of Indigenous & Contemporary Art*, White Hawk explains how her creative process is underpinned by her physical (sensorial and spiritual) playing of "the Great Lakes form of the Indigenous game lacrosse".[12] This holistic connection looks to a medicine game, which, when played in relationship to other Native bodies and in nature, supports health, wellbeing and therefore, her practice. White Hawk strives to make "graceful, and poetic, and poignant" art that she hopes will attract viewers into "conversation through beauty" as an invitation "to talk about the intersectionality of our histories".[13] This is necessary, she explains, as the general population has not been exposed to the histories of Native people. In this way, White Hawk is creating her own web of radical relationality by influencing other Native artists and artists of colour in our community through her work, which is deeply connected to a practice that is based in a holistic relationship with the land, people and other beings of the natural world.

There is a shared connection to the approach that White Hawk describes here in my own work. Although we may work with different mediums, I believe the overlap becomes apparent. Throughout these interventions that White Hawk speaks of, which consider the phenomena of perception, we share a common approach. By deploying a de-centring and unsettling methodology, we share common values in what Dylan Robinson xwélméxw, Stó:lō scholar and settler scholar Keavy Martin describe as "aesthetic actions". "Aesthetic action" stands in for a broad category of the ranges of sensory stimuli that include image, sound and movement. These stimuli have the potential for social and political change through critical and intentional engagement. Martin and Robinson state: "We believe this to be important because of the potential for embodied experiences to go unrecognized or unconsidered, even as they have enormous influence on our understanding of the world".[14]

This intervention between people, spaces and land remains simultaneously dialogic, verbal and corporeal. It remains an investigation, between my body, my people and my own embodied culture. Yet there is an invitation for all to enter into these spaces. Seneca scholar Mishuana Goeman's book, *Mark My Words: Native Women Mapping Our Nations*, "charts women's efforts to define themselves and their communities by interrogating the possibilities of spatial interventions" and

---

12 Dyani White Hawk Polk, personal communication, 2021.
13 Dyani White Hawk Polk, *The Intersection of Indigenous & Contemporary Art*, a Minnesota Original Twin Cities PBS documentary, 2017.
14 Keith Martin and Dylan Robinson, *Arts of Engagement: Taking Aesthetic Action in and Beyond the Truth and Reconciliation Commission of Canada* (Waterloo, Ontario: Wilfrid Laurier University Press, 2016), 89.

discusses the labour of Indigenous artists and scholars who "(re)map" the "communities they write within and about ... to generate new possibilities".[15] Goeman looks to the work of geographer Doreen Massey and her reflections on space, surmising that if place is considered to include a flow or fluidity which extends to the intangible and spiritual notions embedded within Indigenous practices, then for Goeman place possesses the permeability and potential to work "as a meeting place".

Scholars and activists have posited that Indigenous land education must be regarded in its relationship to the legacies of colonial violence, which have in turn created a great need to rebuild relationships to land and to one another. For me, this significance is apparent. I believe it is through "aesthetic action" that I tacitly de-centre and unsettle this connection. As a result, the participants experience through these multiple, nuanced sites of aesthetic action a shock of recognition in which "interest, empathy, relief, confusion, alienation, apathy, and/or shock"[16] becomes manifested, as Menakem has discussed.

Recuperating the archive: *We Wait In The Darkness*

Through living in relationship with and paying attention to these objects, through the practice of deep listening with my senses, the objects began to awaken memories. For me, cultural memories appeared as feelings, thoughts, words, images and colours. Through my practice of creating dance and visual art, the memories become expressions through gesture or physical action, and the weaving together of these movements became the dance.

In 2000, I began a custom of purchasing Seneca-made tourist-trade objects and memorabilia (baskets, beadwork, souvenirs) sold online with the intention of restoring them to my community in our cultural museum. Beginning in 2012, I shifted my focus primarily to maps and other historical documents defining Haudenosaunee territories from the positionality of the dominant European and then United States and Canadian governments.

In 2014, my body, memories, oral stories, familial objects and historical archives were all utilised in the creation of *We Wait In The Darkness*. In collaboration with French composer François Richomme, *We Wait In The Darkness* was a dance performance, a gallery installation and later a museum exhibition. *We Wait In The Darkness*, the dance, was a composition of gestures and generative movement that wove together time and space, to cross dimensions, to heal the historical trauma that scarred the DNA of my grandmother, her mother and our ancestors. The work premiered in Canada at *Montréal Arts Interculturals* (MAI) and

---

15 Mishuana Goeman, *Mark My Words: Native Women Mapping Our Nations* (Minneapolis: University of Minnesota Press, 2013), 3.
16 Goeman, *Mark My Words*, 109.

in the United States at the Red Eye Theater in Minneapolis, Minnesota. The dance toured the US and Canada, and was performed in Marseille, France.

We Wait In The Darkness, the installation, contained textiles, moving images, moving sound and paper sculptures that created an environment in which I performed, as well as historical objects such as maps, and cultural and family artefacts. The installation originated at All My Relations Arts, a Native owned and run gallery in Minneapolis. The installation was shared with communities in Northern Minnesota and became a museum exhibition at the Mitchell Museum of the American Indian in Evanston, Illinois.

The dance and installation were produced simultaneously, each informing the other. My repetitive interactions with living cultural, familial and historical objects became an interactive dialogue generating movement vocabularies that became central to *We Wait In The Darkness* the dance. Choreography, story and memory inspired the contemporary art pieces for the exhibition and set design for the stage. All these physical acts of making dance and visual art guided how the exhibition was installed and contextualised. This work oscillated between the archive/archives, the colonial archive, my body as an archive and the Indigenous archive.

While creating *We Wait In The Darkness*, my body, spirit and mind were interpreting and processing memories and sensations. My body integrated this information in my bones, organs, muscles and memory, and as new neurological pathways. This new intelligence became a part of the architecture of my body and the archive of my body. The completed exhibition was an installation of historical, cultural and family objects that was in dialogue in the gallery with the contemporary art pieces that I created. My intention for the exhibition and dance was to create an experience for the audience from which they could integrate new understandings and sensations.

The exhibition included maps used to create a visual representation of the dwindling of the land of the Seneca over the past 400 years, and I wanted people to understand in a profound way, through their sense of sight, that the Haudenosaunee have experienced massive loss culturally and geographically because of the diminishing of their land. And that we remain deeply impacted by this history of loss to this day. I learned through my practice of pulling together over a hundred family, community, and cultural objects and archives that these material things are embedded with tangible memory and energy. Some of these pieces are living objects.

Each performance featured a 5-foot x 6-foot drawing of a section of a map replicated from a US Corp of Engineers map, which was created to relocate Senecas who would be (who were) displaced by the creation of the Kinzua Dam. Thirty minutes into the dance the sound ceases, and the audience hears me begin to tear the oversized map. The silence preceding the tearing is intentional to draw the audience nearer to me on stage – listening not just with their ears but with their whole beings. I carefully tear the boundary lines of each land plot on the map. I take the pieces and place them in various spots on the stage, distributing some of

Figure 5.1 Rosy Simas tearing up an oversized Seneca Reservation relocation map during a performance of *We Wait In The Darkness*. Photo by Steven Carlino for Rosy Simas Danse, 2015.

the torn plots to the audience. Both Native and non-Native people receive these pieces. Some people wonder what they are to do with this metaphorical gesture, some people are uncomfortable, having to think about what it means for them to hold a piece of Seneca land, plotted by the US government to be redistributed as a commodity, like canned meat, to be consumed.

I remember during the Minneapolis premiere handing two torn paper plots to a Seneca friend who had not inherited land on our reservation. In this exchange, I wished with my gesture that I could return her birthright to her, a place where she can be in relationship with the place of our ancestors. I have collected the torn pieces from the tour of over 30 presentations of the dance. These torn pieces will be repurposed once more and will become paper sculptures for another installation.

Conclusion

I posit that being a Native artist who is working in radical relationality does more than just interconnect me with others in the shared common goal of living in relationship with nature. It is by way of deep intersensorial listening that I awaken the culture stored within my archival body. I posit that in community with others, our collective memory actively contributes to the survivance of our specific Native cultures. I continue to demonstrate this through my own creative practice, and I am seeing it in the practices of other Indigenous artists.

Over the past 20 years, I have researched and developed approaches and methods to cultivate a deep relationship among my senses, physical experience

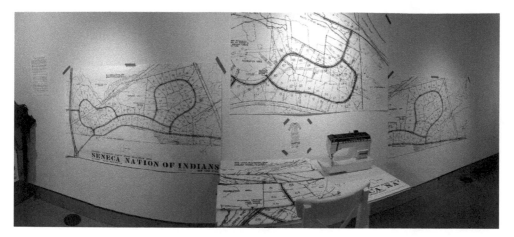

Figure 5.2 Installation of fabric and paper of Seneca relocation maps for a traditional Seneca dress design, *We Wait In The Darkness* exhibition view, All My Relations Arts in Minneapolis. Photo by Rosy Simas, 2014.

Figure 5.3 Rosy Simas in an excerpt of *We Wait In The Darkness* at the Judson Memorial Church. Photo by Ian Douglas, 2015.

and nature, which I use to create dance, sculpture, film and textiles. My research has led to the creation of dance and visual artwork that evokes my ancestors, taps into genetic memory, and brings me and those with whom I work into a vested relationship with the environment, as well as the issues of Native people and other living beings. The senses are key in my practice because it is through the senses that transmission is experienced. The repetition of such transmissions can generate energy which can exponentially grow into a web of radical relationality.

Through my dance-making processes, I have come to experience the ways in which energy works across realms of connectivity and relationality and to understand what this means. Energy is not bound by the same laws of physics as the beings who are confined by gravity seem to be. Energy can impact our bodies' physiological systems. Dance educator and scholar Barbara Mahler discusses how "energy, which is a force that can be channelled through a conduit, when intentionally channelled through the skeleton system, has the potential to actually change the shape of our bones".[17]

As a long-time student of Mahler's, I am living evidence of how this channelling of energy through the skeleton can stabilise and ground the body, despite the years of destabilising postmodern and contemporary dance training I have had. What I have learned with Mahler, coupled with my own research, has made it possible for me to make work that connects with the energy of my ancestors. I am, the earth is, and nature are, the conduits through which the energy of my ancestors flows and connects.

Ancestors, not bound by space and time, are continually interacting with us. Their remains are literally supporting us as they have become a part of the earth we live on. We are not only influenced by these transmissions through the continued practice of deep listening, but we can also create from those experiences. In fact, by multiplying this energy through repetitive movement and actions we can build more energy, which can then be transmitted outward, further influencing the web of radical relationality.

The body, spirit and intellect interpret, process and integrate memories through the very act of creating and sharing. Through multiple *We Wait In The Darkness* performances and installations of the *We Wait In The Darkness* exhibition over four years throughout Turtle Island, an awakening in myself and the audience occurred. Multiple reiterations imitated the recitation of Haudenosaunee teachings that work to heal Native communities and honour our ancestors.

With each performance I was creating movement that generated new energy from an intentional relationship with my senses. The more the dance was shared, the more the story of my grandmother's life and the tragedies that our people experienced were told; it was through this telling that healing has continued for me, the audiences who witnessed it (Native and non-Native) and my ancestors.

What I learned through pulling together over a hundred family, community and cultural objects, as well as paper documents, was that all of these objects are embedded with memory. Like the Haudenosaunee practice of touching and

17   Barbara Mahler, *Klein Technique Workshop* (Minneapolis, Minnesota, 2000).

interpreting the living wampum, when the exhibition artefacts were touched or seen, collective memory was awakened and stored in the archives of our bodies.

References

Goeman, Mishuana. *Mark My Words: Native Women Mapping Our Nations*. Minneapolis: University of Minnesota Press, 2013.

Hamilton, Paula. "Intimate Strangers: Multisensorial Memories of Working in the Home". In *A Cultural History of Sound, Memory, and the Senses*, eds Joy Damousi and Paul Hamilton. New York: Routledge, 2016: 194–211.

Hill, Susan. *The Clay We Are Made Of*. Manitoba, Canada: University of Manitoba Press, 2017.

Mahler, Barbara. *Klein Technique Workshop*. Minneapolis, Minnesota, 2000.

Martin, Keith and Dylan Robinson. *Arts of Engagement: Taking Aesthetic Action in and Beyond the Truth and Reconciliation Commission of Canada*. Waterloo, Ontario: Wilfrid Laurier University Press, 2016.

Menakem, Resmaa. *My Grandmother's Hands: Racialized Trauma and the Pathway to Mending Our Hearts and Bodies*. Las Vegas, NV: Central Recovery Press, 2017.

Miranda, Deborah. *Bad Indians: A Tribal Memoir*. Berkeley, CA: Heyday, 2013.

Moreton-Robinson, Aileen. "Relationality: A Key Presupposition of an Indigenous Social Research Paradigm". In *Sources and Methods in Indigenous Studies*, eds Chris Andersen and Jean O'Brien. New York: Taylor & Francis, 2017: 69–78.

Robinson, Dylan. *Hungry Listening*. Minnesota: University of Minnesota Press, 2020.

Rodriguez, Jeanette with Iakoiane Wakerahkats:teh. *A Clan Mother's Call: Reconstructing Haudenosaunee Cultural Memory*. Albany, NY: State University of New York Press, 2017.

Shenandoah, Joanne and Douglas M. George-Kanentiio. *Skywoman: Legends of the Iroquois*. Santa Fe: Clear Light Publishers, 1998.

Taylor, Diane. *The Archive and the Repertoire: Performing Cultural Memory in the Americas*. Durham: Duke University Press, 2003.

Vizenor, Gerald Robert. *Manifest Manners: Postindian Warriors of Survivance*. Hanover: Wesleyan University Press, 1994.

Whitehawk Polk, Dyani. *The Intersection of Indigenous & Contemporary Art*, a Minnesota Original Twin Cities Public Broadcasting Service (PBS) documentary, 2017.

Yazzie, Melanie and Cutcha Risling Baldy. "Introduction: Indigenous Peoples and the Politics of Water". *Decolonization: Indigeneity, Education & Society* 7, no. 1 (2018): 1–18.

6

Reanimating 1830s Nyungar songs of Miago

Clint Bracknell

Introduction

Miago (also spelled Migeo, Maiago, Migo or Myago) was a Nyungar (also spelled Noongar, Nyoongar or Nyoongah) man from the south-west region of Western Australia (WA) who joined the *HMS Beagle*'s expedition to the north-west of Australia in 1837–38 as an intermediary.[1] His departure, exploits and return inspired the composition of two widely shared local Nyungar songs, the lyrics of which were recorded in the journal of colonist and explorer Sir George Grey.[2] These lyrics are among the earliest records of Nyungar singing. Although the songs about Miago were widely known in the mid-nineteenth century, no musical notation was transcribed, and the melody has not been passed on to contemporary generations of Nyungar people.

The 1829 establishment of the Swan River Colony – today known as Perth, the capital city of WA – was the beginning of British settler-colonial expansion in the state and the subjugation of local Aboriginal people.[3] Throughout the nineteenth century, longstanding Nyungar cultural practices of sharing news and memorialising important events in song nevertheless remained relatively widespread among the Nyungar of Perth and other Aboriginal groups across Australia.[4] By midway through the twentieth century, the increasingly disruptive and restrictive by-products of settler

---

1 Tiffany Shellam, "Miago and the 'Great Northern Men': Indigenous Histories from In Between", in *Indigenous Mobilities: Across and Beyond the Antipodes*, ed. Rachel Standfield (Acton ACT: ANU Press and Aboriginal History Inc., 2018), 185–207.

2 George Grey, *Journals of Two Expeditions of Discovery in North-West and Western Australia: During the Years 1837, 38, and 39* (London: T. & W. Boone, 1841).

3 Patrick Wolfe, "Settler Colonialism and the Elimination of the Native", *Journal of Genocide Research* 8, no. 4 (2006), 387–409.

4 Tamsin Donaldson, "Translating Oral Literature: Aboriginal Song Texts", *Aboriginal History* 3 (1979), 62–83; Clint Bracknell, "Conceptualizing Noongar Song", *Yearbook for Traditional Music* 49 (2017), 93–113.

colonisation had combined to dramatically diminish the vitality of the Nyungar language and many of its attendant singing practices.[5]

Community-directed Nyungar cultural revitalisation efforts since the 1970s have motivated a steady resurgence of Nyungar language and singing, particularly to accompany dance performances or in popular music settings.[6] The 2016 Australian Census recorded just 475 Nyungar language speakers.[7] Although this figure represents just 1.5 per cent of the Nyungar population, it demonstrates increased identification with the language, as only 212 speakers were counted in 2001. The 2020 National Indigenous Languages Report classifies languages into seven categories based on their vitality, from "safe" to "no longer spoken (sleeping)".[8] Based on these categories, the Nyungar language could be described as both "critically endangered", with a few very senior people knowing and using Nyungar vocabulary, and "reviving/revitalising/reawakening", as use of language items among younger speakers has substantially increased since the beginning of concentrated language revitalisation movements in the late 1980s.

Like language revitalisation, much Aboriginal music revitalisation work draws on archival records and audio recordings.[9] Although historical records and contemporary memories frequently characterise Nyungar singing as a communal activity, existing accessible audio recordings of Nyungar song feature only "lone singers".[10] Most are "more akin to elicited memories than fully-fledged performances".[11] Still, Nyungar in recent decades have drawn on sparse archives for inspiration, grafting newly composed melodies onto historically recorded lyrics and developing group performance repertoire from audio recorded in the late twentieth century.[12] Access to much of the written and archival audio record of

---

5   Bracknell, "Conceptualizing Noongar Song".

6   Clint Bracknell and Kim Scott, "Ever-widening circles: Consolidating and enhancing Wirlomin Noongar archival material in the community", in *Archival Returns: Central Australia and Beyond*, eds Linda Barwick, Jennifer Green and Petronella Vaarzon-Morel (LD&C Special Publication 18. Honolulu & Sydney: University of Hawai'i Press and Sydney University Press, 2020), http://hdl.handle.net/10125/24890/, 325–38; Karl Neuenfeldt, "The Kyana Corroboree: Cultural Production of Indigenous Ethnogenesis", *Sociological Inquiry* 65, no. 1 (1995), 21–46; Anna Haebich, *Dancing in Shadows: Histories of Nyungar Performance* (Crawley, WA: UWA Publishing, 2018).

7   Austlang, W41: NOONGAR / NYOONGAR (Canberra, ACT: AIATSIS Collection, n.d.), https://collection.aiatsis.gov.au/austlang/language/w41; *South West Aboriginal Land and Sea Council, Settlement Agreement* (n.d.), https://www.noongar.org.au/about-settlement-agreement.

8   AIATSIS, *National Indigenous Languages Report* (Canberra, ACT: AIATSIS, 2020).

9   James Wafer and Myfany Turpin, eds, *Recirculating Songs: Revitalising the Singing Practices of Indigenous Australia* (Canberra, ACT: Pacific Linguistics, 2017).

10   Luise Hercus and Grace Koch, "Lone Singers: The Others Have All Gone", in *Recirculating Songs: Revitalising the Singing Practices of Indigenous Australia*, eds James Wafer and Myfany Turpin (Canberra, ACT: Pacific Linguistics, 2017), 103–21.

11   Clint Bracknell, "Connecting Indigenous Song Archives to Kin, Country and Language", *Journal of Colonialism and Colonial History* 20, no. 2 (2019), 8.

12   For example, Len Collard singing in Glen Stasiuk, *Weewar* (ABC TV, Australia, 2006); Clint Bracknell, "The Emotional Business of Noongar Song", *Journal of Australian Studies* 44, no. 2 (2020), 140–53.

Source	Original documentation of individual song texts			
	Written lyrics	Lyrics with musical notation	Musical notation with no lyrics	Audio recordings of performance
Grey 1837–39	12			
Salvado 1953			1	
Chauncy 1878			1	
Calvert 1894		4		
Bates 1904–12	65			
Hassell and Davidson 1936	1			
Laves 1931	Unknown (restricted access)			
Hercus 1965	1			
Tindale 1966–68				6
Douglas 1965–67				1
Douglas 1968	1			
Brandenstein 1970				8
Theiberger 1986				2

Table 6.1 Records of Nyungar song 1837–1986.

Nyungar song is presently restricted in various ways, so much so that it is difficult to know the extent of the data. Table 6.1 provides a rough snapshot of the extent of recorded Nyungar songs from 1837 to 1986.

Additionally, from 1999 onwards anthropologist Tim McCabe made recordings of many songs with Nyungar speakers, including the late Cliff Humphries and Lomas Roberts. Although access is restricted to most of this material, some of the songs have emerged via language revitalisation initiatives.[13]

In 2020 I was commissioned by the City of Perth, WA, to compose music for Nyungar singer Gina Williams based on Nyungar lyrics about Miago from Grey's papers (see Figure 6.1).[14] Williams had released three albums of contemporary music with Nyungar lyrics alongside guitarist Guy Ghouse.[15] The three of us had longstanding relationships as performers in WA and I had previously worked on

---

13 Sandra Wooltorton and Glenys Collard, *Noongar Our Way* (Bunbury: Noongar Language and Culture Centre, 1992); Cliff Humphries, *Aalidja Maali Yok Birrla-ngat Kor-iddny (Swan Woman Returns to Her River)* (Noranda: Ngardarrep Kiitj Foundation, 2020).
14 Grey, "Papers of Sir George Grey" (unpublished manuscript, 1838), 573.
15 *Gina Williams & Guy Ghouse*, http://www.ginawilliams.com.au, accessed 1 August 2021.

various projects associated with Nyungar song and language, including *Hecate*, the first Shakespearean theatre production presented entirely in an Aboriginal language of Australia.[16] The Miago project was supported and endorsed by the City of Perth's Nyungar Elders Advisory Group and Edith Cowan University Nyungar Elder-in-Residence Roma Yibiyung Winmar. Its aim was to achieve some degree of fidelity between newly recomposed songs about Miago and conventions of Nyungar singing in the nineteenth century.

The creative process was underpinned by thorough investigation of Nyungar song. Making aesthetic decisions about how to reshape and sustain a musical tradition is fundamental to music revival.[17] Decisions associated with recomposing the Miago songs depended on the development of a contextual, linguistic and musical framework. This chapter will provide an overview of the Nyungar singing culture and the history of Miago's songs, before discussing Nyungar song creation, language and musical aesthetics. This description of the process associated with reanimating songs about Miago may inform future music revitalisation initiatives working with similarly endangered languages and song traditions.

Nyungar song culture

Manifesting in everything from ceremony,[18] to popular music festivals,[19] karaoke[20] and radio requests,[21] song and performance continue to be vital to Nyungar lifeways. Analysis of Nyungar terms for singing and historical records suggests multiple functions of song in Nyungar society of the nineteenth century, including laments, songs for dance and entertainment, news and gossip, identifying oneself, and arrivals and departures.[22] While some Nyungar performance repertoire may be customarily restricted to particular audiences and participants,[23] the wide variety of written descriptions of Nyungar

---

16 Clint Bracknell, "Hecate: Adaptation, Education and Cultural Activism", in *Reimagining Shakespeare Education – Teaching and Learning Through Collaboration*, ed. Liam Selmer (Cambridge: Cambridge University Press, forthcoming).

17 Victoria Lindsay Levine, "Musical Revitalization Among the Choctaw", *American Music* 11, no. 4 (1993), 391–411; Tamara Livingston, "Music Revivals: Towards a General Theory", *Ethnomusicology* 43, no. 1 (1999), 66–85; Caroline Bithell and Juniper Hill, eds, *The Oxford Handbook of Music Revival* (New York: Oxford University Press, 2014).

18 Isobel White, "The Birth and Death of a Ceremony", *Aboriginal History* 4, no. 1 (1980), 33–42.

19 Neuenfeldt, "The Kyana Corroboree".

20 Anna Haebich and Jim Morrison, "From Karaoke to Noongaroke: A Healing Combination of Past and Present", *Griffith Review* 44 (2014), 1–8.

21 Clint Bracknell and Casey Kickett, "Inside Out: An Indigenous Community Radio Response to Incarceration in Western Australia", *Ab-Original: Journal of Indigenous Studies and First Nations* 1, no. 1 (2017), 81–98.

22 Bracknell, "Conceptualizing Noongar Song".

23 Daisy Bates, "Daisy Bates Papers" MS 365, Section XI Dances, Songs (manuscript, 1912); George Grey, *Journals of Two Expeditions*.

performances in the nineteenth century suggests that a range of Nyungar singing practices – and even ceremony associated with maintaining landscapes and kinship – were openly practised and sustained despite the presence of colonists.[24] In the twentieth century, entrenched settler colonisation of Nyungar lands, assimilation policies and an imposed emotional regime inhibited most speaking and singing in the Nyungar language.[25] Up until the early 1970s, access to human rights for Nyungar people inherently depended on avoiding overt public cultural expressions such as song and language.[26] Consequently, from the onset of colonisation until the late 1970s, opportunities to perform, hear and learn Nyungar songs were dramatically diminished.

Today, most Aboriginal performance traditions across Australia face pressing issues of endangerment. Returning archival recordings to their Aboriginal communities of origin has become a common research practice,[27] but few of the communities involved in such work have endured prolonged disruption to song traditions akin to the Nyungar experience. Because Nyungar singing was suppressed and denigrated throughout most of the twentieth century, the contemporary performance of surviving songs carries significant emotional weight.[28] Recirculating Nyungar songs among descendants of the deceased singers who were recorded performing on archival recordings and their broader local Nyungar community supports individual and collective identity maintenance and feelings of connection.[29] In the apparent aftermath of the assimilation era, Nyungar songs – as performative expressions of culture – can also give rise to tensions associated with the politics of Indigenous cultural identity.[30] As a result, some individuals or groups may seek to retroactively impose tight restrictions on previously "open" and unrestricted songs which may have been widely known and shared among Aboriginal and non-Aboriginal people in the past. However, senior Nyungar are generally proud to publicly share old songs today.

Songs of Miago

As part of the City of Perth's online exhibition for the 150th anniversary of Perth Town Hall, the City of Perth's Nyungar Elders Advisory Group decided that

---

24 Bracknell, "Conceptualizing Noongar Song".
25 Bracknell, "The Emotional Business of Noongar Song".
26 Haebich, *Dancing in Shadows*.
27 Linda Barwick, Jennifer Green and Petronella Vaarzon-Morel, eds, *Archival Returns: Central Australia and Beyond. LD&C Special Publication 18* (Honolulu and Sydney: University of Hawai'i Press and Sydney University Press, 2019).
28 Bracknell, "The Emotional Business of Noongar Song".
29 Clint Bracknell, "Rebuilding as Research: Noongar Song, Language and Ways of Knowing", *Journal of Australian Studies* 44, no. 2 (2020), 210–23.
30 Clint Bracknell, "Say You're a Nyungarmusicologist: Indigenous Research on Endangered Music", *Musicology Australia* 37, no. 2 (2015), 199–217.

since the town hall site was recorded as being one of Miago's camping spots,[31] his story – and songs about him – should feature in the exhibition. By 1833, Miago had established himself as a mediator between Nyungar and colonists on the frontier. Historian Tiffany Shellam describes him as:

> a Beeloo Nyungar man from Wurerup country, located around the upper reaches of the Swan River to the north of the Perth township. He had family and kin networks across the Swan and Canning river systems, which made it difficult for settlers to restrict him to a particular tribal group in their census reports and observations.[32]

Such was the ubiquity of song in Nyungar life during the early nineteenth century,[33] singing is frequently mentioned in historical descriptions of Miago. In *Meeting the Waylo*, Shellam describes Miago's song-making and legacy, including how Grey transcribed and interpreted songs performed by Miago and another Nyungar guide, Kaiber.[34]

During the *Beagle*'s Australian survey, assistant surveyor Lieutenant John Lort Stokes described him,

> … gazing steadily and in silence over the sea, and then sometimes, perceiving that I watched him, say to me "Miago sing, by and by northern men wind jump up": then would he station himself for hours at the lee-gangway, and chant to some imaginary deity an incantation or prayer to change the opposing wind … there was a mournful and pathetic air running through the strain, that rendered it by no means unpleasing; though doubtless it owed much of its effect to the concomitant circumstances.[35]

Grey wrote: "if a native [is] afraid, he sings himself full of courage; in fact under all circumstances, he finds aid and comfort from a song".[36] Miago sang not just to quicken his journey home, but also to express frustration and wrath. Stokes observed how after visiting Beagle Bay in the north of WA, Miago considered the way the local Nyul Nyul men examined his body to be:

---

31   Daisy Bates, "Derelicts: The Passing of the Bibbulmun", *The Western Mail*, 25 December 1924, 55.

32   Shellam, "Miago and the 'Great Northern Men'", 186–87.

33   Bracknell, "Conceptualizing Noongar Song".

34   Tiffany Shellam, *Meeting the Waylo: Aboriginal Encounters in the Archipelago* (Crawley, WA: UWA Publishing, 2019).

35   John Lort Stokes, *Discoveries in Australia: With an Account of the Coasts and Rivers Explored and Surveyed During the Voyage of the* Beagle *in the Years 1837–38–39–40–41–42–43* (London: T. & W. Boone) 1/221–22.

36   Grey, *Journals of Two Expeditions of Discovery*, 2/404.

An injury and indignity which, when safe on board, he resented by repeated threats, uttered in a sort of wild chant, of spearing their thighs, backs, loins, and indeed, each individual portion of the frame.[37]

Back at the Swan River colony, Grey transcribed a well-known "war song" likely to have been the same one Stokes described:

The men, when according to their custom they go walking rapidly to and fro, quivering their spears, in order to work themselves up into a passion, chant rapidly as follows:

> U-doo Darr-na
> Kan-do Darr-na
> Miery darr-na
> Goor-doo darr-na
> Boon-galla darr-na
> Gong-oo darr-na
> Dow-all darr-na
> De-mite darr-na
> Nar-ra darr-na

Thus, rapidly communicating all the parts in which they intend to spear their enemies.[38]

Miago would have boarded the *Beagle* with a repertoire of songs from home. During the expedition, he likely composed new songs too.

Stokes questioned Miago regarding the account he intended to give his countrymen about the expedition, writing that:

His description of the ship's sailing and anchoring were most amusing: he used to say, "Ship walk – walk – all night – hard walk – then by and by, anchor tumble down".[39]

It is easy to imagine Miago's composition about the journey delivered in the kind of "loud recitative" song that Grey cites as being the "customary mode of address" among Nyungar recounting current events in group settings.[40] Miago's departure and return also prompted other Nyungar to compose two songs which made "a

---

37   Stokes, *Discoveries in Australia*, 1/59.
38   Grey, *Journals of Two Expeditions of Discovery*, 2/544.
39   Stokes, *Discoveries in Australia*, 1/22.
40   Grey, *Journals of Two Expeditions of Discovery*, 2/253.

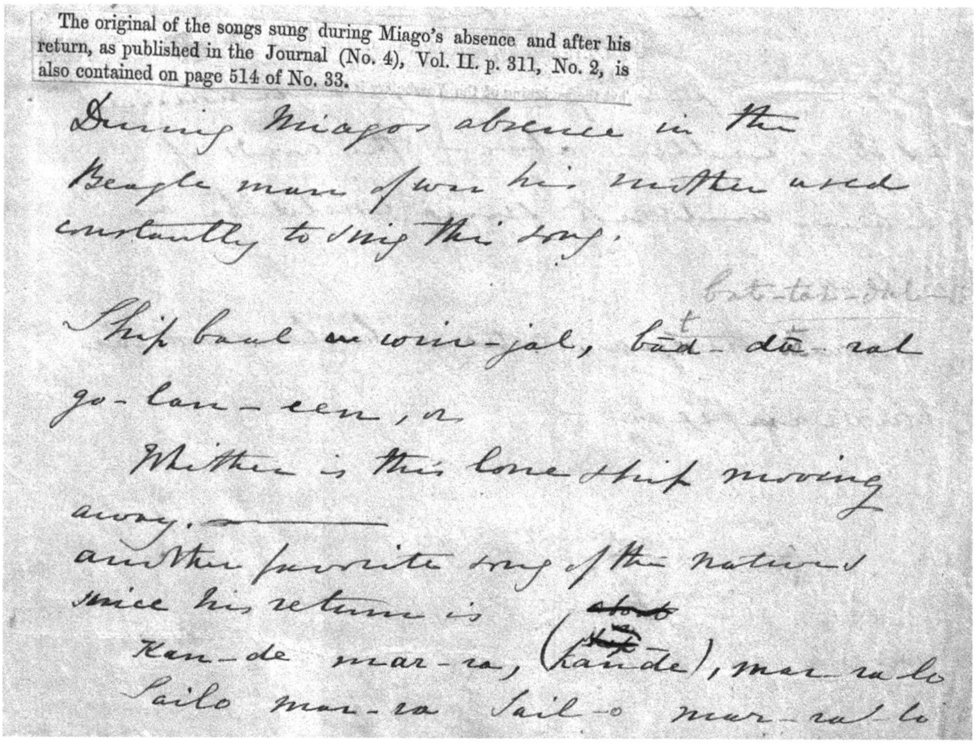
The original of the songs sung during Miago's absence and after his return, as published in the Journal (No. 4), Vol. II. p. 311, No. 2, is also contained on page 514 of No. 33.

During Miagos absence in the Beagle man of war his mother used constantly to sing this song.

Ship baal wiin-jal, bād-dā-ral go-lan-een, or

Whither is this lone ship moving away.—

another favorite song of the natives since his return is

Kan-de mar-ra, (kande), mar-ra-lo Sailo mar-ra Sail-o mar-ral-lo

Figure 6.1 Nyungar song lyrics about Miago in the papers of Sir George Grey. Used with permission from the National Library of South Africa, Cape Town.

great impression on the natives".[41] The lyrics are transcribed in Grey's papers (Figure 6.1):

> During Miago's absence in the *Beagle* man of war his mother used constantly to sing this song:
> Ship baal win-jal, bād-dā-ral
> go-lan-een-
> Whither is this lone ship moving away
> Another favourite song of the natives since his return is
> ~~about a ship~~
> Kan-de mar-ra, (kande), mar-ra-lo
> Sailo mar-ra Sail-o mar-ral-lo
> [Grey does not provide a translation of the second song]

For the purpose of this chapter, I will refer to these two songs as the "ship song" and the "sail song". Considering the apparent popularity of these songs in the

41 Grey, *Journals of Two Expeditions of Discovery*, 2/409–41.

mid-nineteenth century, it seemed fitting to revisit them today as part of a public exhibition focusing on Miago.

However, presenting these songs as mute text in Grey's handwriting seemed to reify them. Ethnomusicologist Gary Tomlinson goes so far as to suggest that the act of writing down an Indigenous song is tantamount to its colonisation; it reduces and enshrines it in written form according to an imperialist's narrow interpretation, and consequently traps it as an artefact of the past.[42] Meaningfully bringing these songs into the present demanded singing them again in a way that paid homage to Nyungar singing aesthetics while simultaneously aligning with contemporary language revitalisation goals in the Nyungar community. Rather than simply lifting something out of an archive, the objective here was to reanimate it with a sense of purpose.

Reanimating the archive

Engagement with the sparse and fragmented Nyungar song archive reveals two interrelated issues. Firstly, the Nyungar song archive is far from comprehensive. Most traces of Nyungar song in historical archives are merely written records of lyrics rendered in a variety of unreliable orthographies.[43] Very little historical music notation of Nyungar song exists and the few accessible audio recordings of Nyungar singing made since the late 1960s feature what would mostly be described as "rememberings" of songs, rather than fully-fledged performances.[44] Despite a few notable exceptions, it is rare for Nyungar people today to sing old Nyungar songs learned from Elders. Without much musical material from which to draw, we cannot be sure exactly how the Nyungar words written down by colonial observers would have sounded when they were originally performed.

Analysis of the small dataset of Nyungar song has resulted in rough conclusions about stylistic conventions typical of Nyungar vocal music.[45] While these ideas could function as a starting point for attempting to graft appropriate melodies onto archival lyrics, operating with so little source data increases the danger of reifying a once dynamic and adaptable song tradition. Consequently, finding ways to sing these lyrics about Miago could not rely on analysis of the archive alone. The task demanded investigation of not just aesthetics but also characteristically Nyungar processes of composition.

---

42 Gary Tomlinson, *The Singing of the New World* (Cambridge: Cambridge University Press, 2007).
43 Bracknell, "Rebuilding as Research".
44 Clint Bracknell, "Maaya Waabiny (Playing with Sound): Nyungar Song Language and Spoken Language", in *Recirculating Songs: Revitalising the Singing Practices of Indigenous Australia*, eds James Wafer and Myfany Turpin (Canberra: Pacific Linguistics, 2017), 45–57.
45 Clint Bracknell, "Natj Waalanginy (What Singing?): Nyungar Song from the South-West of Western Australia" (PhD thesis: University of Western Australia, 2016).

Accounts of Nyungar song and many studies of Aboriginal music elsewhere refer to singers receiving songs while in dream-states.[46] Based on her ethnographic work with Nyungar in the early twentieth century and revealing the esoteric nature of Nyungar songs composed in dreams, Daisy Bates states that in some cases where this occurs, the person who received the song may not be able to reveal its meaning. Bates describes Ngalbaitch of Jerramungup explaining the process of a Nyungar singer trying to find a song, stating:

> they seem to hear it coming into their ears and going away again, coming and going until sometimes they lose it and cannot catch it. The jannuk (spirit) will however fetch it back to their ears.[47]

Providing an example of this process in the early twentieth century, Bates writes of Nyungar singer Bandoor dreaming a song one night, and learning it the following day.[48] Anecdotal reports state that dreams also inspire many classical popular composers;[49] Vogelsang et al. demonstrate that "being creative in waking-life is reflected in creativity in the dream".[50] The general prominence of song in Aboriginal life may partially explain the seemingly high propensity for new songs to reveal themselves in dreams among Aboriginal singers.[51] However, even in recent years, as old Nyungar songs are rarely heard, certain Nyungar individuals occasionally describe receiving or dreaming about old-style Nyungar songs they attribute to ancestors.[52] Employing what could be described as an Indigenous method,[53] perhaps I needed to wait for the music for these old words to reveal itself.

---

46   Meiki Elizabeth Apted, "Songs from the Inyjalarrku: The Use of a Non-Translatable Spirit Language in a Song Set From North-West Arnhem Land, Australia", *Australian Journal of Linguistics* 30, no. 1 (2010); Linda Barwick, Bruce Birch and Nicholas Evans, "Iwaidja Jurtbirrk Songs: Bringing Language and Music Together", *Australian Aboriginal Studies* 2 (2007); Allan Marett, "Ghostly Voices: Some Observations on Song-Creation, Ceremony and Being in Northwest Australia", *Oceania* 71 (2000); Nancy Nancarrow, "What's That Song About?: Interaction of Form and Meaning in Lardil Burdal Songs", *Australian Journal of Linguistics* 30, no. 1 (2010); Bracknell, "Conceptualizing Noongar Song".

47   Bates, "Daisy Bates Papers", 36/208.

48   Bates, "Daisy Bates Papers", 34/408.

49   Robert L. Van de Castle, *Our Dreaming Mind* (New York, NY: Ballentine, 1994); Deirdre Barrett, *The Committee of Sleep: How Artists, Scientists, and Athletes Use Dreams for Creative Problem-Solving – and How You Can Too* (New York, NY: Crown, 2001); Nancy Grace, "Making Dreams into Music: Contemporary Songwriters Carry on an Age-Old Dreaming Tradition", in *Dreams – A Reader on the Religious, Cultural, and Psychological Dimensions of Dreaming*, ed. Kelly Bulkeley (New York, NY: Palgrave Macmillan, 2001).

50   Lukas Vogelsang, Sena Anold, Jannik Schormann, Silja Wübbelmann and Michael Schredl, "The Continuity between Waking-Life Musical Activities and Music Dreams", *Dreaming* 26, no. 2 (2016): 139–40.

51   Jill Stubington, *Singing the Land: The Power of Performance in Aboriginal Life* (Strawberry Hills, NSW: Currency House, 2007); Bracknell, "Conceptualizing Noongar Song".

52   Conversations with Kylie Bracknell, Barry McGuire and Annie Dabb in 2020.

53   Joseph P. Gone, "Considering Indigenous Research Methodologies: Critical Reflections by an Indigenous Knower", *Qualitative Inquiry* 25, no. 1 (2018).

Nyungar song language

Across many regions in Australia, Aboriginal people may readily sing songs originating from distant locations, in languages they may not necessarily comprehend.[54] However, in past work with Nyungar song, senior community members "instructed that the first step in a process to get these songs performed again should involve developing a more solid idea of what the songs mean".[55] In support of this aim, I compiled a dataset of Nyungar wordlists to assist in translating archival songs. Study of Aboriginal languages such as Nyungar – in various states of critical endangerment or revival – frequently involve working with idiosyncratic and inconsistent wordlists originally collected by non-linguists who rarely understood the complexities of the language they were documenting. Working with historical Nyungar language sources also demands consideration of differences due to dialect, orthography, borrowings (the use of English near homonyms), cognates (words with a similar form and meaning),[56] misheard sounds and incorrect glosses.[57]

As part of the process of reanimating the two songs of Miago from Grey's journal, developing a deeper understanding of the lyrics seemed a suitable starting point. Cross-referencing Grey's original and published versions of the songs alongside the Nyungar wordlist dataset revealed both inconsistencies in interpretation of and insights into Nyungar poetics. Grey's original diary entry for the "ship song" provides the English interpretation of the text only as "Whither is this lone ship moving away".[58] His *Journals of Two Expeditions of Discovery* was published in 1841 and expands on this with seemingly greater creative licence:

> Whither does that lone ship wander
> My young son I shall never see again
> Whither does that lone ship wander.[59]

Analysis of the Nyungar language lyrics reveals that Grey has embellished the second line of his interpretation, as the original Nyungar lyric does not mention "seeing" or any kind of temporal concept. The Nyungar lyrics simply ask "win-jal" (where) "baal" (it, the ship – in English) is. The term "bād-dā-ral" is variously translated as

---

54   Myfany Turpin, Brenda Croft, Clint Bracknell and Felicity Meakins, "Aboriginal Australia's Smash Hit That Went Viral", *Conversation*, 20 March 2019, https://bit.ly/3AZrdvD.
55   Bracknell, "Rebuilding as Research", 218.
56   Alan Dench, "Comparative Reconstitution", in *Historical Linguistics 1995: Selected Papers from the 12th International Conference on Historical Linguistics, Manchester, August 1995*, eds John Charles Smith and Delia Bentley (Amsterdam: John Benjamins Publishing Company, 1995).
57   Bracknell, "Rebuilding as Research".
58   Grey, "Papers of Sir George Grey", 573.
59   Grey, *Journals of Two Expeditions of Discovery*, 2/70.

"lone-wild, trackless",[60] a "barren tract of land",[61] "waste, a; barren land utterly destitute of vegetation"[62] and "wild, desolate".[63] The final term, "go-lan-een", based on Grey's interpreted "young son" likely derives from "koolang" (child), with an additional suffix or non-lexical extension "-een". This term could also feasibly be "koorlaniny" (moving continuously). The lexical ambiguity here could be purposely poetic.

In Grey's original record of the "sail song", the words "about a ship" are written and crossed out above the term "kande".[64] Grey's 1839 wordlist has the same term: "kan de: move unsteadily, as a ship". In both cases, "kan" (or "ken") is dance, stomp or step and "de" seems to be a poetic addition.[65] Grey's published journal includes the interpretation "unsteadily shifts the wind-o, unsteadily shifts the wind-o, the sails-o handle, the sails-o handle-ho".[66] It seems like the ship is dancing in the wind. "Mar" or "maar" is both "hand" and "wind" (which may possibly be more accurately rendered as "maarr"), so there may be polysemic poetics at play.

Although there is no recorded audio of the Miago songs, most of the lyrical terms featured in the songs are present on the earliest audio recordings of Nyungar language elicitation from 1960 onwards,[67] and are spoken by experienced Nyungar speakers today, showing no dramatic change in pronunciation over 60 years. Although sibilant sounds are absent from the Nyungar language, they are present in both songs at the onset of English-language words "ship" and "sail". In his original notes, Grey has seemingly corrected these terms to conventional English spelling rather than represent them phonetically in the manner that Nyungar of the 1830s may have pronounced them. In his subsequently published journal, Grey has rendered the lyric "sail" as "tsail", demonstrating Nyungar adaptation of sibilant sounds. While it is difficult to determine exactly how Nyungar of the 1830s would have pronounced the remaining Nyungar-language lyrics, the degree of fidelity between Grey's original notes, the early recorded audio and contemporary speakers does not suggest a significant shift. Nevertheless, as Nyungar language pronunciation is fundamentally different to English, the sounds of the language are crucial to sustaining a classic Nyungar song aesthetic. Whether Aboriginal or not, for anyone who primarily speaks English, a language with mostly front-of-mouth

---

60 George Grey, "Vocabulary of the Aboriginal Language of Western Australia (Continued) (24 August to 12 October)", *Perth Gazette and Western Australian Journal*, 1839, 136.

61 J. Brady, *A Descriptive Vocabulary of the Native Language of W. Australia* (Rome: S. C. DE Propaganda Fide, 1845), 15.

62 G.F. Moore, *A Descriptive Vocabulary of the Language in Common Use Amongst the Aborigines of Western Australia* (London: W.S. Orr and Co, 1842), 167.

63 Moore, *A Descriptive Vocabulary of the Language in Common Use Amongst the Aborigines of Western Australia*, 169.

64 Grey, "Papers of Sir George Grey", 573.

65 Grey, "Vocabulary of the Aboriginal Language", 144.

66 Grey, *Journals of Two Expeditions of Discovery*, vol. 2, 310.

67 Kenneth L. Hale and Geoffrey O'Grady, Balardung and Mirning language elicitation (Canberra: AIATSIS Audiovisual Archive, tape recording. OGRADY-HALE_01. 1960); Wilf H. Douglas, Sound Recordings Collected by Wilf Douglas (Canberra: AIATSIS Audiovisual Archive, tape recording. DOUGLAS_W01. 1965).

sounds, it can be very challenging to create the back-of-mouth sounds typical of Aboriginal languages like Nyungar.[68]

Modes of Nyungar song

After consideration of lexical meaning and pronunciation of the Nyungar text, the next step involved creating an appropriate musical setting for the lyrics. Nyungar music is primarily vocal, so consideration of vocal timbre is equally as important as matching the melodic, rhythmic and structural characteristics of recorded songs from the past in attempts to maintain a distinct Nyungar musical style. According to Hugo Zemp,[69] "nothing is more characteristic of a musical style than vocal timbre, for a few seconds may be more than enough to identify the origin of a song". Grey's early description of singing practices in the early colonial period starkly contrasts European and Nyungar aesthetic vocal preferences:

> A native sings joyously in the most barbarous and savage sounds … while the surrounding natives loudly applaud, as soon as the singer has concluded. But should the astounded European endeavour to charm these wild men by one of his refined and elegant lays, they would laugh at it as a combination of silly and effeminate notes …[70]

Nyungar singers did not strive to produce the forward-projected, restrained vocal sounds common to nineteenth-century music in Britain. Much Aboriginal singing can be characterised as "back-projected", with the resulting sound resonating through the body and sometimes the ground too, when performers are seated. Based on his work with Aboriginal performers at Belyuen in the Northern Territory, ethnomusicologist Allan Marett reveals that "one of the most important things that an apprentice song man learns from his teacher is to imitate the teacher's voice" and describes confusion over the identity of recorded performers due to multiple singers also possessing "the same voice".[71]

Despite the broad divisions applying to classic Aboriginal performance genres from different geographical regions,[72] and the range of musical sub-types associated with cultural and social delineations, classic Aboriginal song styles in Australia are "obviously more related to each other than to anything outside the continent".[73] Indeed, Stephen Wild suggests, "it seems that Aboriginal music across

---

68 Bracknell, "Hecate: Adaptation, Education and Cultural Activism".
69 Hugo Zemp, *Voices of the World: An Anthology of Vocal Expression* (France: Le Chant du Monde, 1995), 119.
70 Grey, *Journals of Two Expeditions of Discovery*, vol. 2, 305.
71 Allan Marett, "Ghostly Voices", 23–24.
72 Marcus Breen, *Our Place, Our Music* (Canberra: Aboriginal Studies Press, 1989).
73 Guy Tunstill cited in Breen, *Our Place, Our Music*, 7.

Australia consists of variants of a common underlying type".[74] Generally, classic Aboriginal music is primarily vocal and most traditional instruments are percussive.[75] Tunstill states that more often than not, this music "needs communal effort to produce it".[76] Furthermore, sung melodies usually begin "high and loud", before "descending to a reiterated low soft note",[77] and vocal rhythm is "most often syllabic".[78]

Despite this general similarity, it would be tokenistic to create new music for archival Nyungar songs relying only on general "superficialities: a descending melody, a regularly repeated stick beat", while remaining ignorant of "structural intricacies".[79] Analysis of historical descriptions of Nyungar performance and 19 more recent examples recorded between 1965 and 2015 distinguish Nyungar songs by a number of features but also suggest a breadth of aesthetic possibilities.[80] Nyungar songs exhibit a range of structural characteristics which imply the existence of multiple song genres and a significant degree of flexibility in the song tradition. Although some of the vocal rhythms in Nyungar songs are syllabic, helping to emphasise a strong regular beat, others are relatively melismatic and rhythmically complex.

The contrast between Nyungar songs that imply a steady "danceable" rhythmic pulse and those that feature far less stable, "expressive" timing suggests the existence of two basic "types" or "modes" of Nyungar song. Those outlining a regular beat would more readily be accompanied by dance and percussive accompaniment and could be performed by a group of singers with minimal need for cues and memorisation. Although no presently accessible archival audio recordings of Nyungar song feature examples of group singing or instrumental accompaniment, historical literature refers to both.[81] As we discovered in singing workshops held across 2017–19,[82] a number of more "expressive" songs in the Nyungar archival collection are difficult for more than one performer to sing as they utilise vocal melisma, significant tempo rubato and complex metre. These features are particularly characteristic of six songs performed solo by renowned Nyungar singer Charlie Dabb and recorded at Esperance, WA, in 1970.[83]

---

74   Stephen Wild, "Ethnomusicology Down Under: A Distinctive Voice in the Antipodes?", *Ethnomusicology* 50, no. 2 (2006), 350.
75   Breen, *Our Place, Our Music*.
76   Tunstill cited in Breen, *Our Place, Our Music*, 8.
77   Tunstill cited in Breen, *Our Place, Our Music*, 7.
78   Schultz cited in Breen, *Our Place, Our Music*, 7.
79   Catherine J. Ellis, "Creating with Traditions", *Sounds Australian* 30 (1991), 14.
80   Bracknell, "Natj Waalanginy (What Singing?)".
81   Hammond, *Winjan's People: The Story of the South-West Australian Aborigines*; Bates, "Daisy Bates Papers".
82   Bracknell, "The Emotional Business of Noongar Song".
83   Von Brandestein, "Sound Recordings Collected by Carl von Brandenstein [tape recording]" (1967–70).

All presently accessible archival recordings of Nyungar song are solo performances – or "rememberings". However, rhythmic features of a particular Nyungar song could characterise it as either a more "danceable" or "expressive" piece and imply the likely corresponding "group" or "solo" nature of its intended performance context. Still, these proposed modes of Nyungar song need not be exclusive. Demonstrating how the "expressive/solo" and "danceable/group" modes may be combined in a single piece, Daisy Bates describes informal performances at night by Nyungar who gathered to perform at the Perth Carnival in 1910. She outlines interactions between Nyungar man Nebinyan, as a "lead" singer, and the rest of the group, who "join in" at specific moments:

> The recitative or song was always commenced by Nebinyan alone, the others only joining in the chorus, so to speak, or keeping up a sort of murmuring accompaniment throughout the melody. Weird and strange they sounded in the stillness and darkness of the night. The natives had rolled themselves in their rugs, but as the old man warmed to his task, and as the memories of early days crowded upon him, lending to his poor cracked voice a fictitious energy, one by one the others sat up and joined their voices to his in harmony. Presently the old voice took a minor key, and I watch the singers literally drone themselves to sleep as the old man's song gradually trailed off into silence.[84]

Although Bates – untrained as a musician – uses the word "harmony",[85] based on the nature of most Aboriginal song I am inclined to interpret this as meaning "unison" or perhaps octave harmony. Furthermore, in light of this description, it is entirely possible in that in "soloist" sections of group performances, "lead" singers utilised the more "expressive" elements of Nyungar song including rubato, increased rhythmic complexity and occasional ornamentation.

Grey describes the songs about Miago as being popular and widely known; however, he describes only solo performances of these songs and never mentions accompanying dance. It is feasible to conclude that both songs about Miago were more likely to have been performed in the more rhythmically complex "expressive/ solo" mode. This informed the decision to feature complex meter in creating new melodies for the songs about Miago. In addition to abiding by the conventions of these theoretical modes of Nyungar song, using complex meter rather than common time automatically distinguishes the songs about Miago from most of the music heard in Australia today.

---

84 Daisy Bates, "Native Shepherding: An Experience of the Perth Carnival", *Western Mail*, 12 February 1910, 44.
85 Bates, "Native Shepherding", 44.

Nyungar tunes

Bates' recollection of Nebinyan switching from singing in what was presumably a major key to a minor key is reasonably significant, given the lack of historical descriptions of Nyungar melodies. The recollection of early Western Australian pastoralist Janet Millett that Nyungar "songs were always in the minor key" is of dubious value,[86] as she also claims to have never observed Nyungar using percussion instruments, suggesting that she witnessed only a few select performance types. Furthermore, the melodic variety evident among recorded examples of Nyungar songs indicates that former Western Australian "Protector of Natives" Jesse Hammond's statements that "[t]hey only had about three of four different chants for their dancing" and "[i]n their ordinary singing too, though they had various words, the tune was nearly always the same",[87] could also reflect narrow experiences with the gamut of Nyungar performance and – as is typical of colonial descriptions of Indigenous performance – limited musical knowledge.

Recorded performances of Nyungar song from 1965 onwards all demonstrate a clear tonal centre and loosely diatonic pitch relationships which would usually suggest a "major" key.[88] Both "major" and "minor" tonalities are suggested by the six pieces of notated music inspired by, or attempting to faithfully record, Nyungar singing in the nineteenth century.[89] Chauncy notates a "morning song" performed by Nyungar on the Swan River in the "key" of C, but the melody features a flattened sixth and seventh, implying a "minor" flavour.[90] While providing a very sparse representation of a musical tradition, these notations support the general conclusions upon listening to audio recordings of Nyungar performances that classic Nyungar songs may evoke major and minor tonalities and feature anything from two or three different repeated pitches to more nuanced melodies employing five or six note "scales". In keeping with the practicalities of the previously discussed solo and group "modes", rhythmically complex Nyungar songs are likely to feature a degree of complementary melodic complexity.

Some of the recorded Nyungar songs with more complex melodies conclude by falling in pitch to an octave below the implied "tonic". Bates provides a

---

86 Janet Millett, *An Australian Parsonage, or, the Settler and the Savage in Western Australia* (London: Edward Standford, 1872), 85.

87 Hammond, *Winjan's People*, 52.

88 Bracknell, "Natj Waalanginy (What Singing?)".

89 Rosendo Salvado, *Memorias Historicas Sobre La Australia: Y Particularmente Acerca La Mision Benedictina de Nueva Nursia y Los Usos y Costumbres de Los Salvajes.*, trans. D.F. De D. (Barcelona: Imprenta de los Herederos de la V. Pla, 1853), https://trove.nla.gov.au/work/ 8489598; Philip Chauncy, "Notes and Anecdotes of the Aborigines of Australia", in *The Aborigines of Victoria: With Notes Relating to the Habits of the Natives of Other Parts of Australia and Tasmania Compiled from Various Sources for the Government of Victoria*, ed. Robert Brough Smyth (Melbourne: Government Printer, 1878), 221–84; Albert Calvert, *The Aborigines of Western Australia* (London: Simpkin, Marshall, Hamilton, Kent & Company, 1894).

90 Philip Chauncy, "Notes and Anecdotes of the Aborigines of Australia", 266.

description for one of Nebinyan's songs about a whaling expedition which closely matches the structural and melodic character of three songs about the sea performed by Charlie Dabb,[91] all of which use complex meter, triplet rhythms and rubato to invoke the flow of the ocean and feature this "octave drop" technique. In her notes, Bates states:

> The tune of this song was in utmost "harmony" with the words of the song. Sung in a low voice, it represented the voices of the great waves, the great seas as they murmured along shores = Goomba warrin in a very low and slow bass ended the song.[92]

Bates' use of the term "harmony" in the context of describing solo vocal performance indicates that she had an affective rather than technical understanding of the term. This form and structure may be characteristic of a song genre Bates implies when stating that "[m]ost of the seacoast tribes have their own songs of the sea".[93] While the "octave drop" is also featured in other Nyungar songs without ocean themes, this melodic feature seems appropriate for the sea-based songs about Miago.

As is common in Aboriginal music of neighbouring regions, examples and descriptions of classic Nyungar song considered in this study indicate the prevalence of repeated melodic contours concluding with a descent in pitch.[94] Most Nyungar songs are relatively isorhythmic, overlaying repeated text and vocal rhythms with different alternating and mostly descending melodic contours. Due to the rarity of strophic songs in the recorded examples of Nyungar song, even lyrically simpler songs with only one or two lines of text, like the songs about Miago, were still likely to have been isorhythmic. The fidelity between audio recordings of one song performed by Nyungar singer Charlie Dabb in 1970 and then Gordon Harris in 1986 provides evidence of the fixed, rather than improvised, nature of at least some Nyungar song items.

Reanimation

Analysis of a broad, scattered sample of Nyungar vocal music captured in audio recordings (1965–2014) and also represented in nineteenth-century musical notation indicates that a significant degree of melodic and structural variety is characteristic of classic Nyungar song genres. As noted by Rosendo Salvado in the early nineteenth century, these constituted "a graceful and beautiful style ... and a grave and serious one ... a war song", along with music to make one "very tearful",

---

91   Von Brandestein, "Sound Recordings Collected by Carl von Brandenstein [tape recording]".
92   Bates, "Daisy Bates Papers", 34/34.
93   Daisy Bates, *The Native Tribes of Western Australia*, ed. Isobel White (Canberra, ACT: National Library of Australia, 1985), 335.
94   Breen, *Our Place, Our Music*.

and up-tempo songs and dance that were "happy and gay and full of life".[95] In light of this, the task of grafting appropriate melodies to archival Nyungar song lyrics and, indeed, creating new songs within a distinct Nyungar musical tradition is a significant challenge. Creative decisions regarding how to reanimate the songs about Miago were underpinned by a thorough understanding of the linguistic, historical and social context of the archival lyrics. I established a framework for composition by identifying apparent "expressive/solo" and "danceable/group" modes of Nyungar song, with "expressive/solo" songs featuring complex meter, utilising a greater number of different pitches and sometimes concluding an octave below the implied tonal centre.

Given that the historical record describes only the songs about Miago being performed solo, it made sense to employ the conventions typical of a "solo/ expressive" Nyungar song. Within that framework, and after years of immersion in the remaining archival and living traces of Nyungar song traditions, the final compositional step involved waiting for the melodies to emerge from a subconscious or dream-like state. The framework helped me remain cognisant of not "straightening-out" complex meter or "imperfect" pitch as I vocalised and recorded melodic ideas when they arrived. The "ship song" (Figure 6.2) ended up with a triplet feel akin to the ocean songs of Charlie Dabb, while the "sail song" (Figure 6.3) included the wide pitch range and complex meter typical of other "solo/ expressive" Nyungar songs. Both songs concluded with an "octave drop". Given the "loosely" diatonic nature of Nyungar song, the importance of pronunciation and timbre, I prepared an audio recording of the song and a lyric sheet with notes about meter for Gina Williams to sing. I also devised a simple harmonic progression for Gina's guitarist, Guy Ghouse.[96] The notation for the songs in Figures 6.2 and 6.3 demonstrates the use of musical conventions described in this paper for illustrative purposes.

Gina and Guy's subsequent recording of the songs about Miago were uploaded as part of the City of Perth's *Kuraree* online exhibition in June 2020.[97] At the time of writing this chapter, fewer than 150 people had engaged with the songs as part of that exhibition. The two songs about Miago were only performed again in January 2021 when I received an impromptu invitation to sing at a Welcome to Country for artists involved in Perth Festival. Noted Nyungar singer Barry McGuire was one of the senior people in charge of the occasion. After the

---

95 Rosendo Salvado, *The Salvado Memoirs*, ed. E.J. Storman (Perth: University of Western Australia Press, 1977), 133.

96 Given the efforts described above to recreate the sound of these songs as faithfully as possible, the inclusion of guitar accompaniment may be surprising. However, Ghouse has been a constant part of Williams' musical activity since 2010 when she began performing in Nyungar language. Consequently, the City of Perth's Nyungar Elders Advisory Group and Williams herself felt most comfortable that the song be recorded in the vocal-and-guitar duo format.

97 "The Heart of Perth, Kuraree", Perth City, https://kuraree.heritageperth.com.au, accessed 1 August 2021.

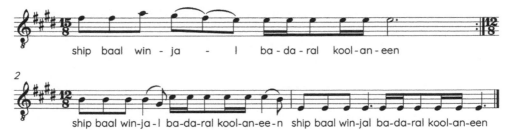

Figure 6.2 Melody for the Nyungar "ship song" about Miago.

Figure 6.3 Melody for the Nyungar "sail song" about Miago.

public part of the event had concluded, he gathered with Gina and me to discuss the processes I undertook to reanimate the songs about Miago described in this chapter. Together, Gina and I sang the songs and the three of us noted how these songs chronicle contemporary events and include English-language terms "sail" and "ship" while remaining consistent with Nyungar traditions of singing. While it is impossible to know how faithful the new melodies for these songs are to the original ones, they did not sound out of place. The songs are a small part of an online resource Roma Yibiyung Winmar and I are building to increase access to Nyungar song and language content and hopefully encourage more singing in our endangered language.[98]

Conclusion

This chapter provides a specific example of how archival records can form the basis for a "reanimation" of songs whose transmission through performance has been broken. It has implications in the fields of archival studies, Aboriginal history and performance practices, and music sustainability. It is significant that the reanimation of these two songs about Miago was requested by a group of senior Nyungar people, undertaken by a Nyungar researcher/composer, and performed

---

98 "Mayakeniny: Restoring on-Country Performance", https://www.mayakeniny.com, accessed 1 August 2021.

by a Nyungar singer. Aboriginal cultural revitalisation can be fraught with tensions associated with the perceived ownership of archival material and how that material should be appropriately shared.[99] In this context, it is important that the lyrics about Miago have long been in the public domain and were once widely known by both men and women, Nyungar and colonists. Although Grey provided interpretations of what these lyrics meant, re-translating them was a worthwhile activity as it shed new light on Nyungar poetics and vocabulary. In endangered language contexts, having a solid evidence-based idea of what archival lyrics mean can build confidence in the community to perform old songs again.[100]

The reanimated versions of the songs about Miago were informed by analysis of historical references to Nyungar musical aesthetics. Nevertheless, the creative process was equally guided by the choice to actively avoid popular music conventions and underpinned by my immersion in archival recordings and remaining singing practices among Nyungar today. Regardless of how much research one can undertake on old song styles, singing old lyrics anew – off the pages of archival texts – is ultimately a creative activity. The perceived success of such an undertaking may be alternately judged in terms of its faithful reproduction of old traditions, its reception among the community of origin today, or its ability to persist into the future.

References

AIATSIS. *National Indigenous Languages Report*. Canberra: AIATSIS, 2020.

Apted, Meiki Elizabeth. "Songs from the Inyjalarrku: The Use of a Non-Translatable Spirit Language in a Song Set From North-West Arnhem Land, Australia". *Australian Journal of Linguistics* 30, no. 1 (2010): 93–103.

Austlang. *W41: NOONGAR / NYOONGAR*. Canberra: AIATSIS Collection, n.d. https://collection.aiatsis.gov.au/austlang/language/w41.

Barrett, Deirdre. *The Committee of Sleep: How Artists, Scientists, and Athletes Use Dreams for Creative Problem-Solving – and How You Can Too*. New York: Crown, 2001.

Barwick, Linda, Bruce Birch and Nicholas Evans. "Iwaidja Jurtbirrk Songs: Bringing Language and Music Together". *Australian Aboriginal Studies* 2 (2007): 6–34.

Barwick, Linda, Jennifer Green and Petronella Vaarzon-Morel, eds. *Archival Returns: Central Australia and Beyond. LD&C Special Publication 18*. Honolulu and Sydney: University of Hawai'i Press and Sydney University Press, 2019.

Bates, Daisy. *The Native Tribes of Western Australia*, ed. by Isobel White. Canberra: National Library of Australia, 1985.

Bates, Daisy. "Derelicts: The Passing of the Bibbulmun". *Western Mail*, 25 December 1924.

Bates, Daisy. "Daisy Bates Papers" (1912): manuscript. MS 365, Section XI Dances, Songs. National Library of Australia, Canberra.

Bates, Daisy. "Native Shepherding: An Experience of the Perth Carnival". *Western Mail*, 12 February 1910.

---

99 Bracknell, "Connecting Indigenous Song Archives".
100 Bracknell, "Rebuilding as Research".

Bithell, Caroline and Juniper Hill, eds. *The Oxford Handbook of Music Revival*. New York: Oxford University Press, 2014.

Bracknell, Clint. "Hecate: Adaptation, Education and Cultural Activism". In *Reimagining Shakespeare Education – Teaching and Learning Through Collaboration*, ed Liam Selmer. Cambridge: Cambridge University Press, forthcoming.

Bracknell, Clint. "Rebuilding as Research: Noongar Song, Language and Ways of Knowing". *Journal of Australian Studies* 44, no. 2 (2020): 210–23.

Bracknell, Clint. "The Emotional Business of Noongar Song". *Journal of Australian Studies* 44, no. 2 (2020): 140–53.

Bracknell, Clint. "Connecting Indigenous Song Archives to Kin, Country and Language". *Journal of Colonialism and Colonial History* 20, no. 2 (2019). DOI: 10.1353/cch.2019.001.

Bracknell, Clint. "Conceptualizing Noongar Song". *Yearbook for Traditional Music* 49 (2017): 93–113.

Bracknell, Clint. "Maaya Waabiny (Playing with Sound): Nyungar Song Language and Spoken Language". In *Recirculating Songs: Revitalising the Singing Practices of Indigenous Australia*, eds James Wafer and Myfany Turpin. Canberra: Pacific Linguistics, 2017: 45–57.

Bracknell, Clint. "Natj Waalanginy (What Singing?): Nyungar Song from the South-West of Western Australia". PhD Thesis, University of Western Australia, 2016.

Bracknell, Clint. "Say You're a Nyungarmusicologist: Indigenous Research on Endangered Music". *Musicology Australia* 37, no. 2 (2015): 199–217.

Bracknell, Clint and Casey Kickett. "Inside Out: An Indigenous Community Radio Response to Incarceration in Western Australia". *Ab-Original: Journal of Indigenous Studies and First Nations* 1, no. 1 (2017): 81–98.

Bracknell, Clint and Kim Scott. "Ever-widening circles: consolidating and enhancing Wirlomin Noongar archival material in the community". In *Language Documentation & Conservation Special Publication No. 18 Archival Returns: Central Australia and Beyond*, eds Linda Barwick, Jennifer Green and Petronella Vaarzon-Morel. Honolulu: University of Hawai'i Press, 2019: 325–338.

Brady, John. *A Descriptive Vocabulary of the Native Language of W. Australia*. Rome: S. C. DE Propaganda Fide, 1845.

Brandestein, Carl Von. *Sound Recordings Collected By Carl Von Brandenstein* (recorded 1967–70): tape recording. VON-BRANDENSTEIN_C04, 1967–70. AIATSIS Audiovisual Archive, Canberra.

Breen, Marcus. *Our Place, Our Music*. Canberra: Aboriginal Studies Press, 1989.

Calvert, Albert. *The Aborigines of Western Australia*. London: Simpkin, Marshall, Hamilton, Kent and Company, 1894.

Castle, Robert L Van de. *Our Dreaming Mind*. New York: Ballentine, 1994.

Chauncy, Philip. "Notes and Anecdotes of the Aborigines of Australia". In *The Aborigines of Victoria: With Notes Relating to the Habits of the Natives of Other Parts of Australia and Tasmania Compiled from Various Sources for the Government of Victoria*, ed. Robert Brough Smyth. Melbourne: Government Printer, 1878: 221–84.

Dench, Alan. "Comparative Reconstitution". In *Historical Linguistics 1995: Selected Papers from the 12th International Conference on Historical Linguistics, Manchester, August 1995*, eds John Charles Smith and Delia Bentley. Amsterdam: John Benjamins Publishing Company, 1995: 57–73.

Donaldson, Tamsin. "Translating Oral Literature: Aboriginal Song Texts". *Aboriginal History* 3 (1979): 62–83.

Douglas, Wilf. *Sound Recordings Collected By Wilf Douglas* (recorded 1965): tape recording. DOUGLAS_W01. 1965. AIATSIS Audiovisual Archive, Canberra.

Douglas, Wilf. *The Aboriginal languages of South-West Australia: speech forms in current use and a technical description of Njungar*. Canberra: Australian Institute of Aboriginal Studies (AIAS), 1968.

Ellis, Catherine. "Creating with Traditions". *Sounds Australian* 30 (1991): 14.

Gone, Joseph. "Considering Indigenous Research Methodologies: Critical Reflections by an Indigenous Knower". *Qualitative Inquiry* 25, no. 1 (2018): 45–56.

Grace, Nancy. "Making Dreams into Music: Contemporary Songwriters Carry on an Age-Old Dreaming Tradition". In *Dreams – A Reader on the Religious, Cultural, and Psychological Dimensions of Dreaming*, ed. Kelly Bulkeley. New York: Palgrave Macmillan, 2001: 167–71.

Grey, George. "Papers of Sir George Grey". Unpublished manuscript, 1838. Cape Town: National Library of South Africa.

Grey, George. "Vocabulary of the Aboriginal Language of Western Australia (Continued) (24 August to 12 October)". *Perth Gazette and Western Australian Journal*, 1839.

Grey, George. *Journals of Two Expeditions of Discovery in North-West and Western Australia: During the Years 1837, 38, and 39, Volume 1 and 2.* London: T. & W. Boone, 1841.

Haebich, Anna. *Dancing in Shadows: Histories of Nyungar Performance.* Crawley, WA: UWA Publishing, 2018.

Haebich, Anna and Jim Morrison. "From Karaoke to Noongaroke: A Healing Combination of Past and Present". *Griffith Review* 44 (2014): 1–8.

Hale, Kenneth L. and Geoffrey O'Grady, *Balardung and Mirning Language Elicitation* (recorded 1960): tape recording. OGRADY-HALE_01. 1960. AIATSIS Audiovisual Archive, Canberra.

Hammond, Jesse. *Winjan's People: The Story of the South-West Australian Aborigines.* Perth: Imperial Printing, 1933.

Hassell, Ethel and Daniel S. Davidson. "Notes on the Ethnology of the Wheelman Tribe of Southwestern Australia". *Anthropos* 31 (1936): 679–711.

Hercus, Luise. *Sound Recordings Collected by Luise Hercus* (recorded 1965): tape recording. HERCUS_L16. 1965. AIATSIS Audiovisual Archive, Canberra.

Hercus, Luise and Grace Koch. "Lone Singers: The Others Have All Gone". In *Recirculating Songs: Revitalising the Singing Practices of Indigenous Australia*, eds James Wafer and Myfany Turpin. Canberra: Pacific Linguistics, 2017: 103–21.

Humphries, Cliff. *Aalidja Maali Yok Birrla-ngat Kor-iddny (Swan Woman Returns to Her River).* Noranda: Ngardarrep Kiitj Foundation, 2020.

Knapp, Albert. Interview by Clint Bracknell, 2015, at Yardup, WA. [Digital Audio Recording].

Laves, Gerhardt. *The Laves Papers: Text in Kurin* (1931). Canberra: AIATSIS.

Levine, Victoria Lindsay. "Musical Revitalization Among the Choctaw". *American Music* 11, no. 4 (1993): 391–411.

Livingston, Tamara. "Music Revivals: Towards a General Theory". *Ethnomusicology* 43, no. 1 (1999): 66–85.

Marett, Allan. "Ghostly Voices: Some Observations on Song-Creation, Ceremony and Being in Northwest Australia". *Oceania* 71 (2000): 18–29.

Millett, Janet. *An Australian Parsonage, or, the Settler and the Savage in Western Australia.* London: Edward Standford, 1872.

Moore, George Fletcher. *A Descriptive Vocabulary of the Language in Common Use Amongst the Aborigines of Western Australia.* London: W.S. Orr and Co., 1842.

Nancarrow, Nancy. "What's That Song About?: Interaction of Form and Meaning in Lardil Burdal Songs". *Australian Journal of Linguistics* 30, no. 1 (2010): 81–92.

Neuenfeldt, Karl. "The Kyana Corroboree: Cultural Production of Indigenous Ethnogenesis". *Sociological Inquiry* 65, no. 1 (1995): 21–46.

Salvado, Rosendo. *Memorias Históricas Sobre La Australia: Y Particularmente Acerca La Misión Benedictina de Nueva Nursia y Los Usos y Costumbres de Los Salvajes.* Translated by D.F. De D. Barcelona: Imprenta de los Herederos de la V. Pla, 1853. https://trove.nla.gov.au/work/8489598.

Salvado, Rosendo. *The Salvado Memoirs.* Ed. E.J. Storman. Perth: University of Western Australia Press, 1977.

Shellam, Tiffany. "Miago and the 'Great Northern Men': Indigenous Histories from In Between". In *Indigenous Mobilities: Across and Beyond the Antipodes*, ed. Rachel Standfield. Acton, ACT: ANU Press and Aboriginal History Inc., 2018: 185–207.

Shellam, Tiffany. *Meeting the Waylo: Aboriginal Encounters in the Archipelago*. Crawley, WA: UWA Publishing, 2019.

South West Aboriginal Land and Sea Council. *South West Native Title Settlement Agreement*. n.d. https://www.noongar.org.au/about-settlement-agreement.

Stasiuk, Glen. "Weewar". ABC TV, Australia, 2006.

Stokes, John Lort. *Discoveries in Australia: With an Account of the Coasts and Rivers Explored and Surveyed During the Voyage of the Beagle in the Years 1837–38–39–40–41–42–43*. London: T. & W. Boone, 1969.

Stubington, Jill. *Singing the Land: The Power of Performance in Aboriginal Life*. Strawberry Hills, NSW: Currency House, 2007.

Thieberger, Nicholas. *Ngatju Project, Language Elicitation and Songs, WA*. (recorded 1986): cassette recording. THIE-YOUNG_01. 1986. AIATSIS Audiovisual Archive, Canberra.

Tindale, Norman. *Site Information, Songs, Cultural Discussions From South-West WA*. (recorded 1966–68): tape recording. TINDALE_N07. 1966–68. AIATSIS Audiovisual Archive, Canberra.

Tomlinson, Gary. *The Singing of the New World*. Cambridge: Cambridge University Press, 2007.

Turpin, Myfany, Brenda Croft, Clint Bracknell and Felicity Meakins. "Aboriginal Australia's Smash Hit That Went Viral". *Conversation*, 20 March 2019. https://bit.ly/3AZrdvD.

Vogelsang, Lukas, Sena Anold, Jannik Schormann, Silja Wübbelmann and Michael Schredl. "The Continuity between Waking-Life Musical Activities and Music Dreams". *Dreaming* 26, no. 2 (2016): 132–41.

Wafer, James and Myfany Turpin, eds. *Recirculating Songs: Revitalising the Singing Practices of Indigenous Australia*. Canberra: Pacific Linguistics, 2017.

White, Isobel. "The Birth and Death of a Ceremony". *Aboriginal History* 4, no. 1 (1980): 33–42.

Wild, Stephen. "Ethnomusicology Down Under: A Distinctive Voice in the Antipodes"? *Ethnomusicology* 50, no. 2 (2006): 345–52.

Wolfe, Patrick. "Settler Colonialism and the Elimination of the Native". *Journal of Genocide Research* 8, no. 4 (2006): 387–409.

Wooltorton, Sandra and Glenys Collard. *Noongar Our Way*. Bunbury: Noongar Language and Culture Centre, 1992.

Zemp, Hugo. *Voices of the World: An Anthology of Vocal Expression*. France: Le Chant du Monde, 1995.

7

Authenticity and illusion: Performing Māori and Pākehā in the early twentieth century

Marianne Schultz

Introduction

During the first two decades of the twentieth century, before radio and "the talkies" established themselves as forms of popular entertainment, vaudeville, the music hall and variety stage served up a huge array of performance events. Anything from acrobats and jugglers, tableaux of famous artworks, musical and dramatic segments, to dancing dogs and performing monkeys could appear on the same playbill. Of especial interest for audiences in Europe and North America were novelty acts that blurred the lines between entertainment and racial taxonomy, between the authentic and the illusion. Between 1910 and 1929 two New Zealand women trod the boards of music halls and appeared on the silent silver screen performing representations of New Zealand to audiences in both the Northern and Southern hemispheres. By adapting and presenting performances that represented and stood for Māori (Indigenous New Zealander) and Pākehā (non-Māori), these women – Princess Iwa and Bathie Stuart – contributed to notions of Māori and Pākehā as separate but related ethnographic entities. This essay shines a light on the archival offerings that uncover moments in their professional careers while also endeavouring to understand how their songs, dances, costumes and embodied expression both created and reflected impressions of a nation/dominion, race and gender. Moreover, by delving into the world of historical performance via photographs, newspaper items, playbills, films and scrapbooks, the evolution of embodied cultural hybridities emerges.

My interest in the archives of these two women and their careers in the performing arts stems from my curiosity on uncovering developments in corporeal expressions of culture both in New Zealand and internationally, from the mid-nineteenth century onwards. Specifically, I wondered how songs and dances, performed by both Indigenous and non-Indigenous peoples on stage and, later, on film, transcended and traversed "traditional" or non-commercial settings and purpose to become shared histories of cultural identities and performing arts. In examining past iterations of representations of race and gender via music and movement, new understandings of cultures emerge, oftentimes disrupting accepted notions of tradition and authenticity, as Tavia Nyong'o states, "hybridity unsettles collective and corporeal memory".[1]

Though all interpretations of historical events rely on scrutiny of primary and secondary sources, performance history demands that the historian imagines movement and sound in the empty spaces on stages, between the lines of sheet music, and behind the static images of facial and bodily expression fixed in photographs. My research aligns with Jane R. Goodall's observation that "performance is not only or even primarily a verbal medium ... communication occurs as much through imagery, movement and expression, all of which leave only partial and secondary traces in the archive".[2] Pertinent to this research, the connections between the performances of a 100 years ago by these two women and the narrative I have constructed of their lives and careers were enhanced by my own personal and embodied history as a dancer and performer. When reading a newspaper review of a performance or analysing a photograph taken on stage, grounded with my own somatic knowledge, I could intuit the flow or force of a movement or gesture. My own experience mirrors that of choreographer and researcher Martin Nachbar when he states that the "body that enters the archive in order to find documents of dance, is itself already a carrier of movement knowledge".[3] Seeing beyond a stationary image, I could sense the excitement or nervousness of these women when standing on stage in front of an audience, feeling the power of communicating through body, eyes and voice as I conjured felt memories of my own past performances.

I also have consulted closely with Iwa's grand-niece, Christchurch-based singer Angela Skerrett Tainui, the two of us sharing our findings on Princess Iwa as we each came upon more material on her life and career.[4] The story of Iwa's career in the UK had faded from memory among some whanau in New Zealand as her contemporaries passed on and with no known surviving recordings to keep her voice present, but Angela has worked tirelessly over the past decade to reintroduce Iwa to them via the surviving archival sources and seeking oral histories from iwi. An audio documentary that she produced, *Whakamarantanga o Iwa*, is held at the Alexander Turnbull Library in Wellington.[5]

---

1   Tavia Nyong'o, *The Amalgamation Waltz: Race, Performance, and the Ruses of Memory* (Minneapolis: University of Minnesota Press, 2009), 13.
2   Jane R. Goodall, *Performance and Evolution in the Age of Darwin* (London: Routledge, 2002), 5.
3   Martin Nachbar, "Tracing Sense/Reading Sensation: An Essay on Imprints and Other Matters", in *The Oxford Handbook of Dance and Reenactment*, ed. Mark Franco (New York: Oxford University Press, 2018), 19–33.
4   I also met and shared my research with Iwa's surviving grandson, Ibsen Barclay, who has lived his entire life in London.
5   Angela Skerrett Tainui, Miri Stacey Flemming, Angela Wanhalla and Paul Diamond, *Princess Iwa, the Maori Contralto, Whakamaharatanga o Iwa*, Kereti Productions, 2011.

Alongside the absence of a recorded voice, dance especially has often been referred to as ephemeral, the "quintessential artform of the immediate", or the "vanishing present".[6] From notation forms being varied and not widely adopted, to the variations in reconstruction/restaging success from photographs, choreographic notes and films, fixing or preserving dance is problematic. Yet, in many ways, archival source material of performers and performances resurrects long forgotten but nonetheless transcendent moments of beautiful musical notes in the air or expressive, evocative gestures of the limbs. Though the extant documents are not the performance itself, they can open the door to the past. Imagination, coupled with a deeply held belief in the centrality of the performing arts in the formation of societies and cultures throughout history, enables the fragile material in folders to breathe.

The archives, if given due respect and attention, can reanimate performance. My research has uncovered musical scores long forgotten and photographs buried in boxes seldom opened. The anticipation of hearing a piece of music not performed in 100 years or viewing a hand-made costume last worn on stages in early twentieth-century London is beyond words. This chapter is an attempt to fill in the gaps of the stories left by those fragments of performance by two remarkable women.

Princess Iwa: The "Maori Nightingale"

The review in the 15 October 1911 edition of *Lloyds Weekly News* enthusiastically stated that "Iwa, the 'Maori Nightingale' is the latest musical star at the Palace Theatre".[7] Headlining an act dubbed the "Dusky Dancers", Princess Iwa appeared as the soloist with a group of young Māori women, the "poi girls". The career of Iwa and her journey from the southernmost point of New Zealand to stages in the United Kingdom reveals the emergent expression of identity of New Zealand as a place where Māori and Pākehā collaborated and coexisted. Princess Iwa first arrived in the UK in 1911 as the soloist in Maggie Papakura's (née Thom) group of Māori performers and carvers. Papakura herself was famous as a tourist guide at the popular hot pools, springs and geysers in Rotorua, in the North Island of New Zealand. In response to a request from financial backers to take a group of entertainers plus a replica whare (house) to Australia and beyond, Papakura directed the group, acutely aware of the lure for Europeans of Māori performing their songs and dances in a "native" environment. She also believed that overseas touring benefited Māori who would

---

6   Mark Franco, "Introduction: The Power of Recall in a Post-Ephemeral Era", in *The Oxford Handbook of Dance and Reenactment*, ed. Mark Franco (New York: Oxford University Press, 2018), 1–19.

7   *Lloyds Weekly News*, 15 October, 1911 n.p., Maggie Papakura – Makereti Papers, Box X – Photocopies of an album of newspaper cuttings, photographs etc., the property of Mr. J.S. Barclay, Pitt Rivers Museum, University of Oxford.

come back to New Zealand and impart "their ideas to those who remained behind".[8] And so, in late 1909 Papakura and her assembled group of "Maori Entertainers" set sail for Sydney. In 1910, performing in Sydney and Melbourne with Papakura's group, Iwa was described by the *Sydney Sunday Sun* as "the star attraction of the Maori village" possessing "a contralto voice of great richness and power" while another Sydney newspaper noted the "fine vocalisation of Iwa, who is known in New Zealand as the 'Glorious Maori contralto'".[9]

Princess Iwa was born Evaline Skerrett (Ngāi Tahu) in 1890 on Stewart Island. She was raised in Bluff, Southland, where she also first started singing. In 1909, Iwa placed second in the Sacred Solo-Contralto category of the Dunedin musical and elocution competitions. The Australian judge cited her as a "contralto with a future" and soon after she came to the attention of Papakura.[10] The young singer proved an ideal symbol of successful Māori assimilation and her association with Papakura provided the springboard for her notoriety in the UK. Indeed, much of the archival material found for my research on Iwa is contained within Papakura's papers held at the Pitt Rivers Museum at the University of Oxford.

The blending of Māori themes, setting and performers with European musical forms and compositional styles constituted new cultural expressions of and for New Zealand, especially as European cultural expression became more prominent within New Zealand society from the end of the nineteenth century as the processes of colonisation solidified and strengthened. Consequently, opportunities for cross-cultural performance events increased for both Māori and Pākehā. Expressions of popular culture in the early twentieth century, particularly songs, stage acts and films also provided platforms for the creation of aesthetic hybrids in the performing arts.

One such instigator of this form of music was composer Alfred Hill.[11] Many of Hill's compositions, championed by some Māori performers including Papakura and Princess Iwa, reflected his quest to rediscover Māori music, alter it and introduce it to a wider audience. Australian-born Hill studied composition at the Leipzig Conservatory of Music, Germany, in the 1880s where his ear for European music was attuned. Hill's 1896 cantata Hinemoa portrayed, via Western musical forms scored for chorus and orchestra, the Te Awara story of mismatched lovers and the triumph of true love. Indeed, following *Hinemoa*'s premiere in Wellington,

---

8   Paul Diamond, *Makereti: Taking Māori to the World* (Auckland: Random House, 2007), 96. At the time Papakura was referred to as "Maggie" publicly. Her archives held at the Pitt Rivers Museum, University of Oxford, are named "Maggie Papakura – Makereti Papers". Her birth name was Margaret Thom. Makereti is the Māori transliteration of Margaret.

9   *Sydney Sunday Sun*, 1 January 1911, n.p. Maggie Papakura – Makereti Papers, newspaper clipping, 25 December, 1910, cuttings and ephemera 1901–10, Box VII, Pitt Rivers Museum, University of Oxford.

10 "Dunedin Competitions", *Otago Daily Times*, 1 October 1909, 6, https://bit.ly/3yPuPiz; "A Contralto with a Future", Evening Post, 1 October 1909, 7, https://bit.ly/3Pb66ul.

11 Hill lived from 1869 to 1960, thus his working life spanned both the ninetenth and twentieth centuries.

Hill was praised in the *Evening Post* for his ability to adapt and manipulate "Maori song" with his "masterly" handling of the Hinemoa legend.[12] However, Sarah Shieff has described Hill's compositions as a "veneer" of Māori laid over European forms of music, keeping the "Western forms intact".[13] His 1917 collection of songs published as Waiata Maori (Waiata meaning song in te reo Māori, the Māori language) have been referred to as "Europeanized Maori songs" and offered advice for singers on pronunciation of te reo Māori.[14] Here Hill suggested that "the pronunciation is practically the same as Italian", thus emphasising the romantic, foreign and "high" cultural element of this music.[15] These European interpretations and imaginings of Māori created a nostalgia for Māori culture, while also assuming ownership of Māori cultural expressions.

The idea that with colonisation the "weaker" of the races would be gradually erased clashed with the inclusion of Māori themes and settings in music and drama. This theory, known as fatal impact, along with the process of assimilation that was imposed on Māori from the mid-nineteenth century onwards, contributed to both a continuing erasure of Māori cultural expressions, including language and spirituality, and a longing to preserve aspects of culture. Māori were kept "alive" in the public's imagination through storytelling, drama and music. The explanation offered by Judith Williamson describes this process of cultural colonisation: "what is taken away in reality, then is re-presented in image and ideology so that *it stands for itself* after it has actually ceased to exist".[16] Hill's compositions clearly illustrate this transformation of Māori music into forms of popular cultural expression in an emerging bicultural society, as do Princess Iwa's and Bathie Stuart's acts.

Hill's most popular song, *Waiata Poi*, illustrates an aspect of the "dying Māori" ideology via his relationship with well-known painter Charles Goldie. Goldie, famous for his portraits of Māori, hoped to capture the essence of the "disappearing" race in his work, with titles of his portraits such as *The Last of the Tohungas* and *A Noble Relic of a Noble Race*. As Hill explained, *Waiata Poi* came to him as he sat in Goldie's studio in the evenings listening to the "old people sing half-remembered chants of the olden days".[17] The early career success of Princess

---

12   "'Hinemoa' and Other Original Works", *Evening Post*, 19 November 1896, 5.
      https://paperspast.natlib.govt.nz/newspapers/EP18961119.2.52.
13   Sarah Shieff, "Magpies: Negotiations of Centre and Periphery in New Zealand Poems by New
      Zealand Composers, 1896 to 1993" (PhD thesis, University of Auckland, 1994), 18, 28–29.
14   Mervyn McLean, *Maori Music* (Auckland: Auckland University Press, 1996), 313.
15   Alfred Hill, *Waiata Maori: Maori Songs Collected and Arranged by Alfred Hill* (Dunedin: John
      McIndoe, 1917).
16   Judith Williamson, "Woman is an Island: Femininity and Colonization", in *Studies in
      Entertainment: Critical Approaches to Mass Culture*, ed. Tania Modleski (Bloomington and
      Indianapolis: Indiana University Press, 1986), 112.
17   John Mansfield Thomson, *A Distant Music: The Life and Times of Alfred Hill
      1870–1960* (Auckland: Oxford University Press, 1980), 81–83. Hill's obituary in the *New
      Zealand Listener* heralded *Waiata Poi* as "the most popular and best-loved of all New Zealand
      songs", *New Zealand Listener*, 18 November 1960, 34.

Iwa relied heavily on the performances of Hill's songs, in particular *Waiata Poi*. While in Australia and later the UK, Iwa performed Hill's *Waiata Poi*, among other works.

In an interview with the *Norwood News* Iwa promoted Hill's talents, expressing "loud praise" for his works, which the reporter concluded as Iwa stating that Hill was the composer "whom English and Maoris alike look upon as their representative musician".[18] A newspaper review appearing five years after she first arrived in the UK confirms that *Waiata Poi* continued to be an important item in her solo repertoire:

> In the Maori song "Waiata Poi" which has been admirably arranged by Alfred Hill, Princess Iwa sang the exhilarating weird melody of her native land – which in some of its strains is reminiscent of Magyar – with fine flair and with just that distinctive suggestion of the bizarre which renders it so stimulating to the imagination.[19]

When she arrived in London in 1911 for the Festival of Empire with Papakura's troupe, Iwa immediately stood out. Personifying cultural hybridity, at once an Indigenous, "authentic" performer and European operatic songstress, the "Maori Nightingale" caught the attention of a public fascinated by her mixed-race heritage and pure, sweet voice. Under Papakura's direction and by association with *Waiata Poi* in particular, Iwa appeared as a performer who crossed cultural lines, appealing to European audiences with her renditions of Pākehā interpretations of Māori music. A showbill in Nottingham listed Iwa as "a British subject of Maori nationality who will sing a typical Maori song in the picturesque costume of her country".[20] It is clear that the Māori soloist resisted categorisation with her embodied difference. Her costume of traditional piupiu (dyed flax reed) skirt and feathered cloaks juxtaposed with her voice, which was that of a European classical singer.[21]

Following their appearances at the Festival of Empire and the Coronation Festival in London in the summer, Iwa and the "poi girls" were offered a contract to perform at the Palace Theatre in the autumn of 1911. The promotional photograph of the Palace season shows Iwa standing on her own wearing her kahu kiwi (cloak of kiwi feathers) with a tāniko (geometric-patterned stitched border) draped across

---

18   *Norwood News*, 30 September 1911, n.p., Maggie Papakura – Makereti Papers, photocopies of an album of newspaper cuttings, photographs etc., the property of Mr. J.S. Barclay, 1984, Box X, Pitt Rivers Museum, University of Oxford.

19   *The Daily Mercury*, 5 October 1916, n.p., Maggie Papakura – Makereti Papers, photocopies of an album of newspaper cuttings, photographs etc., the property of Mr. J.S. Barclay, 1984, Box X, Pitt Rivers Museum, University of Oxford. Magyar refers to native Hungarian.

20   Clipping, n.d. Entertainments: Ayr Burgh Choir Concert, Maggie Papakura – Makereti Papers, photocopies of an album of newspaper cuttings, photographs, etc., property of Mr. J.S. Barclay, 1984, Box X, Pitt Rivers Museum, University of Oxford.

21   Clipping, n.d. Entertainments: Ayr Burgh Choir Concert, Maggie Papakura – Makereti Papers, 67.

her chest. A large hei tiki (greenstone pendant) hangs around her neck. She stands on a korowai whakahekeheke (a woven cloak decorated with tassels and feathers). The accompanying "poi girls", posed in the seated "canoe poi" configuration, wear an assortment of korowai (tasselled cloaks) and piupiu. Aside from their "exotic" dress, these Māori women offered "dances ... weird yet fascinating and totally different from anything seen in London".[22]

The Māori women drew large crowds to the Palace and their act was favourably reviewed. A caption in a London newspaper described how the "songs and dances by the troupe of Maoris, headed by the sweet-voiced Iwa, have proved so popular at the Palace Theatre that their engagement has been indefinitely prolonged".[23] *The Times* singled out Iwa as the "sweet singer of the Maoris", adding that "it is refreshing to come across something rather out of the common run", while the *Croyden Times* called Iwa "the beautiful and extraordinary powerful contralto".[24] All these accounts highlight the contradictory nature of the song and dances that relied upon the embodied combination of "primitive" and "skilled". In the public's mind, Iwa's proficiency as a classical singer contrasted with her costumes and barefoot performances.

Iwa's early musical influence came from both Māori and Pākehā styles of singing. By the 1870s, Ngāi Tahu, Iwa's tribal affiliation in Bluff, had been "regarded as the most 'European' of the Māori tribes" due to the large influx of sealers and whalers and interracial marriage with these predominantly American and European arrivals.[25] Consequently, the ethnomusicologist Mervyn McLean describes how "Maori became bimusical in both the traditional Maori and the European systems" over the years of contact and colonisation.[26] In addition to the songs of whalers, merchants, soldiers and boat builders, the introduction of Christianity and hymn singing all added to the mix of songs among Māori and interracial communities. With this hybridity came new forms of musical expressions, blending melodies, song structure, time signatures and tonality. Iwa's choice of songs, her singing style, and her ability to use both English and te reo Māori in her songs reflect these developments.

---

22 *Bystander*, 1 November 1911, n.p., Maggie Papakura – Makereti Papers, photocopies of an album of newspaper cuttings, photographs etc., the property of Mr. J.S. Barclay, 1984, Box X, Pitt Rivers Museum, University of Oxford.

23 *Bystander*, 1911. Maggie Papakura – Makereti Papers.

24 *The Times*, 17 October 1911; *Croyden Times*, 11 October 1911, Maggie Papakura – Makereti Papers, photocopies of an album of newspaper cuttings, photographs etc, the property of Mr. J.S. Barclay, 1984, Box X, Pitt Rivers Museum, University of Oxford.

25 Angela Wanhalla, *In/Visible Sight: The Mixed-Descent Families of Southern New Zealand* (Wellington: Bridget Williams Books, 2009), 115.

26 Mervyn McLean, *Maori Music* (Auckland: Auckland University Press, 1996), 275. McLean presents several reasons why Māori singing and loss of singing traditions occurred in the wake of colonisation, including a decline in song composition by Māori, loss of cultural practices where singing was integral, fear of incorrect delivery or memory loss of words leading to ill fortune or death, and loss of language. See *Maori Music*, esp. Chapter 18.

Figure 7.1 "Maoriland Love Song", words by Dora Wilcox; music by J. Alexander. London: Beal, Stuttard & Co., 1912. (A-015-001, Fuller, Alfred Walter Francis, 1882–1961. Used with permission of Alexander Turnbull Library/Te Puna Mātauranga o Aotearoa, Wellington).

Unlike most of the group in London, Iwa did not return to New Zealand in 1912. During the Palace season, Iwa received "cheering words" from respected operatic England-based singing teachers and based on their encouragement she decided to "stay and study".[27] Settling in the UK, she developed her performing career as a solo artist and appeared on the variety stage of music halls throughout the country for the next decade. Her repertoire at this time perhaps reflected the influence of her vocal coaches, especially the songs she incorporated into her act that required an operatically trained voice, including "My Treasure", "Nearer My God to Thee" and "I Know a Lovely Garden". Glowing notices, articles and reviews from Birmingham, Edinburgh, Glasgow, Norwich, Plymouth, Manchester, Liverpool and Newcastle appear throughout these years. The sentiment from the review of her performance with the Ayr Burgh Choir concert in Scotland during this time is typical:

> Princess Iwa's appearance on the platform was eagerly awaited by the audience, and she must have been delighted with the warmth of the reception accorded on the grounds of personality alone. She has a voice of great range and power, pure tone, flexibility, and expressional quality, which stamps her as a front rank artist, and her career will be watched by all who had the pleasure of listening to her renderings both of our ballads and her own home gems of song. The effect of her singing was heightened by her appearance in native dress and with bare feet. She will not be soon forgotten.[28]

In the years 1915–18 Iwa performed in numerous benefit concerts in aid of the war effort, sharing the bill with members of the popular Carl Rosa Opera Company. In 1921 the *Glasgow Bulletin* published a photograph of a very stylish Iwa beside her equally sartorially smart husband, tenor Wilson Thornton. Under the headline "Glasgow is Their Choice", the newspaper informed that "Mr. Wilsun [sic] Thornton and his wife (The Maori Princess Iwa) have severed their connection with the Carl Rosa Opera Company. They intend to settle in Glasgow to teach singing".[29] The *Glasgow Evening News* also publicised the couple's move: "Mr. Thornton, it may be recalled, is married to Princess Iwa, a Maori lady in whose bloodline is a Royal strain. She was associated with her husband in opera, and will assist him in his latest enterprise."[30] While conducting this archival research, I travelled to Glasgow and stood outside their home. While Iwa never returned to the land of her birth, having died in London in 1947, I feel that I have helped to bring her story home.

---

27 Mervyn McLean, *Maori Music*, 275.
28 Clipping, n.d. Entertainments: Ayr Burgh Choir Concert, Maggie Papakura – Makereti Papers, Pitt Rivers Museum, University of Oxford.
29 *Glasgow Bulletin*, 25 August 1921, 6.
30 *Glasgow Evening News*, 30 August 1921, Playbills 1921, clipping, Mitchell Library, Special Collections, Glasgow.

Bathie Stuart: "The Girl who Sings the Maori Songs"

While Iwa carved out a niche for herself in the UK as the "Maori Nightingale", a Pākehā woman in New Zealand fashioned a career as a wahine Māori (female) performing songs in te reo Māori, incorporating movements and gestures that mirrored a Māori persona. Billed as "The Girl who Sings the Maori Songs", Bathia (Bathie) Stuart created a racialised caricature both on stage and screen that imitated Māori cultural practice. Contrasting with Princess Iwa, a Māori woman who offered a British-ised version of Māori, Stuart's act relied on her audience's awareness that she was a Pākehā who could conjure "Māori-ness" through song, dance and costume. Reflecting contemporary blackface/ethnic impersonations such as Al Jolson's in the film *The Jazz Singer* (1927), or Toots Paka and Gilda Gray who performed "Hawaiian" dances on mainland United States in the first decades of the twentieth century, audiences knew that Bathie was not Māori. Nonetheless, her unique portrayal of wahine Māori was celebrated and well received.[31] Indeed, so convincing was Stuart's performance that an anonymous reviewer, almost certainly Pākehā, commented Stuart "is a Maori maid in all but colour". The story that emerges from the archives of Stuart's life and career highlights the concepts of the "malleability of ethnicity" and "racial masquerade" so prevalent in early twentieth-century popular entertainment.[32]

Bathie Stuart was born in Hastings on the North Island's east coast in 1893 to parents of Scottish descent. She began her performing career at age 14 when she became a member of Pollard's Juvenile Opera Company, touring operettas on the vaudeville circuit throughout New Zealand and Australia.[33] Having survived being stricken by the 1918 Spanish flu (her husband, unfortunately, did not), by her mid-twenties Stuart developed her own music and comedy act. In a 1984 interview held in her archives, Stuart describes how she believed that she was always "unusual" because she had been so "interested in the Maori lore and could sing Maori songs". She claimed that "no other Pakeha did that in those days. I was the only one".[34] Like Alfred Hill, it seems that Stuart was drawn to Māori songs and felt compelled to promulgate and popularise Māori cultural expression. Unlike Princess Iwa, whose

---

31 See Jane Desmond for a discussion of these non-Indigenous women who performed "Hawaiian" on popular stages in the first two decades of the twentieth century. Jane Desmond, *Staging Tourism: Bodies on Display from Waikiki to Sea World* (Chicago: University of Chicago Press, 1999).

32 Alison M. Kibler explains how, with performances such as Al Jolson's in the 1927 film *The Jazz Singer*, blackface acts "constructed new American identities" as "a link between old and new identities ... and the 'whitewashed' histories of racial unity". This "whitewashing" of history was also present in New Zealand society during Bathie Stuart's career. Alison M. Kibler, *Rank Ladies: Gender and Cultural Hierarchy in American Vaudeville* (Chapel Hill: University of North Carolina Press, 1999), 115.

33 Bathie Stuart Papers, MA 1591, MANS. 0010, Folder 3, New Zealand Film Archive/Ngā Kaitiaki O Ngā Taonga Whitiahua, Wellington.

34 Transcript of interview with Bathie Stuart by Julie Benjamin, Laguna Beach, 1 February 1984, Bathie Stuart Papers, MA 1591, MANS. 0010, Folder 3, New Zealand Film Archives/Ngā Kaitiaki O Ngā Taonga Whitiahua, Wellington.

repertoire consisted of concert and parlour songs reflective of her operatic training, Stuart's songs and dances fit into a comedic, entertaining style.

There is no doubting that opportunities availed themselves to Stuart because she was a white woman. In the early 1920s the Māori population resided primarily in rural and segregated areas of the country. Tourist areas such as Rotorua provided spaces where Pākehā and overseas guests could attend performances of Māori performing arts, such as haka, poi and waiata. These performances allowed for both close proximity to Māori and Māori culture and defined distance from Europeans and everyday life. Therefore, that Stuart was able to create images and representation of Māori for her Pākehā audiences is understandable given the absence of Māori from Pākehā daily life. As historian James Belich has explained, Māori at this time were "isolated from and marginal to, the Pakeha socio-economy" and lived predominantly in the rural environment.[35] The 1923 Census recorded the uneven population of New Zealand, with 1.2 million Europeans/Pākehā compared to roughly 53,000 Māori.[36] Hence, it is not surprising that Māori culture was transplanted and translated onto stage and screen in the early twentieth century in an effort to retain a sense of New Zealand's unique history, minus reminders of the colonial atrocities, disputes over land acquisition, and erasure of spiritual and cultural practices.

There were other vehicles for Māori storytelling by Māori, and one area where the ideologies of some Māori and Pākehā coexisted in this period was within the sphere of the performing arts. However, owing to the constrictions of assimilation, these tended to reflect the growth in hybrid cultural expression. For instance, a decade before Stuart created her vaudeville act, the Māori Opera Company presented a staged version of the Hinemoa story as a three-act opera with a small orchestra and a cast of 30 Māori performers. The music, composed by Englishman Percy Flynn, aimed to showcase Māori culture via European musical settings. This setting of a well-known Māori story in a Western performance form aligned with the views of some Māori, especially men who were educated in Pākehā-led institutions or were associated with the Christian church. Reverend Frederick Bennett, the instigator of the Māori Opera Company, strongly advocated for assimilation. As a man with mixed Māori-Irish ancestry and an ordained Anglican minister, Bennett worked hard to cultivate European sensibilities and practices among Māori. The *Poverty Bay Herald* reported in 1915 that Bennett, as "proprietor", appeared on stage and explained "how the production of the play has been entered upon, so as to create an interest in the Maori mind for the higher

---

35   James Belich, *Paradise Reforged: A History of the New Zealanders from the 1880s to the Year 2000* (Auckland: Penguin Books (NZ) Limited, 2001), 191.

36   *New Zealand Official Yearbook*, 1923, http://www3.stats.govt.nz/New Zealand Official Yearbooks/1923/NZOYP, accessed 29 November 2012.

art".[37] Therefore, Māori and Māori culture had a presence within the realm of popular entertainment in the early twentieth century.

This metamorphosis from traditional and ritual expression by Māori to entertainment by both Māori and Pākehā cast a shadow over cultural production and representation, and it was out of this shadow that Stuart as a "Pakeha Maori" emerged.[38] In 1926 Stuart created a sensation with her act "Bathie Stuart and her Musical Maids". During their four-week run at the Majestic, a vaudeville cinema theatre managed by Henry Hayward in Auckland, Stuart successfully portrayed a Māori woman who, although lacking tribal affiliation or distinct connections to a specific place in New Zealand, entertained on stage. Following this sold-out season, which a reviewer in the *Auckland Star* described as the "instantaneous success of Miss Bathie Stuart and her accompanying native girls", Stuart toured the next incarnation of this group, "Bathie Stuart and her Maori Maids", throughout the Hayward circuit.[39]

Stuart claimed that women from Rotorua taught her the "songs, poi, dances and haka" for her stage show with the "Maori Maids" and that Apirana Ngata, a respected statesman of Māoridom, taught her "many of the Maori songs".[40] The Maids' act consisted of the songs "Hoki Tonu Mai" and "Pokarekare", sung in te reo Māori, in addition to poi dances and haka.[41] Surrounding herself with her "Maori Maids" and performing Māori, through song, dance and dress, Stuart simultaneously highlighted her own non-Māori identity while also celebrating Māori culture. Drawing attention to Māori culture and customs through the phenomenological engagement between audiences and performers reflects a complex cultural exchange between Māori and Pākehā at this time. Stuart assumed both a Māori and non-Māori identity in the moment of performance.

The acceptance and success of Stuart's act mirrors Alison Kibler's description of the "racial masquerade" that was employed by American entertainers in the late nineteenth century. Kibler states that "racial masquerades emboldened some white comediennes by setting them apart from svelte, perky chorus girls".[42] Stuart certainly used her comedic flair and short stature to her advantage. In the 1925

---

37 "Maori Opera Company: *Hinemoa* at the Opera House", *Poverty Bay Herald*, 14 October 1915, 7, https://paperspast.natlib.govt.nz/newspapers/PBH19151014.2.49.

38 Unlike earlier nineteenth-century usage of this term, applied primarily to men who had "turned" Māori and adapted to a Māori way of life and were possibly taking a Māori wife, "Pakeha Maori" as applied to Stuart signified her performance repertoire and stage costumes with the express acknowledgement that she was indeed a Pākehā.

39 "Miss Bathie Stuart and her Maori Maids", *Auckland Star*, 8 May 1926, 18, https://paperspast.natlib.govt.nz/newspapers/AS19260508.2.156.5.

40 Bathie Stuart, Ref TO 1 118 5/3 part 1, Archives New Zealand, Wellington.

41 These are the titles of the songs as referred to at the time. See: Michael Brown, "Hoki Mai Ra", National Library of New Zealand, 11 August 2014, https://natlib.govt.nz/blog/posts/ hoki-mai-ra. More recent popular names of these songs are "Hoki Hoki Tonu Mai" and "Po Karekara Ana".

42 Kibler, 126.

Australian "comedy drama in six reels" *The Adventures of Algy*, Stuart portrayed "Kiwi McGill", a young woman living with her father on a New Zealand farm, whose future is uncertain. Unlike the archival evidence of Princess Iwa's career, found primarily in photographs and newspaper accounts, we are fortunate to be able to view Bathie Stuart in action, as it were.

Viewing the extant copy of *The Adventures of Algy* offers the opportunity to experience Stuart's performance style and movement vocabulary, which is not as readily available when interpreting a static image. Performed and filmed almost 100 years ago, Stuart's dancing in this moving picture draws the viewer towards a deeper comprehension of corporeal expression of past bodies. Unaccompanied by music (this is a silent film), the dance sequences focus attention on the temporal expressions of culture in movement and clothing, via breathing, working, entertaining, bodies. And we witness the energy of the movement: mistakes, reactions, intent.

When the film's Australian director, Beaumont Smith, arrived in New Zealand in early 1925 to conduct a series of screen tests throughout the country seeking *Algy*'s leading lady, a newspaper reported that Stuart, "known throughout the Dominion as 'The Girl who Sings the Maori Songs' is the young New Zealand heroine in support of Claude Dampier [the lead male actor]".[43] The familiar show-within-a-film setup of 1920s motion pictures, seen in movies such as *Golddiggers of Broadway*, is echoed here in this silent film, as Kiwi, a hard-working but unlucky dancer, is discovered by a theatrical producer performing her "Maori" dances with her friends in Rotorua. Troubled by her father's financial hardships, Kiwi visits her Māori friend Mary for advice. Kiwi arrives at the local Māori village dressed in her feathered cloak, when Mary suggests a temporary solution. Mary's caption says, "Dance for us, Kiwi, and forget your troubles". Seeing Kiwi in this environment, surrounded by Māori, viewers are meant to understand that Māori accept Kiwi and her interpretation of Māori haka. Moreover, she is encouraged to dance as wahine Māori by Mary, who *is* wahine Māori. Kiwi acts on Mary's advice and stands, her cloak falling to the ground, revealing her piupiu and woven top draped over one shoulder. She dances, thrusting her hands and hips to the side, circling her wrists and placing one hand near to her ear with a shimmering movement, movements meant to resemble what wahine might perform in a haka or poi dance. As Kiwi dances, a group of European men and women, led by a Māori guide, watches with interest. This is when the Australian theatrical producer discovers the "distinct novelty" for his new revue. Forthwith, Kiwi heads to Australia to headline a new show in Sydney.[44]

---

43 *The Adventures of Algy*, Bathie Stuart Papers, MA 1591, MANS. 0010, Drop folder, New Zealand Film Archive/Ngā Kaitiaki O Ngā Taonga Whitiahua, Wellington.
44 *The Adventures of Algy*, 20007.0072, New Zealand Film Archive/Ngā Kaitiaki O Ngā Taonga Whitiahua, Wellington.

The large-scale stage production number in *Algy*, filmed at Sydney's Palace Theatre, featured Kiwi dancing in front of a chorus of 20 dancing women, all attired in grass skirts, cropped tops and short dark wigs. Their choreography includes typical stage movements of the day – unison lines of turns, kicks and promenades – with the addition of "exotic" gestures, such as hip circles and hand waving, invoking Māori wiriwiri (hand shimmer) or Hawaiian hula hand gestures. This exaggerated "mélange of movements, at times conjuring various ethnicities and time periods" culminates with Kiwi downstage swaying in a crouched position with her raised hand clutching a club.[45] Her triumphant final stance signalled both the power of the imagined "traditional" movements and the female body. Thus, in *The Adventures of Algy*, Bathie Stuart as Kiwi McGill simultaneously represented both an idealised wahine Māori and a Pākehā who had colonised Indigenous expression through her movements and costume.

"How much Maori can you do?"

The illusionary nature of Stuart as an Indigenous New Zealander led to a second career promoting New Zealand to Americans. Having settled in the United States in the late 1920s, she "pioneered adventure/travel film lectures across America", publicising New Zealand as a tourist destination.[46] The events leading up to Stuart's career on the lecture circuit in the United States parallels the story of how Kiwi McGill was discovered by the Australian producer in The Adventures of Algy.[47] In the 1984 interview Stuart explained that after lunching at a women's club in Los Angeles, the host introduced her as "our guest from faraway New Zealand who will speak to us in her native tongue". Explaining that English was her first language, Stuart nonetheless performed her "Maori" dance. Upon witnessing this performance, a booking agent present at the luncheon asked Stuart if she realised what a "remarkable novelty" she possessed, asking, "How much Maori can you do?"[48] From then on her presentations in the United States consisted of showing a tourism film on New Zealand, a short lecture on customs and landmarks, and a performance of her interpretations of waiata, haka and poi. Her publicity flyers promised that Stuart was "as proficient in the rendition of their [Māori] ceremonials and sweet haunting melodies as the natives themselves".[49] These illustrated lectures relied on her ability to perform

---

45   Marianne Schultz, *Performing Indigenous Culture on Stage and Screen: A Harmony of Frenzy* (New York: Palgrave Macmillan, 2016), 147.
46   Bathie Stuart Papers, MA 1591, MANS. 0010, Folder 1, New Zealand Film Archive/ Ngā Kaitiaki O Ngā Taonga Whitiahua, Wellington.
47   Schultz, 151.
48   Transcript of interview with Bathie Stuart by Julie Benjamin, Laguna Beach, 1 February 1984, Bathie Stuart Papers, MA 1591, MANS. 0010, Folder 3, New Zealand Film Archive/ Ngā Kaitiaki O Ngā Taonga Whitiahua, Wellington.
49   Bathie Stuart Papers, TO 1 118 5/3-1, Archives New Zealand, Wellington. Bathie Stuart died in California in 1987, aged 94.

waiata and haka, as she emphasised in a letter to the New Zealand Government Publicity Department in a solicitation for their support: "I am sure that an ordinary lecture on New Zealand could not arouse the enthusiasm that is achieved by a talk embellished with the poetry and rhythmic dances of our 'First New Zealanders'".[50] It is clear that although Stuart never attempted to pass *as* Māori, her careers in show business and tourism nonetheless depended on her convincing portrayal *of* Māori in song and dance.

Conclusion

So what can the microhistories from the archives of these two New Zealand performers reveal about larger phenomena in music, dance and entertainment? The careers of both women slotted into expressions of early twentieth-century popular culture of controlled exoticism, signified by the female form encased in somewhat revealing clothing, often barefoot, performing unfamiliar (to a non-Indigenous audience) rituals, songs and dances on stage or film. Princess Iwa, with her charming, melodic voice, "native" clothing and the regal designation of "Princess" enchanted her audiences by combining songs sung with expertise with the accoutrements of "Other". A Māori woman by birth, the incongruity of an operatic voice coupled with Indigenous clothing only enhanced her popularity in the public's eye.

Bathie Stuart, by enacting Māori through song and dance, while being recognised for her ability as a Pākehā to "interpret" Indigenous culture, transported Māori songs and movement into the realm of popular light entertainment. Importantly, Stuart projected "New Zealand-ness" to audiences who were becoming increasingly aware of their own identities – politically, socially, culturally – as separate from the "home country" of Great Britain. Since 1907 when New Zealand achieved Dominion status from the UK, allowing for self-government at home rather than strict adherence to the rule of the British Crown from a distance, New Zealand visual artists, writers, composers and performing artists sought to create identifications of nationhood via their work.

Significantly, throughout their performing careers, it was essential for both women that they highlighted their origins as New Zealanders; the idea that "authenticity equals ancestry" seems relevant here.[51] Both conjured notions of New Zealand through their corporeal expression. Their uniqueness was also good for business, as reflected in a comment made by the manager of the Palace Theatre in London. Predicting that Princess Iwa's future success relied on her singing "in Maori", the manager emphasised it would be a "fatal mistake" if she sang "the

---

50   Letter to the New Zealand Government Publicity Department, Overseas Publicity Board, Wellington, from Bathie Stuart, 29 October 1929. Bathie Stuart Papers, TO 1 118 5/3-1, Archives New Zealand, Wellington.
51   Charles Lindholm, *Culture and Authenticity* (Malden: Blackwell, 2008), 21.

Figure 7.2 "The only white woman interpreting the unusual folk lore of the Maori people", Miss Bathie Stuart. [TO1 118 5/3 1 R21484799] Archives New Zealand Te Rua Mahara o te Kāwanatanga, used with permission.

usual Pakeha drawing room song".[52] For both women it was through performances of song and dance that their identities as New Zealanders became known. Their different versions of a "New Zealand woman" – Princess Iwa an assimilated Māori, Bathie Stuart a Pākehā interpreting and also celebrating Māori culture – represented modern twentieth-century New Zealand society.

Researching the extant archival material of these two women, it becomes clear that music and choreographed movements can reinforce attachments to place and create notions of race. Princess Iwa's performances, in particular her renditions in te reo Māori of Alfred Hill's *Waiata Poi* and *Hine e Hine* by Te Rangi Pai, substantiated her ancestry, even though her perfectly pitched soprano voice belied her Indigenous heritage in the public's perception of what an Indigenous voice should sound like. The movements of haka and poi, so intrinsically linked to Māori, confirmed Stuart's authenticity as a New Zealander, albeit a Pākehā performing interpretations of Māori culture.

The conflicts of comprehension that arose as I absorbed the material in these archives illuminated the work that historians of performing arts undertake. The archives revealed strongly held beliefs on race, societal hierarchies and acceptability, especially within the realm of popular culture in the early twentieth century. As I have not had access to accounts of either performer in te reo Māori, it is difficult to know how contemporary Māori viewed their "acts". By the early twentieth century te reo Māori was largely confined to Māori communities and all but banned in schools and in public. Though there were newspapers written in te reo at the time, I could find no reference to either performer's acts in these archives.

That sounds and gestures could stand for national identity and racial heritage was an important consideration for both women, reflecting a common phenomenon in the performing arts of the era. By the early twentieth century, cultural hybridity manifested in numerous displays of popular culture, reinforcing the notion that "all cultures are involved in one another; none is single and pure, all are hybrid".[53] Above all else, both Princess Iwa and Bathie Stuart relied on the incongruous but modern nature of their very hybrid beings. As both Māori and Pākehā, their songs and dances shaped expressions and representations of New Zealand and laid the groundwork for future innovations in the evolving and changing nature of bicultural and transcultural performing arts, particularly in later forms of musical and choreographic expression.

References

"A Contralto with a Future". *Evening Post*, 1 October 1909, 7. https://bit.ly/3Pb66ul.
"Alfred Hill Obituary". *New Zealand Listener*, 18 November 1960, 34.

---

52   "Return of the Maoris: Causes of the Failure", *Auckland Star*, 10 January 1912, 8, https://bit.ly/3RgNpHE.
53   Edward Said, *Culture and Imperialism* (New York: Random House, 1994), xxv.

Bathie Stuart. Ref TO 1 118 5/3 part 1. Archives New Zealand, Wellington.

Bathie Stuart Papers. MA 1591, MANS. 0010, Folder 3. New Zealand Film Archive/ Ngā Kaitiaki O Ngā Taonga Whitiāhua, Wellington.

Belich, James. *Paradise Reforged: A History of the New Zealanders from the 1880s to the Year 2000.* Auckland: Penguin Books (NZ) Limited, 2001.

Brown, Michael. "Hoki Mai Ra". National Library of New Zealand. 11 August 2014. https://natlib.govt.nz/blog/posts/hoki-mai-ra.

Desmond, Jane. *Staging Tourism: Bodies on Display from Waikiki to Sea World.* Chicago: University of Chicago Press, 1999.

Diamond, Paul. *Makereti: Taking Māori to the World.* Auckland: Random House, 2007.

"Dunedin Competitions". *Otago Daily Times,* 1 October 1909, 6. https://bit.ly/3yPuPiz.

Franco, Mark. "Introduction: The Power of Recall in a Post-Ephemeral Era". In *The Oxford Handbook of Dance and Reenactment,* ed. by Mark Franco. New York: Oxford University Press, 2018: 1–19.

Goodall, Jane R. *Performance and Evolution in the Age of Darwin.* London: Routledge, 2002.

Hill, Alfred. *Waiata Maori: Maori Songs Collected and Arranged by Alfred Hill.* Dunedin: John McIndoe, 1917.

"'Hinemoa' and Other Original Works". *Evening Post,* 19 November 1896, 5. https://paperspast.natlib.govt.nz/newspapers/EP18961119.2.52.

Kibler, Alison. *Rank Ladies: Gender and Cultural Hierarchy in American Vaudeville.* Chapel Hill: University of North Carolina Press, 1999.

Lindholm, Charles. *Culture and Authenticity.* Malden: Blackwell, 2008.

Maggie Papakura – Makereti Papers (1901–10), cuttings and ephemera. Box VII. Pitt Rivers Museum, University of Oxford.

Maggie Papakura – Makereti Papers, photocopies of an album of newspaper cuttings, photographs etc. Box X. Pitt Rivers Museum, University of Oxford.

"Maori Opera Company: Hinemoa at the Opera House". *Poverty Bay Herald,* 14 October 1915, 7. https://paperspast.natlib.govt.nz/newspapers/PBH19151014.2.49.

McLean, Mervyn. *Maori Music.* Auckland: Auckland University Press, 1996.

"Miss Bathie Stuart and her Maori Maids". *Auckland Star,* 8 May 1926, 18. https://paperspast.natlib.govt.nz/newspapers/AS19260508.2.156.5.

Nachbar, Martin. "Tracing Sense/Reading Sensation: An Essay on Imprints and Other Matters". In *The Oxford Handbook of Dance and Reenactment,* ed. Mark Franco. New York: Oxford University Press, 2018: 19–33.

New Zealand Official Yearbook, 1923, https://bit.ly/3x4dxwN, accessed 29 November 2012.

Nyong'o, Tavia. *The Amalgamation Waltz: Race, Performance, and the Ruses of Memory.* Minneapolis: University of Minnesota Press, 2009.

"Return of the Maoris: Causes of the Failure". *Auckland Star,* 10 January 1912, 8. https://bit.ly/3RgNpHE.

Said, Edward. *Culture and Imperialism.* New York: Random House, 1994.

Schultz, Marianne. *Performing Indigenous Culture on Stage and Screen: A Harmony of Frenzy.* New York: Palgrave Macmillan, 2016.

Shieff, Sarah. "Magpies: Negotiations of Centre and Periphery in New Zealand Poems by New Zealand Composers, 1896 to 1993". PhD thesis, University of Auckland, 1994.

Skerrett Tainui, Angela, dir., Miri Stacey Flemming, Angela Wanhalla and Paul Diamond. *Princess Iwa, the Maori Contralto, Whakamaharatanga o Iwa.* Christchurch: Kereti Productions, 2011. CD.

Smith, Beaumont, dir. *The Adventures of Algy.* Wellington: New Zealand Film Archive/ Ngā Kaitiaki O Ngā Taonga Whitiāhua, 1925. 20007.0072, film.

"*The Adventures of Algy*", Bathie Stuart Papers. MA 1591, MANS. 0010, Drop folder. New Zealand Film Archive/ Ngā Kaitiaki O Ngā Taonga Whitiāhua, Wellington.

Thomson, John Mansfield. *A Distant Music: The Life and Times of Alfred Hill 1870–1960*. Auckland: Oxford University Press, 1980.

Wanhalla, Angela. *In/Visible Sight: The Mixed-Descent Families of Southern New Zealand*. Wellington: Bridget Williams Books, 2009.

Williamson, Judith. "Woman is an Island: Femininity and Colonization". In *Studies in Entertainment: Critical Approaches to Mass Culture*, ed. by Tania Modleski. Bloomington and Indianapolis: Indiana University Press, 1986: 99–119.

8

Bodies of representation and resistance: Archiving and performing culture through contemporary Indigenous theatre in Taiwan

Chi-Fang Chao

Introduction

> Put some more clothes on dancers' bodies? Not now! In the last scene, after the dancers roll into the scene, that's when I will put their traditional costumes back on their bodies before they step out of the curtains. It will then show their most beautiful form.
>
> Bulareyaung Pagarlarva

In front of me sat Taiwanese Indigenous choreographer Bulareyaung Pargalarva, imagining the bodies on the stage. Our conversation was triggered by the concern of a group of cultural specialists and scholars, myself included, who were behind the scenes and worried by the idea and presence of the near-naked bodies of Indigenous dancers on the stage of the National Theatre located in the capital city of Taipei. The choreographer insisted on concretising oppression by using the women's half-naked bodies to symbolise the bitter stigmatisation of young Indigenous sex workers. In his modernistic vision, there seemed to be no better medium to express this issue, other than to reveal the strength of the dancers' bodies in this form.

Later when the scene was shown, the audience was overwhelmed by the presence and sensation of seeing the half-naked bodies, mingling with the feelings of innocence, humiliation and resistance that were all projected on the stage and directed to the oppressed Indigenes. Towards the end, I was finally relieved. Sitting among the audience with applause flooding in, I watched the vivid Indigenous bodies wearing the traditional costumes dancing energetically and holding hands as the curtain fell.

This was a scene from the Indigenous theatrical production Pu'ing: *Searching for the Atayal Route* (2013). It is a contemporary work merging post-colonial voices of resistance with "the repertoire [that] enacts embodied memory",[1] which embraces traditional songs, dances, narratives and costumes.

In the last three decades, theatre has become a vital space for Indigenous peoples in Taiwan to counteract mainstream representations of their histories, social existence and cultural identity. Many of these representations have been stored in official and academic archives, and then reproduced and interpreted to shed light on the political relationship between the producers and objects of knowledge. The archive encapsulates political tones that need to be unravelled, and Indigenous performances either represent or resist these. Situated in the Taiwanese context, this chapter explores the relationship between the lived body and historical objects, and how embodied re-enactment of history, imbued with different knowledge and techniques, can deconstruct and problematise archival realism on the stage.

Archive and performance: Ways of presenting Indigenous culture through bodies

> The archival, from the beginning, sustains power. Archival memory works across distance, over time and space; investigators can go back to re-examine an ancient manuscript, letters find their addresses through time and place, and computer discs at times cough up lost files with the right software.[2]

Arguing for the enduring nature of the archive with the examples of Latin America, Diana Taylor composes an extensive etymological exegesis of the word "archive". She also argues that the archive is "expansionist" and "immunized against alterity". Comments made by scholars such as de Certeau point out the fact that "archival memory succeeds in separating the source of 'knowledge' from the knower [and the known] – in time and/or space". In sum, "[w]hat changes over time is the value, relevance, or meaning of the archive, how the items it contains get interpreted, even embodied".[3]

Indigenous people's social realities have been archived through various embodied, oral and written forms. As Taylor argues, even "in the most literate of societies", cultural practices need both "an archival and an embodied dimension".[4] However, the balance between written and embodied dimensions is skewed by power imbalances between Indigenous subjects and those in control of archiving institutions and practices. Taylor illustrates that writing, which had already existed among Indigenous cultures as an embodied practice to transmit culture, was legitimised over "other epistemic and mnemonic systems".[5] In other words, writing

---

1   Diana Taylor, *The Archive and the Repertoire: Performing Cultural Memory in America* (Durham, NC: Duke University Press, 2003), 20.
2   Taylor, *The Archive and the Repertoire*, 19.
3   de Certeau cited in Taylor, *The Archive and the Repertoire*, 19.
4   Taylor, *The Archive and the Repertoire*, 21.
5   Taylor, *The Archive and the Repertoire*, 18.

does not in itself equal archiving, but has been an essential prerequisite of the latter. Writing is also "easier to control than the embodied culture",[6] because it renders tangible and permanent records. From a technical point of view, writing, along with other ways of inscribing, comprises the majority of archival records – with colonisers being the main producers of archives.

In a recent study, Dee Das suggests important social and political meanings of dancing can be revealed through reading colonial archives. She explores "the embodied archive" on a group of dancers and singers from the Kingdom of Dahomey in Africa, who first performed in Dahomey Village at the World's Fair: Columbian Exposition in 1893. The embodied archive on dance performance can only be deciphered from authors' discourse as in the records about the fair and its follow-ups. Dee Das argues that Dahomey's dancing is "a force of resistance" to the perpetuated discourse, racism and primitivism[7]. Dee Das investigates how to evaluate the expressive freedom in, and the expectation of, performance which is "thought to provide a sense of hope and the possibility for the powerless to speak back, … ,[or] to act out" in response to the coloniser.[8]

Compared to the archive, the notion of performance has enjoyed a rather "democratic" or even decolonised view among scholars. Performances have been seen as "an embodied praxis and episteme", or "a system of learning, sorting and transmitting knowledge".[9] It is especially obvious in terms of Indigenous peoples' actions from a decolonising or post-colonising perspective. Cree theorist and director Floyd Favel argues that, although presentations of songs and dances occurred as a result of the subjugation of North American Native peoples by the settlers' society, still they are "the few places that native peoples could openly practice their cultures".[10] He observes that the Native performances that travel abroad have dual roles for viewers and performers, confirming images of the Native for the former, while at the same time allowing free expression for the latter. By juxtaposing the North American Native performances alongside the Russian folk ones, he concludes:

> [t]he contemporary stage was one of the few places that Native peoples could once again live in freedom and this led to a tradition of performing among many Native peoples, and the stage became the vehicle and the refuge where ancient songs and dance could be kept alive and shared with the world.[11]

---

6   Taylor, *The Archive and the Repertoire*, 17.
7   Ebron cited in Joanna Dee Das, "Dancing Dahomey at the World's Fair: Revising the Archive of African Dance", in *Futures of Dance Studies*, eds Susan Manning, Janice Ross, Rebecca Schneider (Wisconsin: The University of Wisconsin Press, 2020), 57.
8   Ebron cited in Dee Das, "Dancing Dahomey at the World's Fair", 57.
9   Taylor, *The Archive and the Repertoire*, 16–17.
10 Floyd Favel, "Theatre: Younger Brother of Tradition", in *Indigenous North American Drama*, ed. Birgit Däwes (Albany: State University of New York Press, 2013), 115.
11 Favel, "Theatre: Younger Brother of Tradition", 116–17.

Favel names theatre, the contemporary stage for Indigenous performances, "the younger brother of tradition". Favel's notion of "tradition" is concretised as "ways of 'doing' ... songs, dances, narrative structures taking place within the sacred ritual space", while "theatre" is "a set of performative skills" of the above practices "presented in the idealized space for the public at large".[12] Although it is absolutely relevant to contrast contemporary theatre against the notion of tradition for Indigenous peoples, his proposition favours contextualism, in which tradition and theatre are firmly set apart from each other in terms of context, purpose and participants.[13] There is another level of actors' creative and continuous deployment of embodied cultural memory through performance – archival memory:

> Performance genealogies draw on the idea of expressive movements as mnemonic reserves, including patterned movements made and remembered by bodies, residual movements retained implicitly in images or words (or in the silences between them), and imaginary movements dreamed in minds not prior to language but constitutive of it.[14]

As suggested by Joseph Roach, embodiment probes archival memories in our bodies. For Indigenous cultures, the relationship between the archive and performance raises other critical issues on authorship and Indigenous epistemology. The archive and performance are therefore systems of knowledge that are intrinsic to modern societies. For instance, modern institutions, including archives, informed by both ethnic and nationalistic ideologies, usually frame cultural collections in terms of "the past". By comparison, stage performances or the theatre enact the vital practice and process through which cultural memory and Indigenous epistemology are enlivened.[15]

While Indigenous performance gains significance as decolonised action and in building repertoires of Indigenous epistemology, the representation of the past and culture in the archive cannot be overlooked. Archives are not all static, although they are often resistant to change. The rediscovery of archives, whether through remapped geopolitical applications[16] or reidentified key figures,[17] can

---

12 Favel, "Theatre: Younger Brother of Tradition", 118–19.

13 Favel, "Theatre: Younger Brother of Tradition", 119.

14 Joseph Roach, *Cities of the Dead: Circum-Atlantic Performance* (New York: Columbia University Press, 1996), 26. See also Taylor, *The Archive and the Repertoire*, 5.

15 Taylor, *The Archive and the Repertoire*, 16–17.

16 Yuan Shu, "Introduction: Oceanic Archives, Indigenous Epistemologies, and Transpacific American Studies", in *Oceanic Archives, Indigenous Epistemologies, and Transpacific American Studies*, eds Yuan Shu, Otto Heim and Kendall Johnson (Hong Kong: Hong Kong University Press, 2019), 1–21.

17 Anna Haebich, "Aboriginal Families, Knowledge and Archives: A Case Study", in *Colonising the Landscape: Indigenous Cultures in Australia*, eds Beate Neumiere and Kay Schaffer (Amsterdam and NY: Rodopi, 2013), 37–56; Shino Konishi, Maria Nugent and Tiffany Shellam, *Indigenous Intermediaries: New Perspectives on Exploration Archives* (Canberra: Australian National University Press, 2015), http://www.jstor.com/stable/j.ctt19705zg.6.

redefine the scope of history. That is, archives wait to be reinterpreted or rediscovered. Performance enlivens the archive as they sustain each other in relation to their textuality and temporality: the ever-present and the ephemeral.

Taiwanese Indigenous bodies in archives

Globally, the necessity and vitality of Indigenous theatres have been widely discussed,[18] but what is the unique complication or value of understanding their relationship to the archive? Unlike Taylor's case study in Latin America, where writing did exist as a different sort of embodied culture among Indigenous peoples before colonisation, the Taiwanese Indigenous peoples had never developed written languages. Subsequently as written documentation became systematic in Taiwan, Indigenous peoples could only be represented by others.

Representations of Taiwanese Indigenous groups have embedded themselves in the long regional history of East Asia, colonisation and modernisation. In this chapter I mainly discuss four genres of embodied archives representing Indigenous peoples in Taiwan: Chinese historical writings and illustrations; Japanese visual recordings; modern ethnographies and post-colonial reconstructed performances. The different media and techniques of representing the Taiwanese Indigenous groups largely reflect the materiality and institutional priorities of those hegemonic powers, mainly of China and Japan. Each genre also reflects a profound premise of humanity: the "romanticized primitivism" in the Chinese historical documents and the scientific modernism in Japanese colonialism, as far as Indigenous peoples were concerned.

Chinese historical literature

The earliest Chinese account of Indigenous peoples can be dated back to the seventh century. "Record of Liu Chiu" (流求) in *The Book of Sui* (隋書), which is believed to be the earliest writing on Taiwan, depicts a scene of singing and dancing as follows:

---

18 Per Brask and William Morgan eds, *Aboriginal Voices: Amerindian, Inuit and Sami Theatre* (Baltimore and London: Johns Hopkins University Press, 1992); Maryrose Casey, *Creating Frames: Contemporary Indigenous Theatre – 1967–1990* (St Lucia: University of Queensland Press, 2004); Otto Heim, "Recalling Oceanic Communities. The Transnational Theater of John Kneubhul and Victoria Nalani Kneubhul", in *Oceanic Archives, Indigenous Epistemologies, and Transpacific American Studies*, eds Yuan Shu, Otto Heim and Kendall Johnson (Hong Kong: Hong Kong University Press, 2019), 239–60; Marc Maufort, "Voices of Cultural Memory Enacting History in Recent Native Canadian Drama", in *Indigenous North American Drama: A Multivocal History*, ed. Birgit Däwes (Albany: State University of New York Press, 2013), 159–76.

Whenever there was a banquet, people who held the liquor waited for [someone's] name to be called then drank. Those who toasted the King also called his name. They held the same cup and drank it together, as did the Turks. They sang while stamping their feet. One man sang and the other responded. It sounded grievous. [They] held women's arms, shook hands and danced.[19]

Although historians have debated the identities of the people in the "Record of Liu Chiu", this picturesque depiction is strikingly reminiscent of the current scene of singing and dancing in annual rituals among some Taiwanese Indigenous peoples. Hence, contemporary practices testify to the historical archive.

Although bearing the nature of authenticated history, the tradition of Chinese historical writing on "the Others" has a peculiar blending of exoticism and romanticism. Descriptions of customs sometimes reinforce both, as in the above paragraph on singing and dancing. Another example is shown in Chen Di's "Records on the Eastern Barbarians" (東番記), which is a reliable account of Taiwan written in the early seventeenth century. Chen was amazed that Taiwanese Indigenous peoples had no written languages: "They, however, fed themselves and played around happily, enjoyed themselves in satisfaction". Chen even worried that after contact with the Chinese, their simplicity might progressively disappear, including the ritual of "dancing upon singing and making music during the banquet when all drank [liquor] with bamboo cups".

Over the eighteenth century, Chinese officials became increasingly aware of the threat of European "invaders" and so they travelled across the strait in greater numbers to investigate. Historical writings about Taiwan also increased over this time, written mainly by Chinese officers. Their romantic and poetic narratives produced an image of happy, naïve, exotic and uncivilised peoples. For example, a work depicting singing and dancing is called *Sai Shi* (賽戲) (*Game and Play*), which conveys perfectly the tone of joy. Later, the written texts were gradually accompanied with illustrations (Figure 8.1), which further show an idealised life from the Chinese perspective, rather than that of the Indigenous peoples. Both works have been treated as precious historical archives today while their representational undertone has gone largely uninterrogated.

Textual realism in the Japanese archives of Taiwanese Indigenous peoples

If realism was not the main concern in the Chinese historical writings, the Japanese modern technical representation is hard to ignore. The Japanese colonised Taiwan

---

19 Di Chen, "Record of Liu Chiu", in *Book of Sui*, from Chung-Kuo Cher-Hsueh-Shu Tien-Chi-Hua Chi-Hua (Project on Digitalisation of Chinese Philosophy), https://ctext.org/wiki.pl?if=gb&chapter=584840#%E6%B5%81%E6%B1%82%E5%9C%8B. The English translations of Chinese historical accounts are all provided by the author.

Figure 8.1 *Sai Shi* (*Game and Play*) in *Taiwan Fan She Tu* (*Pictures of the Savage Villages in Taiwan*, 1820). [AH001585-004]. National Taiwan Museum, used with permission.

in 1895, a result of Japan's Westernised self-transformation into a modern nation-state. Influenced by British anthropology, Japanese scholars who were hired by the government to study Indigenous peoples not only classified and identified individual ethnic groups using linguistic divides, but also imposed modern knowledge and devices of ethnological collection, such as cameras, and sound and film recorders. It was the first time that bodily images and sounds of Indigenous peoples in Taiwan had ever been recorded, researched and archived. Photography of Taiwanese Indigenous peoples became one of the best media to illustrate "the Other" for the Japanese (Figure 8.2). Famous collectors include Torii Ryūzō (1870–1953),[20] Mori Ushinosuke (1877–1926)[21] and Asa'i Erin (1895–1969).[22] The textual realism then inspired later academic research, resulting in the establishment of the first modern anthropological program in Taiwan in 1928. Taiwanese Indigenous peoples as the ethnic "Other" became the perfect object for academics. Later disciplines such as ethnomusicology collected songs and dances of Taiwanese Indigenous peoples. Renowned Japanese ethnomusicologists such as Kurosawa Takatomo produced findings on Indigenous music and accumulated archives with advanced modern facilities and technology. For instance, Kurosawa sent the recording of the Bunun people's famous ritual song *Pasiputput* to the International Folk Music Council (IFMC) in 1952, based on which he then published his well-known hypothesis exemplifying the origin of music in 1978. He also produced a book that textualised the materials into abstract motifs and notes from the songs and dances of the Indigenous peoples, whom he referred to using the Japanese label of "Takasagozoku".[23] In addition to photos, readers can find scores as well as drawings of movement patterns interpreted from singing and dancing, such as in the section about the Atayal people. The scientific reductionism and academic realism made his account another resource for the contemporary archive.

The missing dancing bodies of Taiwanese Indigenous peoples in post-1945 academic research

Taiwanese anthropology and ethnomusicology in the post-1945 era was primarily influenced by the Japanese legacy and continuous Western influences, mediated with Chinese knowledge systems. While ethnographic investigations among

20 Sung Wen-Hsun et al, *Kua Yueh Shih Chi De Ying Hsiang: Niao Chu Lung Tsang Yen Chung De Taiwan Yuan Chu Ming* (*Images Crossing the Centuries: Indigenous Peoples Viewed by Torii Ryūzō*) (Taipei: Shung Ye Museum of Formosan Aborigines, 1994).
21 Mori Ushinosuke, *Taiwan Fan Tsu Tu Pu* (*Photographs of the Taiwan Indigenes*) Vols 1 & 2 (Taipei: Lin Shih Taiwan Chiu Kuan Tiao Cha Hui, 1915–18).
22 Kurihara Seichi ed., *Taiwan Yuan Chu Min Ying Hsiang Chih: Chien Ching Hui Lun Chiao Shou She Ying Chi* (*Images of Taiwanese Indigenes: Photographs Anthology of Professor Asa'i Erin*), trans. Yang Nan-Chun (Taipei: Nan Tien, 1995).
23 Kurosawa Takatomo, *Music of Taiwanese Takasagozoku* (Tokyo: Yuzankaku, 1973).

Figure 8.2 A postcard illustrating Taiwanese Indigenous peoples (possibly the Rukai) dancing. Photo taken anonymously sometime in the Japanese colonising period, around the 1920s. [AH006858-003] National Taiwan Museum, used with permission.

Indigenous peoples continued to grow, the political relationship between the majority Han and the Indigenous peoples remained extremely imbalanced. Although the two disciplines flourished and were institutionalised further, there was a lack of attention to the dancing bodies of Indigenous peoples. Photos which can only represent still bodies could no longer satisfy the need to capture the moving bodies of Indigenous peoples. This was corrected only when a few dance specialists travelled deep into the mountains and visited the villages to document their dances. The lack of academic attention to Indigenous peoples' dances was a result of the overall difficulty in textualising the moving body. The utilisation of the Westernised tool of reductionist Labanotation to record Indigenous ritualistic dances since the 1990s is a noteworthy exception.[24]

---

24 Madeline Kwok, a University of Hawai'i masters graduate, was one of the earliest to use Labanotation to transcribe the dance of Indigenous peoples (Paiwan) in the 1980s. Taiwanese dance educator Heng Ping then applied its usage to other ethnic groups. Madeline Kwok, "Dance of the Paiwan Aboriginal people of Pingtung County, Taiwan: With Implications of Dance for Tribal Classification" (Master's thesis, University of Hawai'i, 1977). Heng Ping, "Yi-Wan Chu Lo Chih Wu Dao" (*Dances of the Saniwan Village*) in *Taiwan Tu-Chu Chi I Shih Ke Wu Min Su Huo Dong Chih Yen Chiu* (*The Study on Rituals, Songs, Dances, and Folk Activities of Taiwanese Indigenes*), eds Liu Pin Hsiung and Hu Tai Li (Nantou: Taiwan Sheng Min Cheng Ting 1987), 75–99.

Reconceptualising Indigenous dancing bodies as archives

Archives are mostly understood as static objects. In terms of dance, which by its nature moves through time and space, archival records, whether in written or audiovisual forms, can only be a distorted textualisation or partial revelation. Indigenous theatre has then become "the embodied archive" for music and dance.[25] In the following section, I focus on the Formosa Aboriginal Song and Dance Troupe (FASDT), which has become the emblem of reconstruction and revitalisation of Indigenous dance and music in Taiwan since its establishment in 1991. The founding of the troupe, of which the members are exclusively Indigenous peoples, coincides with the Indigenous revitalisation movements of the 1990s. It was formed at a time when threats to the autonomy of Indigenous society and culture were at their peak. The continuous exodus of the population for survival shook the social structure of communities. The standardisation of national languages created a void in communication of cultural memories to younger generations. As Taiwan was introduced to new religions, capitalism and tourism, traditional craft, music and dance were forgotten.

Archiving through performance was embedded in the founding aspirations of FASDT, which intends to preserve gradually disappearing Indigenous music and dance, as well as traditional rituals in which they are largely contained. This would not be possible without the support and actions of a versatile group of professionals, including anthropologists, journalists, dance scholars and theatre managers. The troupe employs a quasi-ethnographic approach for its productions: focusing on single tribes as the cultural unit for productions; troupe members are required to do fieldwork and learn the languages, singing and movement from village Elders; and performances are as loyal to the original forms as possible and for this reason often do not employ musical accompaniment. However, all songs are translated and the presentation, including time scale, is adjusted to today's theatrical conventions.

Between 1991 and 2016, FASDT produced more than 10 productions. Among the 16 officially recognised ethnic groups, FASDT's works have covered Amis, Atayal, Bunun, Paiwan, Rukai, Saaroa, Saisiat, Tsou, Truku and Tao. It has also set a standard for subsequent Indigenous theatrical works of artistic or educational purpose.[26] For instance, since FASDT's first production, performers will sing as well as dance rather than use non-traditional musical accompaniment (instruments), as a nod to theatrical realism.

From an anthropological perspective, Hu argues that the notion of "reality" in performance is more complicated than just transforming music and dance from

---

25 Taylor, *The Archive and the Repertoire*; Dee Das, "Dancing Dahomey at the World's Fair".

26 Many short-term members of FASDT learned and later duplicated the reconstructionist approach of performance when they went back to their colleges or villages. They reproduced and helped spread the FASDT style. FASDT's legacy is still visible in the annual national song and dance competition of Indigenous college students.

tribes onto stage.[27] For instance, the Paiwanese people view singing and dancing for theatre as performance, while the Saisiat believe the reconstructed performance carries ritualistic efficacy. Among the Saisiat people, this has even inspired the younger generations to learn the archaic and abstruse ritual songs that were almost forgotten. In this sense, reconstructed Indigenous performances, while reflecting post-colonial social complications and modernistic technologies, have established themselves as the embodied archive to preserve cultural memories.

Counteracting archiving: Post-colonial Indigenous theatre

Before 2000, FASDT contributed to the revitalisation of language, costumes, music and dance by showcasing traditional Indigenous songs and dances to the Han majority. These efforts, however, have become more and more ambiguous and challenged. Over the past decade, troupe members have recognised the need to produce works beyond an archival purpose. They need to act out their post-colonial conditions rather than merely reciting and repeating "tradition". Several works had been deliberately produced to redefine and reinterpret controversial incidents at the individual, tribal, colonial, national and even global level. These works highlight the tension between the dominators and the dominated, and question the neutrality and distance embedded within the archives of Taiwanese Indigenous peoples.

These works counteract the more traditional archives produced by colonisers. FASDT's new production has invited professionally trained Indigenous artists to direct and choreograph. The professional artistic team also includes composers, a light designer, set designer, costume designer and visual designer. Sophisticated multimedia narratives merge voices of resistance with aesthetic sensibility. In the following sections, I discuss how stage performances invite participants to experience sensations and feelings of struggle and resistance, instead of re-presenting a "naturalistic" archive.

Grotesque scars, patriotic virginity and nudity of oppression: Archives and performances on the Atayal's Indigenous bodies

The work Pu'ing: *Searching for the Atayal Route* premiered in 2013. It was inspired by one of the most controversial figures in Taiwanese modern Indigenous history, an Atayal girl named Sayun Hayun. The Atayal people were known in their traditional culture as hunters and weavers. They were among the fiercest fighters against Japanese rule in the early stages of colonisation in the late nineteenth

---

27 Tai-Li Hu, "Wen Hua Chen Shih Yu Chan Yen: Saisiat Paiwan Ching Yen (*Cultural Reality and Performance: The Experiences with Saisiat and Paiwan*)", in *Wen Hua Chan Yen Yu Taiwan Yuan Chu Min* (*Cultural Performance and the Taiwanese Indigenes*) (Taipei: Lien Ching, 2003), 423–58.

century. One tension between Atayal people and the Japanese was the notion of "civilisation" and its implications. Until the early twentieth century, the Atayal people practised traditional tattooing. Male hunters and female weavers tattooed their faces in recognition of their merits. An Indigenous cultural specialist once told a group of international scholars, myself included, while pointing to a photo of a senior Atayal woman, that she had been forced to remove the tattoo on her forehead when she was a young girl. Her parents were warned by a Japanese policeman that if they didn't send their daughter to hospital for tattoo removal, she would not receive an education nor other civil rights. The girl was sent to the hospital in Taipei where her tattoo was removed without anaesthesia. She was left with a deep scar. Instead of the patterned tattoo carrying cultural import and dignity, she had to bear the grotesque scar on her forehead, which she was unable to remove for the rest of her life.[28] In "civilising" the Atayal girl, the colonisers left an inscription of humiliation on her body.

The extreme hegemonic forces on the bodies of the Atayal was the key theme in the work *Pu'ing: Searching for the Atayal. Pu'ing* is an Atayal lexicon, which means "root" or "tracing the root". This cultural message was chosen during group discussions between the Indigenous director, the Atayal, other Indigenous intellectuals, and anthropologists. The work tells the story of 17-year-old Sayun Hayun. She was born in the village of Liyohen belonging to the Kelisan region deep in the mountains of north-eastern Taiwan. To send off her Japanese teacher who was joining the army, she and her parents carried his luggage all the way from their village in the mountains down to the nearest town. On the night of 27 September 1938, a tropical storm hit the area. As she crossed a bridge, Sayun fell down and was swept away by the furious tide.

While this is a story of an Atayal girl, the Japanese appropriated it for their own narrative. Sayun's death was first reported by the Japanese *Daily News* in Taiwan, and was then deliberately transformed into a propaganda series by the Japanese government to inspire patriotism. Journal reports started to boast of Sayun's "sacrifice". Female patriotic groups spread the spirit of the patriotic virgin Sayun. In 1941, a song entitled "Sayon no Kane", ("The Bell of Sayon") was composed and recited at a memorial held in the famous Taipei Public Hall. Impressed with the recital of Sayun's patriotic sacrifice, months later, the then Japanese Governor General, Hasegawa Kiyoshi, commissioned a heavy bronze bell to be cast and sent to Sayun's village. It was transported all the way to the remote village as a monument to Sayun's "sacrifice" for the nation. Many articles and productions appropriated the image of Sayun, such as journal reports, a paper puppet show and a movie,[29] in which Sayun was portrayed by the famous but controversial Japanese actress Yamaguchi Yoshiko (1920–2014). Famous artist

---

28 Personal communication with Turku cultural specialist Tian Hsiu-shi. December, 2003.
29 The movie can be accessed through the following link, in which Sayun Hayun was depicted as falling in love with the Japanese teacher which accordingly gave her the motivation to see him

Shiotsuki Tōho (1886–1954) painted Sayun holding the bell. Sayun had become probably the best known female icon in both Taiwan and Japan at that time.[30] These Japanese textual productions illustrate how archives can be manipulated and controlled. The Japanese production and reproduction of Sayun-centred narratives reveals the political absurdity of archival accuracy.

Sayun's story spread under Japanese colonisation, and then was silenced once the Chinese Nationalist (KMT) Government took over Taiwan after World War II. As one of the main agnostic powers against Japan during the war, the KMT tried to erase the island's Japanese legacy since 1895. Sayun's narrative, along with the bell, was wiped from public view, although her tribal folk continued to sing the Japanese song "Sayon no Kane". It wasn't until the early twenty-first century that Sayun Hayun's story was rediscovered and recognised as significant to Indigenous lore. Many explorers found people still attracted by her stories as well as the buried trails into what used to be the heart of Kelisan.[31]

FASDT set out to produce *Pu'ing: Searching for the Atayal* by gathering the fragmented and conflicting archives about Sayun, while seeking to reflect cultural and historical nativism. The question is: can the performance deliver a different historiography[32] and cultural memory, or enliven the archive differently? After reviewing Sayun's life and visiting her village and descendants, the production team decided to stage a crisscross narrative to merge the present with the past.

The performance was divided into five scenes:

Prelude

A young Atayal man, Watan, struggles to find his Indigenous identity after living for a long time in the modern urbanised world. He decides to go back to his father's home country in the mountains, but the environment looks very strange to him. He searches for his village with great effort but in vain. When he falls asleep due to tiredness, he dreams and hears faint singing in a peculiar but familiar tone. A group of people approach him in dim light.

---

off. https://youtu.be/eH-soDxfNY4 from 27:50 to 30:00 depicts a scene of Atayal people dancing and singing their traditional songs around the fire.

30 When I did my fieldwork in Okinawa in the late 2000s, I met a senior woman in her eighties. She had lived in Taiwan for her entire adult life before returning to Okinawa in 1945. Upon learning that I was from Taiwan, she immediately sang two songs to me. One was a famous Taiwanese folk song, *Night Flower in the Rain* and the other was the Japanese song *Sayon no Kane*.

31 Lin Ke-Hsiao, *Chao Lu: Yueh Kuang, Sayun, Kelesan (Searching for the Route: Moonlight, Sayun, Kelesan)* (Taipei: Yuan Liu, 2009).

32 Maufort, "Voices of Cultural Memory Enacting History in Recent Native Canadian Drama".

Trials in green

The scene is structured by three traditional Atayal songs featuring the singing style of overlapping polyphony. The repetitive pattern of melody also reinforces the feeling of endlessness. It provides a perfect sound structure for climbing up and moving ahead – the journey that the Atayal ancestors had once taken to found their settlements. The performance visualises how Atayal ancestors migrated and dispersed into three branches, settling in the mountainous areas in north, central and north-eastern Taiwan.

After a number of generations, young tribesmen became curious about where their families had originated. The Elders passed down the story of migration through *lmuhuw*, a genre of epic and narrative songs. The opening scene blends traditional songs and legends of migration with an embodiment of travelling and then settling, using the locomotion of changing floor levels on the stage.

The flaming sun

This scene depicts how the Atayal suffered under bitter political oppression by the Japanese regime during the Japanese colonisation between 1895 and 1945, symbolised by the rising sun. The Atayal men try to riot but fail. Resistance seems in vain. The Japanese eventually send young Indigenous people to the battlefield, condemning them to death. Grieving mothers of Indigenous soldiers dream of bringing the souls of their dead sons home. The Atayal lullaby is sung to comfort their souls, while a special visual effect transforms the flaming sun to a red square pattern, which was typical of Atayal craft. In this scene, Bulareyaung cleverly transplants modern physical military training, which most Taiwanese males undertake, onto the stage to highlight the male body subjected to dominance. The heightened oppression on their bodies finally reaches the climax, provoking fierce but futile resistance through jumping.

While all this is happening, Watan stands off stage and witnesses the battle. Before intermission the dim sound of singing comes from the mother-like woman, which lures Watan, until he becomes lost in the meandering trails.

River in purple

Purple is the colour of dark night, as well as the preferred colour of Liyohen textiles. The scene starts with a group of seated Atayal women scattered and weaving while singing traditional weaving songs. It is the 1930s. Sayun Hayun, the happy teenager from Liyohen, is learning to weave. She and her female friends dance, sing and playfully quarrel. After their group dance, there is an insertion of romantic scenarios accompanied by Atayal love songs, followed by playing of the mouth harp to indicate courting and hunting, cultural meanings related to this unique instrument. Group dances of both genders are reminiscent of scenes from the movie Sayon no Kane. After the climax of the hunters' physical competition,

Figure 8.3 The scene of an Atayal mother holding her son, who fought against the Japanese colonising force, from "The Flaming Sun" in *Pu'ing: Searching for the Atayal Route*. Photo by FASDT, used with permission.

suddenly the pace of the mouth harp speeds up like rapid heartbeats and the stage falls into darkness, conveying a mood of uneasiness. The river that swallowed Sayun is then revealed. There is not just one girl in the river crying for help, but many. The river then turns into the river of time. It not only buried Sayun, who died in 1938, but also the young prostitutes[33] who were ravaged, 50 years later, by the contemporary monetary system. They are drowning, shouting for help and rescue

33 Taiwanese sex brokers often lied to parents and told them that their daughters would be working in factories.

to no avail. "The river turned purple, because it was full of dead people who fought with each other,"[34] is the final message of the purple river.

The final tension focuses on the unsettling and uncomfortable encounter between nearly nude bodies, male and female alike. It is an accusation against the males who have collectively oppressed the female body, with Sayun in the centre symbolising purity and innocence. Then the Japanese song *Sayon no Kane* is sung amid a pacified atmosphere. The original archival memory of colonisation is now overturned as a performance of reconciliation.

The rainbow bridge

According to the Atayal myth, every genuine Atayal person has to obey the norm of *gaga* and fulfil their obligation in order to cross the rainbow bridge and reunite with their ancestors in the afterworld. The stage designer transforms the mountainous trails into a symbolic rainbow. The dancers walk up the rainbow one by one, as the final *lmuhuw* is chanted to guide them into a new world where they can meet their roots and all Atayal, dressed in the most flamboyant costumes, dance together and become one.

Finally, Watan joins the dance with his tribesmen, realising that the rainbow has embraced the colours of cultural trails, the flaming memory and the fluid history of oppression, which contribute to the unique Atayal route that has led him to both his origin and future.

The above description can only loosely depict the narrative centred on the search for history and cultural identity, which blurs the past with the present. It treads through the mythic past, Japanese colonisation, the deceit and social stigmatisation of young Indigenous sex workers, and finally the futuristic reunion with their roots and traditions. The performance is powerfully emotional thanks to the Atayal songs, orchestral music, rhythmic movement, traditional forms of dance and uplifting choreography. The merging of archival memories from different times, genres and cultures is enabled by the bodies, which sang, moved and were narrated as one.

Two scenes are particularly prominent to me. The first is when the Atayal mother washes the body of her son who had died in the battle against the Japanese, while singing the traditional lullaby as a lament. After a series of fierce and high jumps that symbolise the vain resistance of his coup against the Japanese, the male performer (the son) is not always able to hold back his tears, and cries heartily on stage. It is not unusual for audience members to be overheard sobbing throughout. The second prominent scene is when the group of females, whose bodies are barely covered in fitted skin-coloured costumes, jump strenuously only to fall down repeatedly, expressing their struggle for survival against the tide of the river. They do not just replicate the image of Sayun. They are the betrayed innocent. The

---

34   Lin, *Chao Lu*.

women's increasingly heavy breaths provoke uneasiness in the audience, as if we are the oppressors watching them struggle against their destiny.

What the audience does not realise, however, is the real pain and struggle that individual dancers have gone through during the intensive rehearsals over weeks and months. Despite being experienced and talented professionals affiliated with FASDT, most of the performers of *Pu'ing* found it unimaginably tough. They were trained in a way that challenged them far more than the usual constructionist approach; that is, only representing or re-enacting the archive. They needed to embody the oppressed, represented by intense jumping, symbolising resistance to gravity. Embodiment of resistance, which is never visible in the colonial archives, is portrayed by dancing bodies, experienced first by the dancers, then the audience.

I was almost begging Bulareyaung to consider projecting translations of the texts into Chinese on either side of the stage. "No. I want the audience to focus on the dancers, on their bodies, but not extract their attention to read those words." I then surprisingly discovered that the dancers who did not understand Japanese in the beginning strove to memorise the lyrics of *Sayon no Kane*. Towards the end, they were able to sing and move with feeling and imagination as if it were their own language and their own expression. Their dancing bodies relived the archives.

Conclusion

This paper is an enquiry into the archive and performance of Indigenous peoples in Taiwan, whose "pasts" have been mediated by colonial and nationalistic forces. The conversation between the choreographer and me in the opening paragraph reveals the tension between two distinctive foci: performative creativity and established knowledge. This tension can also find its parallel in the dynamic between performance and archive as representation. In the Taiwanese context, the traditions of Indigenous peoples are mostly realised via cultural expression through storytelling, craft, and singing and dancing; however, the archive for them has been mainly produced by colonising rulers and accomplished through the colonial modernisation including photographs, recordings, notation and scholarly writings. These two categories are inherently contrasting but mutually referential; their relationship not only reveals a complicated and hierarchical rationality and power of technologies, but also throws much light on cultural sensibilities for creative forms.

Archives of Indigenous dance and music construct themselves into a complex totality from which the discourse of indigeneity has been rooted and stored. Chinese exoticism and romanticism are visualised through poetic depiction and illustrations. The Japanese exploited realistic yet colonised representations of Indigenous voices and bodies through modern technologies. Western systems of abstraction such as notation, and holistic representation via ethnographic writings, objectify Indigenous peoples' dances and cultures. All have contributed to selecting and shaping the cultural interpretations of Indigenous theatre.

Larger movements of revitalisation are reflected in performance of Indigenous music and dance. The evolution of approaches to theatrical productions parallels post-colonial forces at play in both Indigenous and non-Indigenous communities between the 1990s and 2010s in Taiwan. The theatrical work Pu'ing: *Searching for the Atayal Route* manifests culture and identity, in which multi-layers of narratives and forces are embodied in singing and dancing. With collective professional talents, the performance resists and counters representations sedimented in most archives on Indigenous peoples, on and off the stage.

References

Brask, Per and William Morgan, eds. *Aboriginal Voices: Amerindian, Inuit and Sami Theatre*. Baltimore and London: Johns Hopkins University Press, 1992.

Casey, Maryrose. *Creating Frames: Contemporary Indigenous Theatre – 1967–1990*. St Lucia: University of Queensland Press, 2004.

Chen, Di. "Record of Liu Chiu" in *Book of Sui*, from Chung-Kuo Cher-Hsueh-Shu Tien-Chi-Hua Chi-Hua (Project on Digitalization of Chinese Philosophy), https://ctext.org/wiki.pl?if=gb&chapter=584840#%E6%B5%81%E6%B1%82%E5%9C%8B.

Chen, Zhong-Ren, ed. *Wan Ching Taiwan Fan Su Tu (Paintings of the Indigenous Customs in Late Ching Dynasty)*. Nangang: Centre of Taiwan Study, Academic Sinica, 2013.

Dee Das, Joanna. "Dancing Dahomey at the World's Fair: Revising the Archive of African Dance". In *Futures of Dance Studies*, eds Susan Manning, Janice Ross and Rebecca Schneider. Wisconsin: The University of Wisconsin Press, 2020: 56–73.

Favel, Floyd. "Theatre: Younger Brother of Tradition". In *Indigenous North American Drama*, ed. Birgit Däwes. Albany: State University of New York Press, 2013: 115–22.

Haebich, Anna. "Aboriginal Families, Knowledge and Archives: A Case Study". In *Colonising the Landscape: Indigenous Cultures in Australia*, eds Beate Neumiere and Kay Schaffer. Amsterdam and New York: Rodopi, 2013: 37–56.

Heim, Otto. "Recalling Oceanic Communities: The Transnational Theatre of John Kneubhul and Victoria Nalani Kneubhul". In *Oceanic Archives, Indigenous Epistemologies, and Transpacific American Studies*, eds Yuan Shu, Otto Heim and Kendall Johnson. Hong Kong: Hong Kong University Press, 2019: 239–60.

Hu, Tai-Li. "Wen Hua Cheng Shih Yu Chan Yen: Saisiat Paiwan Ching Yen (Cultural Reality and Performance: The Experiences with Saisiat and Paiwan)". In *Wen Hua Chan Yen Yu Taiwan Yuan Chu Min* (Cultural Performance and the Taiwanese Indigenes). Taipei: Lien Ching, 2003: 423–58.

Konishi, Shino, Maria Nugent and Tiffany Shellam. *Indigenous Intermediaries: New Perspectives on Exploration Archives*. Canberra: Australia National University Press, 2015.

Kurihara, Seichi, ed. *Taiwan Yuan Chu Min Ying Hsiang Chih: Chien Ching Hui Lun Chiao Shou She Ying Chi (Images of Taiwanese Indigenes: Photographs Anthology of Professor Asa'i Erin)*. Translated by Yang Nan-Chun. Taipei: Nan Tien, 1995.

Kurosawa, Takatomo. *Taiwan Takasagozoku no Oongaku (Music of Taiwanese Takasagozoku)*. Tokyo: Yuzankaku, 1973.

Kwok, Madeline. "Dance of the Paiwan Aboriginal People of Pingtung County, Taiwan: With Implications of Dance for Tribal Classification". Master's thesis, University of Hawai'i, 1977.

Lin, Ke-Hsiao. *Chao Lu: Yueh Kuang, Sayun, Kelesan (Searching for the Route: Moonlight, Sayun, Kelesan)*. Taipei: Yuan Liu, 2009.

Maufort, Marc. "Voices of Cultural Memory Enacting History in Recent Native Canadian Drama". In *Indigenous North American Drama*, ed. Birgit Däwes. Albany: State University of New York Press, 2013: 159–76.

Ping, Heng. "Yi-Wan Chu Lo Chih Wu Dao (Dances of the Saniwan Village)". In *Taiwan Tu-Chu Chi I Shih Ke Wu Dao Min Su Huo Dong Chih Yen Chiu (The Study on Rituals, Songs, Dances, and Folk Activities of Taiwanese Indigenes)*, eds Liu Pin Hsiung and Hu Tai-Li. Nantou: Taiwan Sheng Min Cheng Ting, 1987: 5–99.

Roach, Joseph. *Cities of the Dead: Circum-Atlantic Performance*. New York: Columbia University Press, 1996.

Shimizu, Hiroshi. *Sayon No Kane (The Bell of Sayon)*, black and white, 75 min. Taipei: Matsutake films, 1943. https://youtu.be/eH-soDxfNY4.

Shu, Yuan, "Introduction: Oceanic Archives, Indigenous Epistemologies, and Transpacific American Studies". In *Oceanic Archives, Indigenous Epistemologies, and Transpacific American Studies*, eds Yuan Shu, Otto Heim and Kendall Johnson. Hong Kong: Hong Kong University Press, 2019: 1–21.

Sung Wen-Hsun. *Kua Yueh Shih Chi De Ying Hsiang: Niao Ju Lung Tsang Yen Chung De Taiwan Yuan Chu Ming (Images Crossing the Centuries: Indigenous Peoples Viewed by Torii Ryūzō)*. Taipei: Shung Ye Museum of Formosan Aborigines, 1994.

Taylor, Diana. *The Archive and the Repertoire: Performing Cultural Memory in America*. North Carolina: Duke University Press, 2003.

Ushinosuke, Mori. *Taiwan Fan Tsu Tu Pu (Photographs of the Taiwan Indigenes), Volumes 1 & 2*. Taipei: Lin Shih Taiwan Chiu Kuan Tiao Cha Hui, 1915–18.

9

Mermaids and cockle shells: Innovation and tradition in the "Diyama" song of Arnhem Land

Jodie Kell and Cindy Jinmarabynana

Introduction

In the Western Arnhem Land community of Maningrida, 500 kilometres east of Darwin, the recent creative expression of the all-female Ripple Effect Band has reignited interest in the origins of the "Diyama" song. As the first women in their community to take up instruments and form a band, their innovative musical practices have prompted recollection and discussion of cultural practices among women of the region, particularly An-barra family members of band member Stephanie Maxwell James. Their perspective provides new knowledge that contests the descriptions of song practice in archives and historical records. The new interpretations of the "Diyama" song and its origin story challenge the fixity of archival objects, recognising the law held in oral traditions and the prerogative of song custodians to respond creatively to changing contexts over time.

"Diyama" is a song written by Stephanie Maxwell James.[1] Sung in the Burarra language, it is named after the cockle shells that are found in the surrounding coastal regions. The song tells the story of the mermaids that inhabit the waters of the An-barra homeland of Gupanga, 40 kilometres east of Maningrida. Stephanie is among the few women from the region to compose and perform songs in public, as a member of the Ripple Effect Band. She is also part of a lineage of An-barra musicians who have performed versions of this song over three generations.

---

1   Stephanie Maxwell James, "Diyama" [song], recorded June 2018 on *Wárrwarra* (Ripple Effect Band), streaming audio accessed 9 July 2021, https://open.spotify.com/track/0YZ7618tj3ZZUNfztpC0cT?si=9f9a4194faeb44af.

The title "Diyama" is shared with a songset of the traditional kun-borrk genre,[2] an Indigenous song style known across Western Arnhem Land. The kun-borrk called "Diyama" is attributed to the creative powers of mermaid spirits as received in a dream, which is typical of kun-borrk songs across Western Arnhem Land.[3] In 1960, anthropologist Lester Hiatt made the first recording of "Diyama" sung by Stephanie's grandfather, Mulumbuk, with a description of how Mulumbuk first received the song.[4] The recordings and liner notes are held in the archive of the Australian Institute of Aboriginal and Torres Strait Islander Studies (AIATSIS).

In 2017, An-barra Elder Mary Dadbalag gave an alternative account of the origins of the "Diyama" kun-borrk, explaining that it was her eldest sister who saw the ancestral spirits come out of the water and sing and dance "Diyama", instructing her to pass the songset to her younger brothers, Harry Mulumbuk and Barney Geridruwanga. In the 1960s, it was very unusual for a woman to receive kun-borrk and this may have directed non-Indigenous researchers away from asking women about the song's origins. Men are responsible for singing and playing the musical accompaniment of kun-borrk and therefore other aspects of song knowledge discharged by women, such as dance instruction, correcting the singers and providing authoritative accounts of song origins and meanings, were arguably overlooked. It was also a time of social change and there may have been other circumstances that prevented women from claiming ownership of the song.

This chapter contends that a multiplicity of truths and narratives can exist in archives, oral stories and historical narratives, and examines how reinterpretations of stories and songs can be used to construct identity. We suggest that at the time the origins of the "Diyama" song were recorded, there were social factors contributing to the dominance of the male perspective. Drawing upon archival theory that questions the permanence of historical storytelling and archival objects, we take into consideration the perspectives of An-barra women, who are responding to and reinterpreting the story of "Diyama" in narrative and in song.

This chapter arose out of conversations between An-barra educator Cindy Jinmarabynana and Ripple Effect Band member Jodie Kell. It will focus on two

---

2   Kun-borrk is a genre of individually owned songs accompanied by didjeridu and clapsticks, with associated public ceremonial dances. They are called manyardi in Mawng and Iwaidja and sometimes referred to as borrk. Unlike totemic songs of many other Arnhem Land song styles, kun-borrk focus on gossip and human emotion though they can also be concerned with ancestral spirits. They commonly use a haiku-like sparse lyrical poetry. See Murray Garde, "The Language of Kun-borrk in Western Arnhem Land", *Musicology Australia* 28, no. 1 (2005), 59–89.

3   See Allan Marett, *Songs, Dreamings, and Ghosts: The Wangga of North Australia* (Middletown, CT: Wesleyan University Press, 2005); Reuben Brown, "The Role of Songs in Connecting the Living and the Dead: A Funeral Ceremony for Nakodjok in Western Arnhem Land", in *Circulating Cultures: Exchanges of Australian Indigenous Music, Dance and Media*, ed. Amanda Harris (Canberra: ANU Press, 2014), 169–202.

4   The "Diyama" song appears as "Borg Song" performed by Mulumbug on the vinyl LP; Betty Hiatt and L.R. Hiatt, *Songs from Arnhem Land* (Canberra, ACT: Australian Institute of Aboriginal Studies, 1966). The story appears in the accompanying booklet, "Notes on Songs of Arnhem Land".

cases of engagement with the 1960 audio recording and accompanying written notes of the "Diyama" song; an alternative version of the origins of the song recorded in an interview in 2017 and the reinterpretation of the song in a contemporary setting by a descendant and her band.

Cindy Jinmarabynana is an An-barra woman currently living in Maningrida and teaching at the Maningrida school. Her patrilineal clan group is Marrarrich/ Anagawbama and her homeland, Ji-bena, stretches across the floodplains to the south-east of Maningrida. Cindy is a junggay (B: cultural manager)[5] for the An-barra estate of Gupanga on the mouth of the Blyth River, where she grew up, learning from her Elders in a traditional way.

> When I hear the "Diyama" song, it makes me cry. It makes me cry because, the way I see it, I have knowledge from when I was a little kid in Blyth River, in my own mother's country. That's where I got my knowledge by sitting down and listening to the old people. Especially the old man Frank Gurrmanamana, Betty's father. He taught me that knowledge.[6]

Jodie Kell is a non-Indigenous woman who grew up on Darramuragal Country, part of the Eora Nation, in the north of Sydney. She worked as a teacher at Maningrida College from 2002 to 2006, starting a long connection with the people of the Maningrida region. She currently manages and performs in the Ripple Effect Band. She has accompanied Cindy and her family to her estate of Ji-bena, hunting in the rich fertile floodplains as far as Gupanga, learning about the culture and stories connected to the An-barra clan and Country.

Jodie collated this chapter, reviewing literature and archival recordings and working with Cindy to conduct interviews, discuss issues of archives, and research and document knowledge of the "Diyama" song and story for future generations. We wanted to record and publish Cindy's mother's story of the song's origin, being aware of the power of the written word and archival objects, such as the recording of "Diyama" on the 1966 album. We hope that this story will shed light on the changing social structures for women in relation to kun-borrk and music-making in Maningrida, and the history of the "Diyama" song which led to the Ripple Effect Band's song about the mermaids who inhabit the waters of the An-barra homelands. By analysing a recent performance and recording of this song, we seek to demonstrate how the history of the "Diyama" song is interwoven in the Ripple Effect Band's popular music performance. We will examine how these contemporary iterations are both influenced by and depart from the version held

---

5   This study uses a range of languages from the Maningrida region, using the specific language relevant to the context. Words in language are followed by an English translation and the language group in brackets. The languages used are Burarra (B), Yolngu Matha (Y), Ndjébbana (Ndj) and Gun-nartpa (G).

6   Cindy Jinmarabynana, interview by Jodie Kell, Maningrida, 18 May 2020. (Available as JK1-DY006 at https://catalog.paradisec.org.au/collections/JK1/items/DY006, 15:12.)

in the archive. We will comment on how this pertains to the negotiation of agency and construction of identity, particularly from the standpoint of women.

We also hope to add to the existing archival recordings, song recordings and writing about the "Diyama" song, with Cindy, as a junggay (B: cultural manager), wanting to document important knowledge about the "Diyama" story and song for the future of the An-barra clan.

> I want to bring that evidence back. That evidence tells us who we are, what is our clan and where we come from.[7]

An-barra people

The An-barra people are part of the Burarra-speaking language group that also includes the Martay people to the east. Their language is closely related to Gun-nartpa from the inland floodplains, and they are close relatives of their western neighbours the Na-kara.

The Burarra estates lie to the east of Maningrida as marked on the Maningrida Language Map (Figure 9.1). The Blyth River, called An-gatja Wana (B: Big River), runs through the heart of Burarra territory, starting in the sandstone plateau country to the south through eucalyptus forest, until it reaches the saltwater fringed by mangroves and many small creeks from the floodplains that exit past the sand spit at Lalarr Gu-jirrapa.

The An-barra estate is situated along the coast and the mouth of the river, and An-barra people refer to themselves as Saltwater people (see Figure 9.2). Anthropologist Lester Hiatt explains that the estate boundaries are not fixed; rather, the differentiation of estate land is based around important sites.[8] The "Diyama" song refers to two sites, Gupanga on the western bank and Lalarr Gu-jirrapa at the mouth of the river, and it is in the waters between the two sites at the river mouth where the mermaids are found.

In more recent times, An-barra and Burarra people have moved to live in the community of Maningrida. Originally set up as a government trading post in the 1950s, Maningrida is now home to one of the most linguistically diverse communities in the world, with 15 languages spoken or signed every day among only a few thousand people.[9] Living away from their homelands has intensified a

---

7   Jinmarabynana, interview, 2020. (Available as JK1-DY006 at https://catalog.paradisec.org.au/ collections/JK1/items/DY006, 00:05.)

8   Lester Hiatt, *Kinship and Conflict: A Study of an Aboriginal Community in Northern Arnhem Land* (Canberra: Australian National University, 1965), 27–28.

9   Jill Vaughn, "Meet the Remote Indigenous Community Where A Few Thousand People Use 15 Different Languages", *Conversation*, 5 December 2018, accessed 9 July 2021, https://bit.ly/ 3uwDMuF.

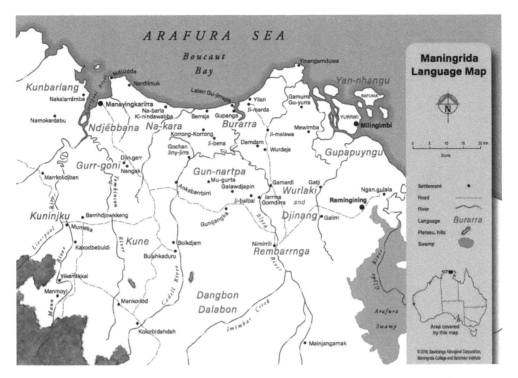

Figure 9.1 Language map of the Manayingkarírra (Maningrida) region (2016). Courtesy of Bawinanga Aboriginal Corporation, Maningrida College and Batchelor Institute. Map by Brenda Thornley.

sense of longing and nostalgia for their Country which has become a focus for musical expression among An-barra and neighbouring Na-kara musicians.

Like other groups across Arnhem Land, An-barra people divide the world into two patrifilial moieties, Yirrchinga and Jowunga. People, animals, plants and places belong to one of these moieties. This is the basis for the kinship system that dictates how people relate to each other, to Country, and to ancestral stories, songs and dances. The two moieties are exogamous and the kinship system that binds them, called the skin system, regulates whom people can or cannot marry and governs social interaction based on eight classificatory subsections. People inherit their bapururr (B: clan) from their father and they are seen as responsible for their mother-clan's Country, songs and stories. There are about a dozen An-barra patrilineal clans, with the Ana-wulja clan central to the story of the "Diyama" song.

Diyama

The song title, "Diyama", refers to the striped cockle shellfish, *tapes hiantina*, which stands out as a prolific food source for Burarra people and other groups of the

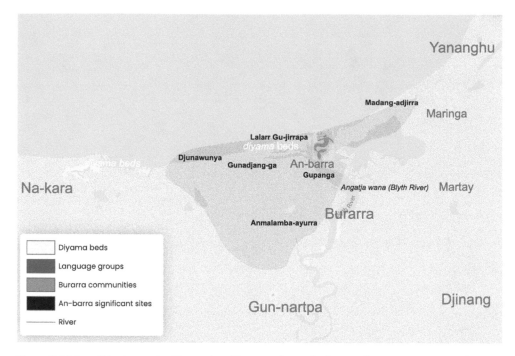

Figure 9.2 Map of An-barra significant sites. The map shows the Burarra language groups An-barra, Martay and Marawuraba (these two groups tend to call themselves Martay), and Maringa (also known as Gulula). This map is based on conversations and travels with Cindy Jinmarabynana and An-barra Burarra people, and maps by Lester Hiatt, *Kinship and Conflict*, 1–19 and Betty Meehan, *Shell Bed to Shell Midden* (Canberra: Australian Institute of Aboriginal Studies, 1982).

region, both in quantity and consistency throughout the year. The shellfish are collected in the sandy river mouths along the coast, where hunters stand in the shallow saltwater and dig into the sandy bed to a depth of between 1 and 15 centimetres. The diyama tend to aggregate, so each dig reveals a handful of the shells. These are then cooked either in the coals of a fire or boiled in water, or they can be kept alive in damp cool storage for days.

In the 1970s, anthropologist Betty Meehan lived with the An-barra people and documented details of their shellfish harvest between July 1972 and July 1973. She noted that, over the year, the An-barra community of around 34 people collected at least 6,700 kilograms of shellfish. Out of the 29 different species collected, Meehan rated diyama as the most important because it was collected consistently throughout the year and made just over 60 per cent of the total annual yield.[10]

For the An-barra people, the abundance of the diyama shellfish is associated with a unique origin story about werrgepa (B: mermaids), who dig underwater

---

10   Betty Meehan, *Shell Bed to Shell Midden* (Canberra: Australian Institute of Aboriginal Studies, 1982) 69–74.

Figure 9.3 Diyama shells (*Tapes hiantina*) of the marrambai or "black duck" pattern with radiating dark bars across the shell. This is differentiated from the an-gedjidimiya or "whistle duck" pattern. Photo by Jodie Kell.

diyama beds in the mouth of the Blyth River.[11] Their song has the ancestral power to put flesh inside the shells. While diyama are not found at Gupanga itself, it is there that the mermaids live and assure a bountiful supply through their song. Cindy describes how diyama are formed through a metaphysical connection to the An-barra estate of Gupanga, where white clay is found. Rrakal (B) is white pipeclay used for ritual body paintings and bark paintings. Given by the original ancestors, this substance of ceremonial significance is an intrinsic part of the Diyama story.

> This diyama comes from white clay. They call it rrakal. It is the rrakal that junggay
> (B: cultural managers), like me or my sisters, spread out and say the name of
> the country to form that diyama. Towards the end of the dry, when the rain is
> forming, then the rrakal spreads and forms into diyama. When it forms, we hear
> this dilartila (B: Australian magpie lark). It's a black and white bird Dreaming. Our
> totem, dilartila, who says "dill, dill". Every year, from the ending of the dry season

---

11   Betty Hiatt and Lester Hiatt, "Notes on Songs of Arnhem Land", companion booklet to
      disc (Canberra: Australian Institute of Aboriginal Studies, 1966), 13–14.

Figure 9.4 Members of the Ripple Effect Band and families hunting for diyama on the Na-kara estate of Na-meyarra. From left to right: Rona Lawrence, Marita Wilton, Zara Wilton and Tara Rostron. Photo by Jodie Kell.

to the starting of the rain, the junggay will get the clay and say the name of the country – for example, Lalarr Gu-jirripa or Djunawunya – and by spreading that clay, they form the diyama from the song line.[12]

This story is connected to the practice of dalkarra (G: the singing out of called names of sacred sites by ceremonial leaders of public ceremonies).[13] In Eastern Arnhem Land, the singing of place or clan names is an important part of mortuary and other public ceremonies.[14] In this case, the clay is a physical embodiment of the metaphysical power of creation, where the calling out of names of Country causes the proliferation of diyama seashells in the underwater beds. It also relates to the story of the mermaids, who appeared in a dream, singing the name of the diyama shellfish, ensuring their continued harvest.

12   Cindy Jinmarabynana. Interview by Jodie Kell, 14 October 2017. (Audio interview and transcript available as JK1-DY003-04 at https://catalog.paradisec.org.au/collections/JK1/items/DY003, 14:39.)

13   Crusoe Batara England et al., *Gun-Ngaypa Rrawa: My Country* (Batchelor, NT: Batchelor Press, 2014).

14   Margaret Clunies Ross, "The Aesthetics and Politics of an Arnhem Land Ritual", *TDR: Drama Review* 33, no. 4 (1989), 124.

Where did the "Diyama" song come from?

The origins of the "Diyama" song date back to the 1950s, when a new kun-borrk emerged from the An-barra homelands on the mouth of the Blyth River. The singer was Mulumbuk, also known as Harry Diyama.[15] Lester Hiatt described Mulumbuk as a major figure in the establishment of the Maningrida community in the 1950s.[16] He later featured in the 1980 ethnographic film by Hiatt and Kim McKenzie called *Waiting for Harry* that documented a funeral ceremony on the An-barra estate of Djunawunya.[17]

In 1960, Hiatt recorded Mulumbuk singing a kun-borrk style song that was later included on the 1966 Australian Institute of Aboriginal Studies vinyl record,[18] *Songs from Arnhem Land*.[19] Side A of the album consists of songs in the Eastern Arnhem Land style called manikay (B). Side B consists of Western Arnhem Land kun-borrk-style songs, and the opening kun-borrk song is sung by Mulumbuk. As is usual for songs of the kun-borrk genre, Mulumbuk told Hiatt that he learned the songs from the spirits of the deceased:

> One night during a dream his deceased brother took him to the bottom of the Blyth River, and there they heard spirits of the dead singing it.[20]

Nearly 60 years later, another version of the origin story has emerged. In 2017, we sat in Cindy's daughter's yard in Maningrida and recorded her mother, An-barra Elder Mary Dadbalag, the last of the generation to have lived at Gupanga when "Diyama" was first performed. Unlike the story recorded by Hiatt, she asserts that it was her mother's sister, Elizabeth, instead of Mulumbuk, who learned the songs from ancestral spirits in a dream.

> One of her [Mary's mother's] eldest sisters, Elizabeth, had a dream. All these people came out from the river, and it was low tide at night. They came up with strings and dilly-bags full of diyama, and they were talking to her. They said to her, "Hey, wake up sister. Wake up. We're full of diyama here. We've got diyama clay here. You tell our kids that they're the ones who are responsible for this

---

15   Betty Hiatt and Lester Hiatt spelled this name as Diama. Here, we are using the current orthography convention of Diyama.
16   Hiatt, *Kinship and Conflict*, 148–54.
17   Lester Hiatt and Kim McKenzie, *Waiting for Harry* (Canberra: Australian Institute of Aboriginal and Torres Islander Studies, 1980).
18   Now known as the Australian Institute of Aboriginal and Torres Strait Islander Studies (AIATSIS).
19   Betty and Lester Hiatt, *Songs from Arnhem Land* (Canberra: Australian Institute of Aboriginal Studies, 1966).
20   Hiatt and Hiatt, "Notes on Songs of Arnhem Land", 14.

diyama. They're the ones who will say the names of the places and spread that diyama like junggay."[21]

According to this story, rather than the dreamer being taken to the bottom of the river, the mermaids came out of the water wearing ceremonial objects such as rrawka (B: ceremonial feathered armbands), and they sang and danced the song for Elizabeth, telling her to pass it on to her younger brothers, Harry Mulumbuk and Barney Geridruwanga. "She had to give [it to] them because, if she would have been a man, she would have been taking over singing this song."[22] As women are not allowed to sing kun-borrk songs, Cindy explained that Elizabeth needed to give the song to her male relatives.

> She told my two uncles – that is, David Maxwell's father, old man Harry Mulumbuk and my uncle Barney Geridruwanga – "I'm the eldest sister. You two sit down. I had a dream." They sat down next to the fire and she started to sing that song, "Diyama". She said, "Our ancestors of the Ana-wulja clan, An-barra people, I had a dream and they gave me this song, so I'll pass it on."
>
> That was what they had told her to do. She was singing at the same time she told those two boys to get the clapsticks and they started to sing, and they were starting to sing what she told them to sing, "Aa-aa-aa an-diyama," like that and they picked it up really quickly. They were aburr-delipa (B: small children), ten or eleven years old.[23]

It is significant that a woman received a song in a dream, as there are very few accounts of the transmission of songs from women to men in this region. One example is the wangga song "Yendili No. 2", which was received in a dream by Marri Ngarr woman Maudie Attaying Dumoo, who gave it to her husband, Wagon Dumoo, to perform.[24] Musicologist Allan Marett described the song as "almost unique among the various wangga repertoires in that it was composed by a woman".[25]

Mary's memory of the origin of the song, as told to her, tells a story of women as composers, sharing their dreams and the songs heard in them, so they could be performed in public. Her perspective sheds light on the role of women in the

---

21 Jinmarabynana, interview, 2017. (Audio interview and transcript available as JK1-DY003-04 at https://catalog.paradisec.org.au/collections/JK1/items/DY003, 06:11.) In this interview, Cindy interpreted the stories and words of Mary Dadbalag whom she had just interviewed.
22 Jinmarabynana, interview, 2020. (Audio interview and transcript available as JK1-DY006 at https://catalog.paradisec.org.au/collections/JK1/items/DY006, 03:41.)
23 Jinmarabynana, interview, 2017. (Audio interview and transcript available as JK1-DY003-04 at https://catalog.paradisec.org.au/collections/JK1/items/DY003, 08:43.)
24 See Allan Marett, Linda Barwick and Lysbeth Julie Ford, *For the Sake of a Song: Wangga Songmen and Their Repertories* (Sydney: Sydney University Press, 2012); Marett, *Songs, Dreamings, and Ghosts*.
25 Marett, *Songs, Dreamings, and Ghosts*, 66.

Figure 9.5 Mary Dadbalag (left) and her daughter, Cindy Jinmarabynana, discussing the story of "Diyama". Photo by Jodie Kell.

composition and transmission of this region's music in the past and the present. The story documented by Hiatt suggests a sense of the dreamer, Mulumbuk, looking upon the mermaids and hearing their song and then taking it back and singing it himself. Mary's version describes a more active role for the mermaid spirits who came out of the water to wake the dreamer and give her the song, directing her to pass it on to her family members, while also demonstrating and passing on its associated dances.

> The ancestor spirits, they came out from that water, walking on the beach. But that other one she saw is like a mermaid with arm band around her – you know, like traditional costume. In that dream, my mum said to my sisters, "In dream dje! Awurr-bony diyama, awurr-banyjinga (B: they have gone to get diyama shells under the water)." They already put that [flesh inside the] diyama, the spirit people, and that slow dance – you know, the one when we dig and dance and then we put it on our head swinging. What we are putting on our head is string bags full of diyama.[26]

While Mulumbuk is undisputed as the first person to sing this song in public, Dadbalag's version of events raises questions about its origins. Rather than seeing these stories as conflicted, it is useful to explore what these different perspectives tell us about how historical events are remembered and recorded. In Aboriginal and

---

26 Jinmarabynana, interview, 2020. (Audio interview and transcript available as JK1-DY006 at https://catalog.paradisec.org.au/collections/JK1/items/DY006, 09:10.)

Torres Strait Islander communities, the transmission of knowledge is enacted orally through songs and stories, and visually through dance and painting. This leads to multiple narratives that shape collective memory, influencing the construction of community and individual identity. This origin story paints a picture of women actively involved in communication with ancestral spirits, and its recent emergence suggests that women are ready to share their stories to strengthen the right of women to compose and perform songs.

Archivists such as Eric Ketelaar and Terry Cook question the relative fixity of historical understanding. Ketelaar comments that subsequent events, new interpretations and sources of history are all valid and have the effect of changing the view and reopening historical cases.[27] Cook states that many historians are now seeing that:

> identity in the past is shaped by common or shared or collective memory animating invented traditions and that such identities, once formed or embraced, are not fixed, but very fluid, contingent on time, space, and circumstances, ever being re-invented to suit the present, continually being re-imagined.[28]

The omission of a woman's perspective on the "Diyama" song could be in part because of the status of women at the time. As women did not sing or perform music in public, researchers may not have thought to ask them about this song, or perhaps women themselves did not feel empowered to tell the story of a woman receiving a men's song in a dream. The 1960s were a time when the recordist was seen as a guardian protecting the static archival object, suggesting one "truth". This dominance of the documented narrative tended to reflect the gender bias embedded in society, with archives becoming "active sites where social power is negotiated, contested and confirmed".[29]

When Jodie asked Cindy why she thought this story had not surfaced before, Cindy said:

> Well, Betty and Les [Hiatt], they don't know that story. Those women, they hid that story. Les only knew the song and story when Harry sang it. He didn't know the history about the song. Because I heard that story when my grandmother told me, when I was age ... six or seven. I took that story in my heart when this old lady told me the story, because she had been carrying that story from her sister.[30]

---

27 Eric Ketelaar, "Archives as Spaces of Memory", *Journal of the Society of Archivists* 29, no. 1 (2008), 11.

28 Terry Cook, "Evidence, Memory, Identity, and Community: Four Shifting Archival Paradigms", *Archival Science* 13 (2–3) (2012), 96.

29 Terry Cook and Joan Schwartz, "Archives, Records and Power: From (Postmodern) Theory to (Archival) Performance", *Archival Science* 2 (2002), 172.

30 Jinmarabynana, interview, 2020. (Audio interview and transcript available as JK1-DY006 at https://catalog.paradisec.org.au/collections/JK1/items/DY006, 00:10.)

Figure 9.6 The Ripple Effect Band performing "Diyama" at the Darwin Festival in 2020. From left to right: Jodie Kell, Jolene Lawrence, Marita Wilton, Lakita Taylor (Stephanie's daughter) and Stephanie Maxwell James. Photo by Benjamin Warlngundu Bayliss.

Our approach seeks to allow for the possibility of multiple narratives and perspectives through recognising a diversity of sources of knowledge. Faulkhead et al. see this as "acknowledging Indigenous frameworks of knowledge, memory and evidence".[31] This brings us back to Cindy's desire to share her mother's story and document it as evidence before it is too late. Her mother had been carrying this story and now it is recorded as part of the archival corroboration of the "Diyama" song, adding to a rich and complex history documented through oral storytelling and song that continues to this day.

Transmission, re-creation and innovation

The impetus for the recording of the "Diyama" origin story came about because of the Ripple Effect Band's new iteration of the "Diyama" song. The Ripple Effect Band are an all-women's rockband that emerged out of Maningrida in 2017, singing in five Aboriginal languages of the region.

31   Shannon Faulkhead, Livia Iacovino, Sue McKemmish and Kirsten Thorpe, "Australian Indigenous Knowledge and the Archives: Embracing Multiple Ways of Knowing and Keeping", *Archives and Manuscripts* 38, no. 1 (2010), 29.

When Stephanie Maxwell James, an An-barra woman of the Ana-wulja clan, composed "Diyama" and performed it with the band, this was the first time in living memory that a group of women was singing about the mermaids that live in the waters off Gupanga. Following our debut performances at Maningrida, the Bak'bididi Festival in Ramingining and the Milingimbi Gatjirrk Cultural Festival, the band recorded the song as part of the *Wárrwarra* (Ndj: the sun) EP released in 2018.[32]

While distinctive, this new version of the song is one of many reinterpretations of the "Diyama" song over three generations as shown in Table 9.1. Popular bands such as the Letterstick Band and Wildwater preceded the Ripple Effect Band with recordings and performances of songs that directly reference the "Diyama" kun-borrk. Many of these songs can be found on CDs or online streaming services. As well as this, copies of the original 1960 recording circulate around the community as people Bluetooth the songs from phone to phone, listening to the kun-borrk as readily as more contemporary versions of the song.

Listening to archival objects, such as heritage recordings, enables engagement with knowledge held in cultural performance and song and can lead to the reinvigoration of contemporary performance practices. There are many examples across Australia, such as the work of the Wirlomin Noongar Language and Stories Project in Western Australia documented by Clint Bracknell and the collaboration between a team of researchers and the Manmurulu family of the Arrarrkpi (Mawng-speaking people) of the Northern Territory.[33] In discussing the repatriation of junba songs of the Kimberley region of north-west Australia, Matthew Denbal Martin sees the value of the recordings for teaching and learning. He comments that the recordings hold the spirits of the old people whose voices are heard in the recordings:

> Listening to the songs reminded me of all the old people and it was like they were in me. They were sitting beside me, you know. And I picked them songs up. It was like they was telling me "that way. Sing this song that way". It was like they were telling me which way to sing.[34]

---

32 Ripple Effect Band, *Wárrwarra*. Sydney: Ripple Effect Band, 2018. Available at https://www.ripple-effect-band.com/music, accessed 14 March 2021. Recorded at Sydney Conservatorium of Music, produced by Paul Mac, Clint Bracknell and Jodie Kell, the four-track EP *Wárrwarra* was independently released in July 2018. It features four songs in four languages, Burarra, Kune, Ndjébbana and Na-kara.

33 Clint Bracknell, "Connecting Indigenous Song Archives to Kin, Country and Language", *Journal of Colonialism & Colonial History* 20, no. 2 (2019), DOI: 10.1353/cch.2019.0016; Reuben Brown, David Manmurulu, Jenny Manmurulu and Isabel O'Keeffe, "Dialogues with the Archives: Arrarrkpi Responses to Recordings as Part of the Living Song Tradition of Manyardi", *Preservation, Digital Technology & Culture* 47, no. 3 (2018), 102–14.

34 Sally Treloyn, Matthew Dembal Martin and Rona Goonginda Charles, "Moving Songs: Repatriating Audiovisual Recordings of Aboriginal Australian Dance and Song (Kimberley Region, Northwestern Australia)", in *The Oxford Handbook of Musical Repatriation*, 1st edn. (New York: Oxford University Press, 2019), 10.

This form of engagement is apparent in re-creations of the song of the mermaids through an inherited lineage of An-barra musicians, leading to the proliferation of the song in a range of media.

Musical innovation is an integral aspect of the story of the "Diyama" song, starting back at the emergence of the kun-borrk from the An-barra homelands. Betty and Lester Hiatt describe "Diyama" as the "easternmost example of the borg [kun-borrk] style" and claim Mulumbuk as the only Burarra person who sang a kun-borrk-style song.[35] Usually, the more easterly Burarra-speaking groups would own and sing manikay (B: clan songs).[36] They go on to suggest that:

> [b]ecause of marriage irregularities in the previous generations, Mulumbuk and several other members of his clan have changed their moiety affiliations in order to bring their own marriages into conformity with the rule of moiety exogamy. This has entailed a serious disturbance of their ritual status, including loss of recognition as joint owners of any mortuary song.[37]

Mulumbuk was a Yirrchinga man. Gupanga is a Jowunga estate and so he would not have been able to sing the associated manikay due to the rules of exogamous moieties. Using the medium of kun-borrk enabled him to own and compose original songs, receiving them in dreams and passing them on to his descendants. Expressing direct communication with ancestral spirits, the song strengthened his rights to the Gupanga estate. He subsequently gained status travelling to other clan estates across the region as a jalakan (B: song leader) with a ceremonial troupe to perform the "Diyama" kun-borrk and associated bunggul (B: dances).[38]

As well as adopting an atypical song genre, Mulumbuk recorded the song with Lester Hiatt on a battery-powered tape recorder in 1960, demonstrating his ability to utilise new technologies and extrinsic knowledge to create an enduring record of his singing that can be played again and again after his passing. Ethnomusicologist Paul Greene comments that modern recording technologies have opened up "new directions for musical expressions and evolution, inspiring new logics of music creation and empowering local cultural and expressive values".[39] The innovative development of creating a permanent audio record of the "Diyama" kun-borrk has contributed to the continuation of realisations of the "Diyama" narrative as told in song.

---

35   Hiatt and Hiatt, "Notes on Songs of Arnhem Land", 14.
36   Betty and Les Hiatt use the spelling manakay, but we use the orthography of Yolngu-matha language.
37   Hiatt and Hiatt, "Notes on Songs of Arnhem Land", 14.
38   Aaron Corn, "Burr-Gi Wargugu ngu-Ninya Rrawa: Expressions of Ancestry and Country in Songs by the Letterstick Band", *Musicology Australia* 25, no. 1 (2002), 166; Jinmarabynana, interview, 2020.
39   Paul Greene, "Introduction: Wired Sound and Sonic Culture", in *Wired for Sound: Engineering and Technologies in Sonic Culture*, eds Paul D. Greene and Thomas Porcello (Middletown, CT: Wesleyan University Press, 2005), 3.

Table 9.1 Documented representations of the "Diyama" song and/or story. This does not include many informal and unrecorded ceremonial performances such as the opening of the local health clinic, school concerts and festivals. (See References for further information on the recordings in this table.)

Song/film title	Singer/performer	Year	Style	Media format (Publisher)
"Diyama"	Mulumbuk	1966	borrk	*Songs of Arnhem Land* (AIAS) vinyl
Waiting for Harry	Mulumbuk	1979	documentary film	AIAS, film
"An-barra Clan"	Letterstick Band	1994	borrk sung over reggae	(CAAMA Music) CD
"Rrawa"	Letterstick Band	1995	reggae	*Demurru Hits* CD
"Bartpa"	Letterstick Band	1995		*Demurru Hits* CD
"Diyama"	David Maxwell and others	1997		
"Diyama"	David Maxwell	2004	borrk	*Diyama* CD
"Diyama/ Mimi"	David Maxwell and Crusoe Kurrtal	2004	borrk with samples and synthesiser	*Diyama* CD
"Gupanga"	Letterstick Band	2004	reggae	*Diyama* CD
"Blyth River"	Letterstick Band	2004	country rock	*Diyama* CD
Soundtracks of Maningrida	Letterstick Band	2004	documentary film	(CAAMA Music) film
"Ngarnji Mamurrng"	David Maxwell and others	2006	borrk	Mamurrng ceremony, live
"Rrawa"	Wild Water	2007	reggae	*Rrawa* CD
"Maningrida Diyama"	Wild Water	2007	borrk sung over reggae	*Rrawa* CD
"Make it Through"	Elston Maxwell, Djolpa Mackenzie, Cindy Jinmarabynana, Marita Wilton, Patricia Gibson	2016	hip-hop	Indigenous Hip Hop Projects film clip
"Blyth River"	Ripple Effect Band	2017	country rock with borrk	Live performance at Ramingining Festival

Song/film title	Singer/performer	Year	Style	Media format (Publisher)
"Diyama"	Ripple Effect Band	2017	country rock with borrk	*Wárrwarra* EP
"Jarracharra"	Ripple Effect Band with Bábbarra Women's Centre Jess Gunjul Phillips	2019	sound installation	Exhibition at the Australian Embassy, Paris

Sustained engagement with the "Diyama" kun-borrk and the 1960 recording has contributed to a proliferation of the song and its themes among the subsequent generations of An-barra and Na-kara musicians. After Mulumbuk passed away, his sons, David and Colin Maxwell, followed in their father's footsteps, taking on responsibility for the performance of the "Diyama" ceremony and travelling across Arnhem Land to perform at ceremonial events. Like their father, they also adopted new technologies in the expression of their An-barra identity. They formed the Letterstick Band, playing a distinctive style of rock-reggae, fusing elements of their inherited kun-borrk song series with globalised popular music styles.

In her article about music technology at Wadeye, Linda Barwick proposes that the emerging non-traditional musical forms and their dissemination through digital means "continue to develop a strategic assertion of cultural and territorial autonomy and identity through song that was and is also fundamental to traditional musical forms in the area".[40] This "strategic blend of traditionalism and innovation"[41] is a feature of the Letterstick Band, as they used contemporary music practices and documentary film-making to assert clan affiliation and continue the innovative legacy of their father.

The many different versions of this song over time are an example of what is called intertextuality. Burns and Lacasse define intertextuality as "a network of songs, styles, artists and consumers influenced, directly or indirectly, by the music and artists that came before".[42] This can be applied to the intricate network of relationships that link An-barra musicians and their estates to the "Diyama" song and its association with Gupanga. Linguist Ken Hale used the phrase "the persistence of entities through transformation"[43] in his article on song as

40 Linda Barwick, "Keepsakes and Surrogates: Hijacking Music Technology at Wadeye (Northwest Australia)", in *Music, Indigeneity, Digital Media*, eds Thomas Hilder, Shzr Ee Tan and Henry Stobart (Rochester, NY: University of Rochester Press, 2017), 156.
41 Barwick, "Keepsakes and Surrogates: Hijacking Music Technology at Wadeye (Northwest Australia)", 157.
42 Lori Burns and Serge Lacasse, "Introduction", in *The Pop Palimpsest: Intertextuality in Recorded Popular Music*, eds Lori Burns and Serge Lacasse (Ann Arbor: University of Michigan Press, 2018), 4.
43 Ken Hale, "Remarks on Creativity in Aboriginal Verse", in *Problems and Solutions: Occasional Essays in Musicology Presented to Alice M. Moyle*, eds Jamie C. Kassler and Jill Stubington (Sydney: Hale & Iremonger, 1984), 260.

re-creation. Cindy comments that the range of styles that encompass performances of "Diyama" has contributed to the lasting popularity of this kun-borrk:

> Everybody sings it now. They all enjoy with our young people. This is one other thing we get to see growing, you know. We have passed that song up to our future generations.[44]

This song that was originally accompanied by only two traditional instruments, the an-gujaparndiya (B: clapsticks) and ngorla (B: didjeridu), can still be heard today in kun-borrk style, but also with contemporary instrumentation and mixed media. Musicians like David Maxwell from the Letterstick Band, and now his daughter Stephanie, have followed in the footsteps of Mulumbuk, adopting new technologies and musical practices to reinterpret the song of the mermaids in different forms. In so doing, they assert their cultural identity in the changing social structures of modernity.

A new performance of "Diyama"

> I do a lot of dance: Black Crow, Shark and Crocodile dance, and Diyama. I have traditional and then play in a band. Because my dads,[45] you know, they played in a band, so I am following in their footsteps.[46]

> My daughter wrote a song for the mermaids. It's my dreaming. We call it werrgapa "mermaid" (B), the spirit and the land for the An-barra people staying in one place called Gupanga on the Blyth River.[47]

The performance at the Bak'bididi Festival in Ramingining in 2017 was the first public performance of the song by the Ripple Effect Band outside of the Maningrida community. We were joined by David Maxwell on stage. This was the first time any kun-borrk song had been sung by a man accompanied by a group of women. The contrast between his vocal style and that of his daughter brought great excitement to the crowd and across Arnhem Land, as social media enabled the spread of this historic moment. Through his participation, he confirmed his daughter's cultural identity and bestowed authority on the changing social structures that are now allowing women to perform music in public.

---

44   Jinmarabynana, interview, 2020. (Audio interview and transcript available as JK1-DY006 at https://catalog.paradisec.org.au/collections/JK1/items/DY006, 11:34.)
45   In the Maningrida region kinship systems, a person's father's brother is also called their "father".
46   Stephanie Maxwell James et al. Interview by Spotify at Barunga Festival, 3 June 2018. (Interview and transcript available as JK1-NG003 at https://catalog.paradisec.org.au/collections/JK1/items/NG003, 18:33.)
47   David Maxwell. Interview by Jodie Kell, 28 October 2017. (Audio interview and transcript available as JK1-DY002 at https://catalog.paradisec.org.au/collections/JK1/items/DY002, 02:34.)

Figure 9.7 David Maxwell (left) on stage with his daughter, Stephanie Maxwell James (right), at the Bak'bididi Festival in Ramingining in 2017. Behind is Rona Lawrence on bass guitar and Tara Rostron on electric guitar. Photo by Eve Pawley.

Writing about the Letterstick Band's setting of Mulumbuk's "Diyama" kun-borrk in "An-barra Clan", Aaron Corn says that brothers David and Colin Maxwell were able to balance the "continuity of musical traditions against creative engagement with new musical media and technology".[48] Similarly, the use of contemporary instrumentation can be seen to bypass some of the gendered restrictions and allow women to play instruments and accompany a senior songman singing traditional songs. In this extraordinary moment, a song re-created and performed by father and daughter was made possible by the context of its contemporary musical setting.

The subsequent recording of the "Diyama" song by the Ripple Effect Band included the voice of David Maxwell.[49] In the middle of the song and at its ending, he sings the "Diyama" kun-borrk. This was recorded in the Wiwa Music and Media studio in Maningrida on a Zoom H6 audio recorder when he sang two iterations of this kun-borrk, one for the middle section and one for the ending of the recorded song. As will be shown later in our analysis of this song, David based his song on the 1960 recording, re-creating the melodies and phrasing of his father.

---

48   Corn, "Burr-Gi Wargugu ngu-Ninya Rrawa", 76.
49   James, "Diyama".

David passed away before he could hear the final recording of the song. But when we placed the audio recording of his kun-borrk song over the tracks, it fitted and it felt like he was there in the room with us. By allowing us to include his voice in both live and recorded performances of the song, David was reinforcing his daughter's legitimacy and endorsing a new modality of women's singing in a way that was as innovative as the Letterstick Band was in the 1990s or Mulumbuk in singing kun-borrk in 1960. The Ripple Effect Band's rendering of the "Diyama" song enables a new voice, a female voice, and a new expression of tradition.

In recording these songs, we have also enabled the creation of new archival artefacts in the form of audio and film recordings of song and performance that can enhance the oral histories, heritage recordings, and accounts of song and dance performance by An-barra people and surrounding communities.

Music analysis

In this section, musical analysis of the 2018 recording from the *Wárrwarra* EP shows how Stephanie and her father allude to Mulumbuk's song, using contemporary production techniques to bring new perspectives to the "Diyama" song.

"Diyama" (Transcription by Stephanie Maxwell James, Jodie Kell and Margaret Carew.)	Stephanie Maxwell James, David Maxwell and Jodie Kell Ripple Effect Band
VERSE 1	
Ana-munya gaba ng-garlmana	*I got up in the morning*
Ngi-jarl ngu-bamana	*I hurried along*
Nga-nana bartpa	*I saw the waves*
Gu-buna gu-jinyja	*The waves were hitting the shore*
Lika warrgugu ngu-ni	*I couldn't stop thinking about my country*
Nga-nana Lalarr Gu-jirrapa	*I saw the place, Lalarr Gu-jirrapa*
Gu-nachichiya gu-jinyjirra rrawa Gupanga	*Facing across from my country, Gupanga*
CHORUS	
Aa Diyama	*Ah Diyama*
Aa Diyama	*Ah Diyama*
Aa Diyama	*Ah Diyama*

"Diyama" (Transcription by Stephanie Maxwell James, Jodie Kell and Margaret Carew.)	Stephanie Maxwell James, David Maxwell and Jodie Kell Ripple Effect Band
VERSE 2	
Jungurda a-wena apula	*My grandfather told me*
Awurr-merdawa yerrcha	*About the mermaid spirits*
Ana-munya gu-nirra	*At night time*
Jina-beya jina-workiya	*They always come out*
Gala ngu-yinmiya ng-galiya	*I can't hear them*
Ngu-marngi awurr-gatiya	*I know they are there*
Ya Gupanga rrawa gun-molamola	*In my beautiful country, Gupanga*
CHORUS	
Aa Diyama	*Ah Diyama*
Aa Diyama	*Ah Diyama*
Aa Diyama	*Ah Diyama*
VERSE 2	
Jungurda a-wena apula	*My grandfather told me*
Awurr-merdawa yerrcha	*About the mermaid spirits*
Ana-munya gu-nirra	*At night time*
Jina-beya jina-workiya	*They always come out*
Gala ngu-yinmiya ng-galiya	*I can't hear them*
Ngu-marngi awurr-gatiya	*I know they are there*
Ya Gupanga rrawa gun-molamola	*In my beautiful country, Gupanga*

Table 9.2 "Diyama" (Transcription by Stephanie Maxwell James, Jodie Kell and Margaret Carew).

The use of spirit language is common to the kun-borrk songs of Western Arnhem Land.[50] In the 1960 recording of "Diyama", Betty and Les Hiatt describe how Mulumbuk sings in the spirit language of the mermaids:[51]

> The only sounds to which Mulumbuk attributes meaning are the initial "Aa" suggesting the ebb and flow of the tide, "andiya mara [an-diyama rra] (shellfish sowing)" – the magical words used by spirits of the dead to put flesh inside the diyama shells, "aa aa aa, ee ee ee" signifying the movements of the spirits as they rake the shells into localised beds and the final "*Aa*" expressing nostalgia amongst the spirits as they think of their living kinsfolk.[52]

---

50 See Murray Garde, 2005; Kevin Djimarr, 2008; Reuben Brown, 2014; Isabel O'Keeffe, 2016.
51 Hiatt and Hiatt, "Notes on Songs of Arnhem Land", 13–14.
52 Hiatt and Hiatt, "Notes on Songs of Arnhem Land", 13.

David Maxwell also sang the words of the spirits inherited from his father, both in ceremonial performances and with popular bands accompanied by contemporary instrumentation in songs such as "An-barra Clan". Stephanie's version of the song has no spirit language in its verses and offers a more narrative perspective than the original kun-borrk. It is the chorus that imitates the mermaids' song, using the sustained "*Aa*" vocable that is a prominent feature of the "Diyama" kun-borrk. This communicates nostalgia and sorrow for the spirits of the deceased. Vocables are units of non-translatable language that are commonly found across different song genres. Their usage can contribute to a sense of solidarity. As part of ritual language, they serve as a means of connection and spirituality.[53]

Linguist Murray Garde, in writing about the music of Western Arnhem Land, comments that the ability to compose songs, perform your father's songs and receive songs from supernatural beings establishes authority over song repertoires and raises the status of songmen.[54] In the case of the "Diyama" song, the use of vocables indicates communication with ancestral spirits, reinforcing Stephanie's hereditary rights to sing "Diyama".

The sustained "Aa" vocable is followed by calling out the name "Diyama". Originally, Stephanie had called the song "Blyth River" and we sang this in the chorus at our performance at the Bak'bididi Festival. After her father's death, she changed the chorus and the name of the song in a deliberate declaration of her inherited rights to the "Diyama" kun-borrk. Singing diyama in the chorus associates the song with the An-barra tradition of calling out the name of the shellfish, diyama, in order for the diyama ancestors to form themselves across the land.[55]

The synthesis of different iterations of this song are apparent in the kun-borrk that David sings over the song's middle section and coda. Drawing upon his father's interpretation of the mermaids' song, he reinterprets its melodic phrasing. Figures 9.8 and 9.9 are transcriptions of father and son singing "Diyama" kun-borrk. In the part recorded for Stephanie's song, even though David contributes his own slightly differentiated rhythms, he mimics his father's rhythmic motif as highlighted in the transcriptions. They also show that both men start with the "Aa" declamatory vocable that calls out to the spirits and announces the singers' presence. This intertextuality of songs within songs links three generations of singers as echoes of Mulumbuk's song are heard in the iterations sung by his son and embedded in a recording made by his granddaughter.

When Stephanie's father enters singing "Diyama" kun-borrk after the second chorus, the intermusicality apparent in this over-layering of two very different musical cultures creates an intensification increased by his vigorous singing. As

---

53   Leanne Hinton, *Havasupai Songs: A Linguistic Perspective* (Amsterdam: John Benjamins Publishing Company, 1984).

54   Garde, "The Language of Kun-borrk in Western Arnhem Land", 86.

55   Jinmarabynana, interview, 2017. (Audio interview and transcript available as JK1-DY003-04 at https://catalog.paradisec.org.au/collections/JK1/items/DY003, 07:46.)

Figure 9.8 David's vocals (highlighted) in the middle section of the Ripple Effect Band's recording of "Diyama". Transcription by Jodie Kell.

David sings the song of the werrgepa (B: mermaids), we the listeners are asked to suspend our judgement and believe we are hearing their voices. His vocal mastery plays into the surprise audiences feel when they first hear a women's band accompanying his expression of ancestral beings.

Production elements of the song reinforce this effect with long organ chords and backing vocalists intensifying the texture into the chorus. Throughout the song, Stephanie's vocals have been doubled with a more natural track using reverb and a chorused track that suggests a spirit's vocal quality. As the song draws to a close, the rhythmic pulse drops out, leaving only a sustained organ note and vocals singing the "Diyama" kun-borrk song. This change in rhythmic density and musical timbre creates an intensification that combines with the intermusicality of the incorporation of the kun-borrk song to evoke an emotional response, "taking it to another level".[56]

---

56   Ingrid Monson, *Saying Something: Jazz Improvisation and Interaction* (Chicago: University of Chicago Press, 1996), 39.

Vocable

Figure 9.9 Mulumbuk's original "Diyama" song recorded in 1960. Transcription by Jodie Kell, based on transcription by Aaron Corn. (Aaron Corn, "Dreamtime Wisdom, Modern-time Vision: Tradition and Innovation in the Popular Band Movement of Arnhem Land, Australia" (PhD thesis, University of Melbourne, 2002), 125–26.)

Over the tremulous organ elongated through a slow delay and extended sustain, David Maxwell sings his last kun-borrk. His vocals convey a sense of longing for the past, for people and place, directly referencing the song recorded by his father Mulumbuk in 1960, but also marking his own place in the history of the "Diyama" song.

Conclusion

Analysis of the "Diyama" song and its associated musical practices demonstrates how musical innovation enables song custodians to respond to changing contexts. We have examined how three generations of An-barra musicians have transformed the expression of ancestral spirits using new musical forms and utilising music technology. Stephanie's grandfather, Mulumbuk, recorded a Western Arnhem Land kun-borrk. His sons incorporated his song into popular music forms in the Letterstick Band, influenced by the archival recording. In recent times, Stephanie and the members of the Ripple Effect Band are the first women to compose and sing their own version of the song, using popular music practice to negotiate agency as women musicians. Including Stephanie's interpretation of the original kun-borrk in their recording gives authority to the new expression of the mermaid song by women musicians and affirms Stephanie's An-barra heritage.

We have presented new knowledge that challenges the descriptions of cultural practices in archival recordings and written texts. Cindy's mother told her version of the origins of the "Diyama" song as a narrative of a woman visited by mermaids in a dream who taught her the song and the dance associated with the diyama seashells. The possibility that a woman composed the well-known An-barra song will now coincide with the historical account recorded in the 1960s that places a man as the receiver of the dream. We have suggested that the status of women at the time prevented the recording of the women's story and now Cindy feels strongly that it is time to document her mother's story and rebalance the dominant narrative. By including both stories, we acknowledge archival theories that question the invariability of archival objects and historical accounts. This comes from an understanding that collective or shared memories are not fixed but are fluid and contingent on changing social structures that shape notions of identity.

The story of the "Diyama" song demonstrates how a historical recording can contribute to the sustaining of cultural practices. At the same time, its reinterpretation contains elements of innovation that both reflect and influence changing social structures and the construction of identity. In composing a new version of the song, performed by women musicians, Stephanie Maxwell James has rekindled interest in the origins of the song, opening up possibilities for the inclusion of women's perspectives in the expression of An-barra culture.

References

Barwick, Linda. "Keepsakes and Surrogates: Hijacking Music Technology at Wadeye (Northwest Australia)". In *Music, Indigeneity, Digital Media*, eds Thomas Hilder, Shzr Ee Tan and Henry Stobart. Rochester, NY: University of Rochester Press, 2017: 156–75.
Bawinanga Aboriginal Corporation. *Bawinanga Aboriginal Corporation Annual Report, 2016–2017*. Maningrida 2017, accessed January 2021, https://www.bawinanga.cm/wp-content/uploads/sites/26/Bawinanga_Annual_Report_201617_Web.pdf.
Bracknell, Clint. "Connecting Indigenous Song Archives to Kin, Country and Language". *Journal of Colonialism & Colonial History* 20, no. 2 (2019). DOI: 10.1353/cch.2019.0016.
Brown, Reuben. "The Role of Songs in Connecting the Living and the Dead: A Funeral Ceremony for Nakodjok in Western Arnhem Land". In *Circulating Cultures: Exchanges of Australian Indigenous Music, Dance and Media*, ed. Amanda Harris. Canberra: ANU Press, 2014: 169–202.
Brown, Reuben, David Manmurulu, Jenny Manmurulu and Isabel O'Keeffe. "Dialogues with the Archives: Arrarrkpi Responses to Recordings as Part of the Living Song Tradition of Manyardi". *Preservation, Digital Technology & Culture* 47, no. 3 (2018): 102–14.

Burns, Lori and Serge Lacasse. "Introduction". In *The Pop Palimpsest: Intertextuality in Recorded Popular Music*, eds Lori Burns and Serge Lacasse. Ann Arbor: University of Michigan Press, 2018: 1–5.

Cook, Terry. "Evidence, Memory, Identity, and Community: Four Shifting Archival Paradigms". *Archival Science*, 13, no. 2–3 (2012): 95–120.

Cook, Terry and Joan M. Schwartz. "Archives, Records and Power: From (Postmodern) Theory to (Archival) Performance". *Archival Science* 2, (2002): 171–85.

Corn, Aaron. "Dreamtime Wisdom, Modern-time Vision: Tradition and Innovation in the Popular Band Movement of Arnhem Land, Australia". PhD thesis, University of Melbourne, 2002.

Corn, Aaron. "Burr-Gi Wargugu ngu-Ninya Rrawa: Expressions of Ancestry and Country in Songs by the Letterstick Band". *Musicology Australia* 25, no. 1 (2002): 76–101.

Dadbalag, Mary. Interview by Cindy Jinmarabynana, 14 October 2017. Interview available as JK1-DY003-01 at https://catalog.paradisec.org.au/collections/JK1/items/DY003.

Dadbalag, Mary. English interpretation of JK1-DY003-01 by Cindy Jinmarabynana, 14 October 2017. Interview available as JK1-DY003-03 at https://catalog.paradisec.org.au/collections/JK1/items/DY003.

Djimarr, Kevin. *Wurrurrumi Kun-Borrk: Songs from Western Arnhem Land, the Indigenous Music of Australia*. Sydney: Sydney University Press, 2008.

England, Crusoe Batara, Patrick Muchana Litchfield, Raymond Walanggay England and Margaret Carew. *Gun-Ngaypa Rrawa: My Country*. Batchelor, NT: Batchelor Press, 2014.

Faulkhead, Shannon, Livia Iacovino, Sue McKemmish and Kirsten Thorpe. "Australian Indigenous Knowledge and the Archives: Embracing Multiple Ways of Knowing and Keeping". *Archives and Manuscripts* 38, no. 1 (2010): 27–50.

Garde, Murray. "The Language of Kun-borrk in Western Arnhem Land". *Musicology Australia* 28, no. 1 (2005): 59–89.

Glasgow, Kathy. *Burarra – Gun-Nartpa Dictionary: With English Finder List*. Darwin: Summer Institute of Linguistics, Australian Aborigines and Islanders Branch, 1994.

Greene, Paul. "Introduction: Wired Sound and Sonic Culture". In *Wired for Sound: Engineering and Technologies in Sonic Culture*, eds Paul Greene and Thomas Porcello. Middletown, CT: Wesleyan University Press, 2005: 1–22.

Hale, Ken. "Remarks on Creativity in Aboriginal Verse". In *Problems and Solutions: Occasional Essays in Musicology Presented to Alice M. Moyle*, eds Jamie C. Kassler and Jill Stubington. Sydney: Hale & Iremonger, 1984: 254–62.

Hiatt, Betty and Lester Hiatt. "Notes on Songs of Arnhem Land". Canberra, ACT: Australian Institute of Aboriginal Studies, 1966.

Hiatt, Betty and Lester Hiatt. *Songs from Arnhem Land*. Canberra, ACT: Australian Institute of Aboriginal Studies, 1966.

Hiatt, Lester. *Kinship and Conflict: A Study of an Aboriginal Community in Northern Arnhem Land*. Canberra: Australian National University, 1965.

Hiatt, Lester and Kim McKenzie. *Waiting for Harry: Tensions Behind the Scenes of a Ritual Event in Central Arnhem Land, Northern Territory* [film]. Canberra: Australian Institute of Aboriginal and Torres Strait Islander Studies, 1980.

Hinton, Leanne. *Havasupai Songs: A Linguistic Perspective*. Amsterdam: John Benjamins Publishing Company, 1984.

Indigenous Hip Hop Projects. *Make it Through* [music video], 2016. Available at https://www.youtube.com/watch?v=T85KkTms-XE&ab_channel=IndigenousHipHopProjects, accessed 30 March 2021.

James, Stephanie Maxwell. "Diyama" [song], *Wárrwarra* [album] Ripple Effect Band, 2018. Sydney Conservatorium of Music. Independent Release, https://spoti.fi/3Da9mmW.

James, Stephanie Maxwell, Jodie Kell, Jolene Lawrence, Rona Lawrence, Patricia Gibson, Rachel Thomas and Tara Rostron. Interview by Spotify at Barunga Festival, 3 June 2018. Interview and transcript available as JK1-NG003 at https://catalog.paradisec.org.au/collections/JK1/items/NG003.

Jinmarabynana, Cindy. Interview by Jodie Kell, 18 May 2020. Audio interview and transcript available as JK1-DY006 at https://catalog.paradisec.org.au/collections/JK1/items/DY006.

Jinmarabynana, Cindy. Interview by Jodie Kell, 14 October 2017. Audio interview and transcript available as JK1-DY003-04 at https://catalog.paradisec.org.au/collections/JK1/items/DY003.

Keen, Ian. *Knowledge and Secrecy in an Aboriginal Religion*. Oxford: Clarendon Press, 1994.

Kell, Jodie, Janet Marawarr, Deborah Wurrkidj and Jennifer Wurrkidj. "Jarracharra" recorded 2019, exhibited with Bábbarra Women's Centre at *Jarracharra* exhibition, Australian Embassy, Paris, France, 2019–20, https://catalog.paradisec.org.au/collections/JK1/items/J001, accessed 9 July 2021.

Ketelaar, Eric. "Archives as Spaces of Memory". *Journal of the Society of Archivists* 29, no. 1 (2008): 9–27.

Letterstick Band. *An-barra Clan* [album]. Alice Springs: CAAMA Music, 2004. Available at https://caamamusic.com.au/caama-music-artists/letterstick-band/, accessed 14 March 2021.

Letterstick Band. *Diyama* [album]. Alice Springs: CAAMA Music, 2003. Available at https://caamamusic.com.au/caama-music-artists/letterstick-band/, accessed 14 March 2021.

Letterstick Band, Sunrize Band, Wildwater. *Demurru Hits*. Maningrida, NT: Maningrida Arts, 1995.

Marett, Allan. *Songs, Dreamings, and Ghosts: The Wangga of North Australia*. Middletown, CT: Wesleyan University Press, 2005.

Marett, Allan, Linda Barwick and Lysbeth Julie Ford. *For the Sake of a Song: Wangga Songmen and Their Repertories*. Sydney: Sydney University Press, 2012.

Maxwell, David. Interview by Jodie Kell, 28 October 2017. Audio interview and transcript available as JK1-DY002 at https://catalog.paradisec.org.au/collections/JK1/items/DY002.

Meehan, Betty. *Shell Bed to Shell Midden*. Canberra: Australian Institute of Aboriginal Studies, 1982.

Monson, Ingrid. *Saying Something: Jazz Improvisation and Interaction*. Chicago: University of Chicago Press, 1996.

Murphy, Allen, dir. *Diyama: Soundtracks of Maningrida* [film]. Alice Springs: Central Australian Aboriginal Media Association (CAAMA) Productions Pty Ltd, 2003.

O'Keeffe, Isabel. "Multilingual Manyardi/Kun-borrk: Manifestations of Multilingualism in the Manyardi/Kun-borrk Song Traditions of Western Arnhem Land". PhD thesis, University of Melbourne, 2016.

Ripple Effect Band. *Wárrwarra* [album]. Sydney: Ripple Effect Band, 2018. Available at https://www.ripple-effect-band.com, accessed 14 March 2021.

Ross, Margaret Clunies. "The Aesthetics and Politics of an Arnhem Land Ritual". *TDR: Drama Review* 33, no. 4 (1989): 107–27.

Treloyn, Sally, Matthew Dembal Martin and Rona Goonginda Charles. "Moving Songs: Repatriating Audiovisual Recordings of Aboriginal Australian Dance and Song (Kimberley Region, Northwestern Australia)". In *The Oxford Handbook of Musical Repatriation*, 1st edn. New York: Oxford University Press, 2019.

Vaughn, Jill. "Meet the Remote Indigenous Community Where a Few Thousand People Use 15 Different Languages". *Conversation*, 5 December 2018, accessed 9 July 2021. https://bit.ly/3uwDMuF.

Vogler, Dalton. "Is Pop Music Addicted to Hand Clapping?" *Cue point*, 31 August 2016, accessed 9 July 2021. https://bit.ly/3Q22sD0.

Wildwater. *Rrawa* [album]. Darwin, NT: Wildwater, 2007.

Wildwater. *Bartpa* [album]. Darwin, NT: Wildwater, 1996.

Index

Printed in the USA
CPSIA information can be obtained
at www.ICGtesting.com
LVHW060852051223
765558LV00012BA/230